Postwar America

The United States since 1945

Postwar America
The United States since 1945

IRWIN UNGER

DEBI UNGER

ST. MARTIN'S PRESS   NEW YORK

To

Anthony, Brooke, Elizabeth, Miles and Jody, Paul and Eszter
and Layla
with love

Senior editor: **Don Reisman**
Development editor: **Michael Weber**
Project editor: **Beverly Hinton**
Text design: **Leon Bolognese and Associates**
Graphics: **Vantage Art**
Photo researcher: **Lynn Goldberg Biderman**
Cover design: **Darby Downey**

Library of Congress Catalog Card Number: 89-60982
Copyright © 1990 by St. Martin's Press, Inc.

Manufactured in the United States of America.
43210
fedcba

For information, write:
St. Martin's Press, Inc.
175 Fifth Avenue
New York, NY 10010

ISBN: 0-312-03217-x

Preface

As we approach the final years of the twentieth century, it becomes increasingly clear that the era since 1945 represents a coherent segment of American history. Not that during this period the United States became a world power—it had been that since 1898. In 1945 America became the unchallenged leader of the entire Western world and a political and economic colossus unmatched in history. At the same time America's leadership came up against a major adversary: the Soviet Union and its sometime allies in the Third World. *Postwar America: The United States since 1945* describes this confrontation and shows as well how in recent years the United States has encountered major challenges from its own allies and has been forced to take stock of its world role.

But in the pages that follow we seek to tell an even broader story of American life in the post–1945 period. We emphasize the term "life" because *Postwar America* is not merely a history of elites and the political decisions they made. Rather it is a survey of America in all its diversity of class, race, culture, thought, and ideology. And yet the text is not, we believe, a shapeless mass of unrelated facts. We have tried to weave the social, political, cultural, and intellectual threads into coherent patterns so that the student can see where the parts relate to the whole.

We would like to refer instructors who need a text covering the entire twentieth century to the "parent" work of this one: our *Twentieth-Century America,* also published by St. Martin's Press.

Every book is to some extent a cooperative effort—a text like this, inevitably, even more than most. We have reason to be grateful to a number of skilled and generous people for help in bringing it to completion. First, we would like to thank our editor at St. Martin's Press, Michael Weber. Michael's keenly attuned ear and remarkable knowledge of American history placed him far beyond the ordinary editor in his contribution to the final product. We would also like to thank senior editor Don Reisman and project editor Beverly Hinton. Finally, we would like to thank our agent, Gerrard McCauley, who helped to launch the book and has expedited the process of bringing it to a successful conclusion in a number of significant ways.

Irwin Unger
Debi Unger

Contents

―――――――

MAPS AND CHARTS

Prologue:
From 1900 to 1945

Americans went wild on August 15, 1945. It was V-J Day, Victory over Japan Day, and it marked the triumphant end of World War II, the most expensive and savage war in history. On that glorious day Americans looked ahead to the blessings of peace and prosperity. Few, certainly, considered what had preceded during the twentieth century, now almost half over. Yet such a backward glance would have explained the four hard years just past and revealed to the happy crowds how their world had come to be the way it was.

America in 1900

The twentieth century began with the nation in the full throes of modernization. Technology was transforming the way Americans worked and played. By 1900 cities had electric lights; factories used electric motors. The automobile had begun to appear on city streets. Businesses and richer householders used the telephone to communicate. Here and there in crowded downtowns enterprising showmen had put chairs in empty stores and were showing flickering images on a screen to dazzled audiences. In 1901 Gugliemo Marconi had sent the first wireless signals across the Atlantic; modern radio was not far down the road. Meanwhile, on the windswept dunes at Kitty Hawk, North Carolina, two Ohio brothers, Wilbur and Orville Wright, were experimenting with gliders. Three years later they would launch the first heavier-than-air flight, fulfilling the dream of ages.

Many of these innovations had already begun to alter the daily life of Americans; their impact in the decades ahead would be revolutionary. In 1900, however, most Americans were grappling with problems carried over from the nineteenth century, and it was the solutions to these that took first place on the national agenda.

By 1900 the United States had become the most powerful industrial society on earth, with a total output several times that of its closest competitors. Americans, on average, were also the richest people on earth. Yet the glowing aggregate statistics disguised serious economic and social problems.

Industrial progress had created a nation of cities. In 1900 over 45 million Americans out of a total population of 75 million still lived in villages and on farms. But the cities and towns were growing much faster than the rural regions and by 1920 would be home to a majority of Americans.

Early twentieth-century cities were places of wonder and opportunity. Thousands of rural Americans were drawn to them by the lure of jobs. Others were pulled by the dazzle of city lights, city amusements, city dissipations. Millions of immigrants added to the flood. The immigrants of the early twentieth century, unlike their predecessors, came primarily from Europe's southern and eastern portions. Proportionately many more were Catholic and Jewish, and they seemed to contemporary native-born Americans more alien than earlier immigrants.

The communities that accepted the flood of newcomers experienced severe growing pains. Sewage, sanitation, transit, water supplies, housing, schools, police, government—all were overloaded as the nineteenth century approached its conclusion. Also strained were social relations: within families, between neighbors, among groups, between individuals and the larger society. During the early twentieth century the stressed communities by and large rose to the challenge.

The solutions, however imperfect, came from a mobilization of both private and public energies and resources. Clergymen, reformers, and social workers all sought to address the problems of city people. Through the churches, settlement houses, and numerous voluntary societies they tried to educate the city poor, improve their health and hygiene, and provide them with job and language skills. Many of the same clergymen, civic-minded reformers, and social workers also entered city politics as supporters of reform mayors. The new city administrations were not only economical and honest; at their best they were also sensitive to the social needs of the cities' working class. Within two decades American cities were relatively well governed places that had met many of the physical and social challenges brought about by rapid growth and technological change.

But city problems were only a portion of the nation's social and political concerns. The breakneck pace of economic growth had been costly. For decades after the Civil War the country had manufactured millionaires almost as quickly as steel. It had also expanded its middle class of professionals, managers, and white-collar workers. But in addition it had created a class of industrial workers whose daily rounds were governed by the screech of factory whistles and the clamor of machines and whose lives were arduous and insecure.

The Progressive Movement

The inequalities of wealth and power had grave implications. How could America's democratic political system, inherited from a more economically egalitarian era, continue to function in a world of economic giants and pygmies? The industrial changes since the Civil War—national markets dominated by a small number of centrally located giant firms—also threatened serious abuses of consumers. In an increasingly urbanized society, more and more Americans had come to depend on distant producers for everything they ate, wore, and took for their health. In the new century a new class of exposé journalists and novelists—the *muckrakers*—would make clear how the new arrangements endangered the health and pocketbooks of consumers and how the new aggregations of economic power threatened to convert a democratic republic into a plutocracy, a nation ruled by the rich.

The response was a political movement called *progressivism,* a movement that borrowed much from the Populist fear of monopoly and unregulated private power but avoided some of the suspicion and provincialism of the 1890s People's, or Populist, party. Urban, rather than rural, progressivism was a broad-based movement that sought to protect the vulnerable—industrial workers, women, children, middle-class consumers, small business people, and others—from the uncertainties and hazards of modern life. Operating within both major parties, the progressives first launched their attack on privilege and exploitation in the state capitals. In Wisconsin, Oregon, New York, Ohio, Iowa, New Jersey, and even in the conservative and racist South, progressive governors and legislators passed railroad and utility regulation bills; laws to compensate workers for job injuries, to protect women workers, to outlaw child labor; and to bypass or replace corrupt officials by means of "direct democracy": primaries, the initiative, referenda, and the recall. From the state capitals the progressive impulse soon moved to Washington to create a powerful current of national reform.

The front man for the national progressive movement would be the exuberant Theodore Roosevelt. "TR" abruptly became the nation's youngest chief executive in 1901 after an anarchist assassinated President William McKinley. Roosevelt was a patrician New Yorker who evolved over time from good government reformer into a true progressive. He became progressivism's chief publicist, employing his high office as a "bully pulpit" for the reform cause.

Roosevelt deplored the "malefactors of great wealth." But he did not believe that it was possible to turn back the clock to the mid-nineteenth century, before the age of big business. In the 1902 Northern Securities suit and other antitrust actions he rejuvenated the virtually dead Sherman Anti-Trust Act. But his preferred solution to business abuses was government regulation rather than break-up. Under his auspices the government tightened its control over the railroads (Elkins Act and Hepburn Act, 1903 and 1906) and imposed health standards on meatpackers (Meat Inspection Act of 1906) and packaged food and drug manufacturers (Pure Food and Drug Act of 1906).

Roosevelt was also a dedicated conservationist who sought to protect the nation's natural resources from private despoilers and preserve it for long-term public use. He encouraged passage of the Newlands Act of 1902, removed millions of acres of public land from private exploitation, and established several national parks and national monuments. His efforts for conservation were seconded by his close friend, Gifford Pinchot, the nation's chief forester. Roosevelt also befriended organized labor, most notably during the 1902 anthracite coal strike when he intervened to support the aggrieved miners against the arrogant and arbitrary coal mine operators.

TR was reelected to a full term in 1904 but declined to run once more in 1908. Instead, he successfully orchestrated the Republican nomination for his protegé, Secretary of War William Howard Taft, who easily won the presidential contest.

As president, Taft disappointed TR's friends. Although he sponsored several antitrust suits and some progressive legislation, he failed to support the Republican progressives in Congress who wanted a lower tariff. He also offended the conservationists when he took the part of Interior Secretary Richard Ballinger against Chief Forester Pinchot in disputes over the sale to private interests of western water power sites and Alaskan coal lands. By the time Roosevelt returned home in 1910 from a year-long safari trip to Africa, Taft had lost the support of an important group of Republican Midwestern insurgents and faced the prospect of a renomination battle with TR in 1912.

In the end Taft secured the Republican renomination but at the price of dividing the party. After being rebuffed at the Chicago convention, TR's progressive supporters walked out and reassembled to create the Progressive party (the "Bull Moose" party), with Roosevelt as its nominee and one of the most advanced platforms of social reform to date. The 1912 Democratic candidate was the progressive governor of New Jersey, Woodrow Wilson, a former president of Princeton University. The campaign soon boiled down to a choice between Roosevelt and Wilson, as Taft lagged behind. The two leaders were both progressives, but with a difference: Roosevelt's *New Nationalism* endorsed government control of big business; Wilson's *New Freedom* advocated a Jeffersonian restoration of competition by the breakup of large economic units. Wilson won with a plurality of the popular vote.

As president, Wilson was a forceful leader. Abandoning the precedent of over a century, he appeared personally before Congress to present his program and effectively intervened to goad the members to action when they balked. Under his prodding Congress passed the Underwood Tariff (1913), lowering tariff duties for the first time since the Civil War. Attached to the measure was the nation's first income tax in a generation, authorized under the newly adopted Sixteenth Amendment. He also sponsored the Federal Trade Commission Act and the Clayton Antitrust Act (1914), strengthening federal control over business practices and outlawing those designed to reduce competition or to deceive or defraud the public. The Federal Reserve Act (1913) established a new banking system intended to enhance the nation's financial structure and provide a flexible national currency.

By 1914 Wilson's initial reform zeal was exhausted, but as the 1916 election approached, he gained a second wind. To improve his reelection chances in 1916, Wilson sponsored a final burst of progressive legislation closer to TR's New Nationalism than his own New Freedom. By this time the entire European world was two years into World War I and the presidential campaign turned as much on Wilson's foreign policy leadership as on his domestic policies. Running on the slogan "He Kept Us Out Of War" as well as on his newly reinforced progressive record, Wilson won a narrow victory over his Republican opponent, Charles Evans Hughes.

Foreign Relations and World War I

Wilson's second term was dominated by international problems. During his first four years he had bungled relations with Mexico by applying his moralistic principles to the chaotic internal affairs that followed Mexico's 1911 revolution. At one point, seeking to prevent the return of an authoritarian regime south of the border, Wilson stumbled into a military confrontation with the Mexican leader Victoriano Huerta at Vera Cruz. War was barely averted. In 1916, following an attack by Mexican revolutionary Pancho Villa on American citizens on the U.S. side of the border, Wilson dispatched troops under General John Pershing to pursue the rebel leader through Mexico's northern provinces. But Villa was never captured.

By the fall of 1914 the great powers of Europe, grouped in two rival blocs—the Allies (France, Russia, Great Britain, and Italy after 1915) and the Central Powers (Austria-Hungary, Germany, and later Turkey)—were at war, and millions of men were struggling and dying in Europe, Africa, and Asia and on the high seas. Wilson initially advised Americans to avoid partisanship, but it proved impossible. From the outset Germany had its American supporters; Britain had its American enemies. But a majority of Americans, including the president, favored the Allies. This attachment was reinforced by effective Allied propaganda that painted the Germans as brutal aggressors in Belgium.

Even more effective in molding American opinion was the German U-boat campaign against Allied shipping. Since the United States was a major supplier of arms and raw materials to the Allies, American ocean commerce quickly fell prey to German submarines, with resulting loss of life as well as property. The sinking in 1915 of the British liners *Lusitania,* with the deaths of 128 Americans, and *Arabic,* with the loss of two more Americans, produced a major German-American diplomatic crisis that was resolved by Germany's pledge to desist from sinking passenger ships. In February 1917, however, the German government resumed unrestricted submarine warfare. On April 2 the United States declared war on Germany for the avowed purpose of defending freedom of the seas and making the world "safe for democracy."

American manpower and supplies revived Allied morale and contributed to the collapse of the Central Powers. So did Wilson's Fourteen Points, promising a just peace and a new world order that would avoid the destructive conflicts of the past. The Central Powers gave up, and the guns fell silent on November 11, 1918.

Wilson went to Versailles, France, for the peace conference and succeeded in getting the victorious Allied powers to accept his idea of a League of Nations to resolve international disputes peaceably. He could not prevent the victors from imposing harsh terms on defeated Germany, however, and the treaty poisoned the European political atmosphere for the next twenty years. Wilson was also not able to get the U.S. Senate to accept the principle of continued American involvement in cooperative efforts to maintain international stability. In the end the Senate refused to ratify the Treaty of Versailles, and the United States never joined the League of Nations.

Wilson suffered a stroke in 1919 while campaigning for the League and never regained his health. In 1920, Republican Warren G. Harding, expressing the isolationist and conservative mood of the postwar period, swept into office as the man who would replace twenty years of noble reform and dedication with "normalcy."

The Twenties

Elements of reform survived during the 1920s, but by and large the decade was one of political conservatism as the concerns of business and businessmen came to the fore. During these years the labor movement receded and the political left—anarchists, syndicalists, socialists, Bolsheviks—came under attack by private vigilantes and government officials alike. The twenties were also years of deep social and cultural rifts that pitted the values and interests of urban and cosmopolitan America against those of rural and provincial America. The two sides joined battle over a wide range of issues including evolution teaching, prohibition of alcoholic beverages, race, immigration, radicals, morals, and religion. During the era the Ku Klux Klan revived as the most extreme expression of the rural, provincial mood. Meanwhile, one of the symbols of the other side were the *flappers*: young women, newly enfranchised by the Nineteenth Amendment, who expressed their dissent from traditional social and moral constraints by smoking, necking, wearing their hair and their skirts short, and leading independent lives.

During the twenties the economy boomed. The war had made the United States the world's major creditor nation. It had also lifted consumer incomes and helped rationalize American industrial technology. National income surged as investment in new industries connected with automobiles and other consumer durable goods lifted American living standards to new levels. By the end of the decade millions of Americans owned cars, radios, washing machines, and other appliances. America had become the first mass consumption society in the world.

But some groups had been left behind. Agriculture was depressed in the 1920s. So were mining, railroads, and portions of the textile industry. Much of the decade's benefits accrued to the urban middle class, with rural people and unskilled wage earners getting less. By 1927 the forward thrust of the economy had slowed, in part because of income inequality, but the glow of prosperity continued in the form of a speculative stock market boom. Fueled by easy bank credit and limitless optimism, the Wall Street Bull Market of 1928–29 dominated the economy.

Crash, Depression, and New Deal

In the fall of 1929 the stock market crashed, wiping out billions of paper profits. President Herbert Hoover sought to reassure the public, but his optimistic pronouncements failed. Investment and consumption dropped. Thousands of businesses went bankrupt; thousands of factories closed. The Federal Reserve System could have helped ease the downward pressure by making credit cheaper. Instead it foolishly tightened the money supply. By 1933 there would be almost 13 million unemployed, an unprecedented 25 percent of the labor force.

Hoover refused to allow the federal government to provide relief for the unemployed and their families, but he supported loans to business through the Reconstruction Finance Corporation to prevent further bankruptcies. His opponents called this approach to mass economic distress the "trickle down theory."

Despite the widespread suffering that accompanied the Great Depression, most Americans retained their faith in the political system. In 1932 they turned to the Democrats under Franklin D. Roosevelt ("FDR"), governor of New York, rather than parties that promised revolutionary change. A former progressive (and distantly related to TR), Roosevelt had no clearly defined plan to conquer the Depression, but he represented a chance for change, and the public found his promise of a *New Deal* reassuring. Roosevelt and the Democratic ticket won a resounding victory.

What followed was the greatest flood of significant legislation in any presidential administration. Roosevelt came into office in the midst of a bank crisis that threatened to shut down an already shaky financial structure. One of his first acts was to declare a national bank holiday to allow banks to shut their doors while the government put their affairs in order. He next induced Congress to pass an economy act to reduce the federal budget and a bill to allow again the production of beer and light wine. These first measures were not significant in themselves, but they established the president as a man of action and immensely cheered the fearful public.

During the remainder of its first "Hundred Days," the new administration tackled one by one the major symptoms of collapse, hoping to find a cure. Included in the bold legislative program was the Agricultural Adjustment Act to raise farm prices and income by restricting food and fiber output; a Civilian Conservation Corps to provide jobs for unemployed young men on conservation projects; the Federal Emergency Relief Act to provide federal money to the states for relief for the unemployed; a Banking Act to detach commercial banks from the business of selling securities; a Tennessee Valley Authority to develop the waterpower potential of the Tennessee River and to aid regional conservation; the Home Owners Loan Corporation to rescue home owners from mortgage foreclosure; and a National Industrial Recovery Act (NIRA) to revive industrial production through industry-wide "fair-competition" codes while at the same time protecting labor's right to collective bargaining. Many of these measures were concocted by the president's inner group of advisers, the "Brain Trust," composed largely of Columbia University professors.

These early measures produced mixed results. The bank crisis eased; farm prices and farm income rose; home mortgage foreclosures dwindled; thousands of youths found healthful work in national forests and parks; millions of Americans were kept from hunger and total destitution; unions increased their membership; business confidence rebounded; and the economy turned up. But the Depression did not end. In 1935 there were still 10.6 million Americans without jobs, and gross national product was still less than three-fourths its 1929 level. Clearly the Great Depression still had not released its frigid grip.

One thing the president failed to do that economists now believe would have made a difference was deliberately run large budget deficits. The federal government's spending did exceed its income during FDR's first term, but the excess was moderate and incidental to the need to provide relief for the unemployed. In 1937, when the economy seemed to be moving strongly toward full recovery, the government cut spending back sharply. Employment, investment, and sales dropped sharply, threatening to undo the progress of the previous four years.

But the New Deal balance sheet did show large improvements. In the so-called Second Hundred Days (Second New Deal) following 1934, Roosevelt succeeded in winning passage of a collection of reform measures that permanently changed American society. The National Labor Relations Act (Wagner Act) expanded and made permanent labor's collective bargaining rights conferred initially in the NIRA; the Banking Act of 1935 increased the power of the Federal Reserve System over the nation's money and credit; the Social Security Act of 1935 established a combined state-federal system of unemployment insurance, created a program of old-age payments to retired people over sixty-five, and appropriated federal money to help states support the destitute blind as well as homeless, crippled, and dependent children. The Social Security Act was the most massive intrusion ever of federal power into the daily lives of Americans and marked a watershed in U.S. history.

However mixed the results, millions of blue-collar workers, intellectuals, small-business people, immigrants and their children, and small farmers gave the New Deal and the Democrats their enthusiastic support. Among the party's newest supporters were thousands of northern African-American voters who had previously voted Republican but were grateful for the jobs and relief provided by the Roosevelt administration. In the anti-Roosevelt camp were small groups of radicals, strong traditional Republicans, and conservative business leaders who hated Roosevelt as "a traitor to his class." Running against Governor Alfred Landon of Kansas in 1936, FDR racked up one of the most monumental presidential victories of all time. The political coalition forged by 1936 would remain a powerful voting bloc in American politics for an entire generation.

Ironically, FDR's landslide only brought political frustration. To bypass the conservative-dominated Supreme Court that had already struck down important New Deal legislation, the president proposed soon after his second inauguration that Congress give him the power to appoint new justices to offset those over seventy who refused to retire. The "Court packing" plan offended moderates and conservatives alike and hurt Roosevelt politically. After this setback conservative Southern Democrats in Congress felt free to join with Republicans to defeat New Deal legislation. During the 1938 congressional primary campaign the President attacked the party conservatives and asked the voters to support their liberal opponents. His "purge" of the Democratic conservatives failed, further damaging his political power. Thereafter to all intents and purposes the New Deal was dead.

The World Scene

By this time Roosevelt's attention had already shifted to what was happening abroad. His 1933 inauguration had coincided with the coming to power in Germany of Adolf Hitler, leader of the antidemocratic, anti-Semitic, anti-Communist, militaristic Nazi party. Hitler soon launched a reign of terror against Germany's Jews, liberals, and radicals, repudiated the Versailles Treaty, and began to rearm his nation. In 1936 he joined with Europe's other major dictator, Italy's Benito Mussolini, to form the Rome-Berlin Axis. In 1936–39 both countries intervened in the Spanish Civil War on the side of the far-right rebels under Francisco Franco. In 1938 Germany absorbed Austria into the Greater German Reich. Soon after, Hitler's territorial demands on democratic Czechoslovakia precipitated an international crisis with France and Great Britain. In the end, France's Edouard Daladier and Britain's Neville Chamberlain met with Hitler and Mussolini at Munich, Germany, in September 1938 and sold the Czechs down the river for the sake of avoiding a general European war. Violating his promises, Hitler then occupied the entire Czech republic in March 1939. Shortly after he made demands on Poland. By this time the French and British, determined to stop further Nazi gains, had concluded an alliance with Poland to guarantee its territorial integrity.

In the Far East too an aggressor was on the move. There Japan, convinced that it had been excluded from the "have nations'" imperial feast, had begun to gnaw away at huge but feeble China. In 1932 Japan tore Manchuria away from China and converted it into a puppet state. In 1937 the Japanese began a major war of conquest against China in which Japanese forces were pitted against both the nationalist regime of Chiang Kai-shek and the Chinese Communists under Mao-Tse-tung (Mao Zedong).

In 1940 Japan joined in a loose relationship with the Axis nations of Germany and Italy.

Americans worried about the rise of the aggressors in Europe and Asia. But they also, by and large, had no intention of allowing their nation to become directly involved. By the mid 1930s a mood of profound disillusionment with America's role in World War I had set in, fueled by the 1934 congressional Nye Committee hearings which seemed to demonstrate that the United States had been pushed into the war by munitions makers, bankers, and other "merchants of death." Those who resisted American involvement with overseas disputes were called *isolationists*. Between 1935 and 1939 they induced Congress to pass measures (the Neutrality Acts) forbidding arms sales and loans to belligerent nations and restricting travel by U.S. citizens on belligerent ships.

Roosevelt was not an isolationist. An old Wilsonian internationalist, as early as October 1937 he had called for "peace-loving" nations to "quarantine" aggressors. But FDR was aware of the powerful hold on Americans of isolationist sentiments and moved slowly against the aggressors.

Meanwhile, in the late summer of 1939, after concluding a nonaggression treaty with the Soviet Union, Germany attacked Poland. Soon after, in accordance with their guarantees to Poland, Great Britain and France declared war on Germany. But Poland was quickly defeated and the Germans established on its territory a regime of unimaginable brutality.

With Poland's defeat major fighting ceased for many months. During the "phony war" an ominous calm settled over Europe. Then in April 1940 German forces invaded Norway and Denmark. The British sought to help the Norwegians, but the Germans quickly overwhelmed them. The Norwegian defeat led to the replacement of Chamberlain, the ineffectual British prime minister, by the bold and inspiring Winston Churchill. In May 1940 German forces invaded Holland, Belgium, and France and, with lightening speed, overran all three. In June France surrendered to both the Germans and the Italians, who had joined the war weeks earlier to help share the victor's spoils.

Americans watched European events in dismay, and many began to believe that the United States could not continue to ignore the possible dangers. In October 1939 the United States had repealed the arms embargo and permitted the Allies to buy American war matériel if they paid cash and carried the goods in their own ships. After the fall of France Congress appropriated billions for rearmament and enacted the first peace-time military draft.

Roosevelt ran for an unprecedented third term in 1940 on the promise that he would make America strong but would avoid sending American troops to fight in a foreign war. FDR won a decisive victory over his Republican rival Wendell Wilkie, a Wall Street lawyer from Indiana.

Despite the promise, during the next year the United States became a virtual cobelligerent with Britain and its remaining allies. America sent a steady stream of arms to Britain under the cash and carry law and, when Britain could no longer pay, Congress passed the Lend-Lease Act extending generous credit. In June 1941 Germany invaded the Soviet Union. Roosevelt quickly offered lend-lease aid to Hitler's new enemy. Meanwhile, to guarantee that U.S. aid arrived safely, the American navy began to escort convoys across the North Atlantic and fire at German submarines. Although a majority of Americans supported each of these successive steps toward full participation, isolationism, expressed through the American First Committee, remained powerful.

In the Far East, in the meantime, Japan was taking advantage of Europe's preoccupations to expand its power and influence. After the fall of France the Japanese occupied French Indochina and were soon demanding access to much needed raw materials from the Dutch East Indies. The American government responded by freezing Japanese assets in the United States and embargoing oil to Japan. By the summer of 1941 the Japanese leaders had decided that if an agreement could not soon be reached with America they would rather attack the United States than wait until they ran out of vital fuel supplies for their military and naval forces. On December 7, 1941, while Japanese representatives in Washington were conducting negotiations with Secretary of State Cordell Hull, Japanese planes attacked without warning the American naval base at Pearl Harbor, Hawaii, and destroyed a large part of the American Pacific fleet.

The Japanese attack immediately ended the isolationist-interventionist argument. On December 8 the United States declared war on the Japanese Empire. Several days later Germany and Italy declared war on the United States. The United States was now an ally of Britain and the Soviet Union in the most destructive war in history.

America Fights World War II

The war at first did not go well for the United States. In the Pacific the Japanese invaded the Philippines, a U.S. possession, and quickly overran it. They also conquered the British colonies of Singapore and Malaya and the Dutch East Indies. By early 1942 they were threatening Australia and India. In the Atlantic, meanwhile, German submarines were sending thousands of tons of American shipping to the bottom.

From the outset the British and Americans agreed on a coordinated strategy of achieving victory in Europe first. The first fruits of this strategy were a successful operation against the German and Italians in North Africa in late 1942 followed by an invasion of Sicily and the Italian "boot" in July 1943. Although Italy officially surrendered in September, Mussolini escaped and fled behind the German lines.

Nineteen forty-two also saw the turning of the tide in the Soviet Union and the Pacific. In the Pacific the Japanese advance was checked at the Battle of Midway, where American carrier-based planes devastated a Japanese naval task force intent on seizing the vital Midway island base. At the city of Stalingrad, on the plains of Southern Russia, in the winter of 1942–43 the German army suffered a major defeat. The Russians then went on the offensive.

Meanwhile, Europe suffered grievously under the Nazi heel. In the Soviet Union—and throughout the German-occupied continent of Europe—Germany's brutality toward its millions of subject people marked the extremity of modern barbarism. Most bestial of all was the *Final Solution* (the "Holocaust"): the systematic murder of six million of Europe's Jewish population.

In June 1944 British-American forces finally opened the long awaited "second front" against Germany in France. Hemmed in initially in Normandy, they soon broke out and swept across France and the Low countries into Germany itself, while the Soviets continued to advance from the east. on April 24, 1945, the Soviet army entered Berlin. On April 30 Hitler committed suicide in his underground bunker. Germany surrendered to the Allies in early May.

The members of the anti-Axis coalition had already been planning for peace. In 1943 at Casablanca in Morocco Britain and the United States agreed to make their war goal the "unconditional surrender" of the enemy. At the Tehran Conference of late 1943 in Iran the "Big Three"—Roosevelt of the United States, Churchill of Great Britain, and Joseph Stalin of the Soviet Union—formulated a plan to establish an international peace-keeping organization after the war. The following year lower-level conferences in the United States at Bretton Woods and Dumbarton Oaks, respectively, sought to establish a new postwar economic order and laid out the charter of the postwar international body, the United Nations.

At the Soviet resort of Yalta in early 1945 the three Allied leaders worked out plans for the Soviet Union to enter the war against Japan when Germany was defeated. Disagreement had long been festering, however, between the Soviets and the other Allies over postwar Poland. At Yalta Britain and the United States assented to the Soviet annexation of part of eastern Poland; Poland would be compensated by territory from Germany. The Soviet Union in turn agreed to allow noncommunists to join the Polish government-in-exile it had established and also accepted a British-American demand that the postwar governments established in occupied Europe be chosen by popular elections. Clearly, however, the Soviets had no intention of allowing unfriendly governments on their borders.

In June 1945 a United Nations European Advisory Commission established occupation zones in Germany administered by Britain, France, the United States and the Soviet Union. Berlin too was divided among the four nations. The final major conference of the anti-Axis powers was held in Potsdam, Germany, in July. Roosevelt had died in April and the chief American negotiator was his successor, Harry Truman.

Meanwhile, in the Pacific, island-hopping American troops under General Douglas MacArthur slowly pushed the Japanese back to their home islands. The enemy employed suicide tactics against American ships and troops and inflicted severe casualties. For a number of years the United States had been secretly developing an atom bomb to be used against the Axis. On July 16, 1945, the first bomb was successfully tested in New Mexico. By this time Germany was out of the war, and some of the scientists who had worked on the bomb believed it should not be used. The administration, however, feared that the Japanese would fight for their home islands to the last man. After the Allies warned Japan that failure to accept "unconditional surrender" would lead to "prompt and utter destruction," the signal was given to proceed. On August 6 a U.S. B–29 dropped an atom bomb on Hiroshima; three days later a second bomb was released over Nagasaki. Almost one hundred thousand people died in the attacks. On August 14, after receiving assurances that the emperor would be allowed to retain his throne, Japan accepted the Allies' surrender terms.

The war was over, and the crowds went wild on the streets of American cities. A new era had begun.

1
Postwar and Cold War America

Suburbia, U.S.A.—a home in a community like this was the aspiration of many Americans in the immediate post–World War II years. (Library of Congress)

War's Aftermath

In the immediate excitement and joy at victory few Americans could have thought seriously about the postwar world. If they considered the future in those heady days of mid-August they probably focused on resuming normal life, greeting returning family and friends, buying new cars, and going back to school. If they thought about more general matters they probably worried about the economy: would good times continue? Surely few spent much time pondering the future world international order. Fewer still could have envisaged an era where superpower rivalry would profoundly affect many aspects of daily life.

The New Internationalism

The war destroyed isolationism, and long before V-J Day most Americans had concluded that this time, unlike 1918, the United States must remain an active player on the world stage. To some extent the new internationalism reflected a new collective national egotism. Through its might and will it had destroyed the most vicious enemies the world had ever seen and had emerged more powerful than ever. The United States now had a responsibility to lead the world in the ways of peace and prosperity. In 1941 Henry Luce, head of the powerful Time-Life publishing empire, coined the phrase "the American century" to describe his vision of a new international order under benevolent American leadership.

There were also more practical motives for avoiding isolationism this time: world peace. Without American participation in collective security arrangements the United States would find itself forced once more to rescue the world from an oppressor. Shortly before his death FDR summed up this view, "We shall have to take responsibility for world collaboration or we shall have to bear the responsibility for another world conflict."

The new internationalism was embodied in a supernational peacekeeping organization to succeed the old, defunct League of Nations. Called the United Nations (UN) after the wartime anti-Axis alliance and meeting first in San Francisco in April 1945, the new body was given a structure similar to the League: a powerful Security Council composed of the major powers, an Assembly representing all the member nations, a new International Court of Justice, and a cluster of agencies to help publicize and ameliorate world social and medical problems. Despite some effort to give the UN teeth and an independent voice, time would show that, like the League, it could not replace the long-standing system of power politics or settle major international differences when these involved the great powers.

Yet for a time Americans supported the UN enthusiastically as a symbol of the nation's new commitment to collective security and a long-overdue atonement for rejecting the League of Nations. On July 23, 1945, the United States Senate by a historic vote of eighty-nine to two passed the UN Treaty, making this country the first nation to formally sign the charter. American ardor for the new international body was reinforced when the decision was made to locate its permanent headquarters in New York.

The public commitment to activism in world affairs must not be exaggerated. There was a countercurrent, reflecting a desire to get on with ordinary living and resume day-to-day life, that resembled the retreat to privatism of the 1920s. This attitude would brook no delay in getting "the boys" home as soon as possible regardless of America's international responsibilities and the needs of the occupation forces in Japan and Germany. Spouses, parents, and other relatives bombarded members of Congress, administration officials, and military brass with demands that discharges be speeded up. Encouraged by tearful or peevish letters, GIs themselves staged "Wanna-Go-Home" riots in major military centers from the Philippines to France. Under such pressure it proved politically impossible to follow demobilization procedures that met America's military and occupation needs. Within months the armed forces of the United States had virtually melted away.

Readjustment

Once home former GIs faced wrenching problems of readjustment. Unlike Vietnam War veterans in the 1970s returning service men and women in 1945–46 were given heroes' welcomes. Johnnie, or Joe, or Jane came home to celebrating relatives and friends and huge "Welcome Home" banners stretched across the doorway. Most took time off, living on their military discharge pay, while they considered how to resume civilian life. In 1944 Congress had passed the Servicemen's

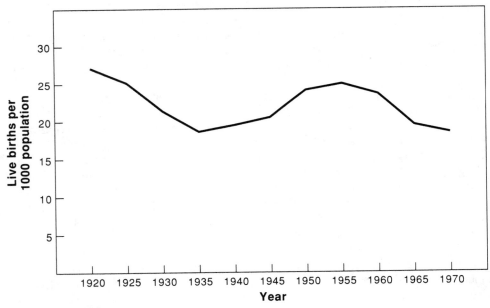

Figure 1–1 Birthrates, 1920–1970

Source: Historical Statistics of the United States (Washington: U.S. Bureau of the Census, 1975), p. 49.

Readjustment Act guaranteeing a year's unemployment pay of $20 a week to returned service personnel, providing money for tuition and maintenance for veterans who wanted to resume or begin schooling, and offering loans to buy homes or start businesses. This "GI Bill of Rights" helped enormously to ease the transition to civil life once the veteran had decided what to do.

And yet despite the psychological and material aid many World War II veterans struggled with serious personal difficulties. Some had been physically or emotionally scarred by their experiences and found it difficult to adjust to the humdrum routines of peacetime. Others returned to find that stored up problems were now free to boil over. There had been many hasty wartime marriages of ardent young men and women who scarcely knew one another. Often these could not stand the strain of everyday existence once peace returned. In 1946 the divorce rate rose dramatically.

Yet for every former GI who regretted a wartime marriage, there were a dozen who looked forward to one in the near future. Thousands of young people had postponed matrimony for the duration of the war and now quickly tied the knot. If the divorce rate soared, so did the marriage rate.

And so did the birthrate. For many years population experts had noted the decline in American fertility. During the Depression it fell still further. Long-term population projections of the late 1930s predicted ever-fewer children and ever-smaller families. But then came the war and the peace. Birthrates leaped. (See Figure 1–1.) During the next twenty years there would be a startling "baby boom" that would mold American values and alter American life for a generation.

Togetherness

In part this upward tilt of the fertility curve represented ex-servicemen and their wives making up for lost time. It also represented a remarkable shift in values.

Many women had enjoyed the work experience of the war period and sought to stay in the labor force after 1945. Some did, but others were forced out by employers who either disliked women workers or felt they must make room for returning veterans. But many women also welcomed the opportunity to get back to home and family.

Such attitudes made a deep impression on national values. The later forties and the fifties would be the era of "togetherness," when all the popular media, led by *McCall's,* the *Ladies Home Journal,* and other women's magazines, beat the drums for family cohesion and traditional domestic values. Life, they said, should revolve around the home and children. Women must renounce careers outside the home. Domesticity, the opinion-makers proclaimed, must be women's chief end. As journalist Agnes Meyer wrote in 1950, "woman must boldly announce that no job is more exacting, more necessary, or more rewarding than that of housewife and mother." The advice was intended to apply to both sexes, and to some extent it did. Men too in the postwar years sought satisfactions in family life and activities around the home. Do-it-yourself home repairs and the garage workshop became a prominent feature of the new life-style.

Suburbia

With millions of men returning from Europe and the Far East, getting married, and planning families, no problem after 1945 seemed more urgent than housing. Hard times during the 1930s had hurt the construction industry and left the nation with a severe housing deficit. During the war home construction had been suspended to conserve scarce building materials and labor. Now, after 1945, everyone wanted a place to live—and as quickly as possible.

But providing the millions of new homes and apartments needed was difficult. Resources had to be shifted from military production to civilian construction, land had to be bought, and loans had to be negotiated. The process was glacial, and the housing shortage quickly became a scandal. In the months after V-J Day thousands of veterans either moved in with their families or made do with makeshifts. Some lived in garages, cellars, or even automobiles. In Chicago the city turned over 250 old streetcars to veterans to make into dwellings.

Everyone had a plan for ending the housing shortage quickly. Seemingly plausible were schemes to build houses on assembly lines, like ships, cars, and planes during the war. But the idea simply did not work. Local housing ordinances, labor union rules, and most of all, traditional personal tastes, quickly punctured the "prefab" balloon. By 1949 or 1950 the answer was found in the "Levittown" suburb, named after William Levitt, a Long Island, New York, builder whose approach was soon widely imitated.

Levittown and its equivalents confirmed the triumph of suburbia over the cities. Levitt and Sons avoided the cities where land and labor were expensive. Instead, they bought up potato and cornfields close to major roads and commuter rail lines. Although the houses did not actually roll off assembly lines, Levitt used the latest mass-production, low-cost construction technology. One Levitt crew would descend on the building tract with bulldozers to clear and grade; another would pour hundreds of slab foundations; another crew would erect precut walls. The lumber and hardware for the houses were prepared in Levitt mills. The structures were two-bedroom houses available in only a limited number of models. But by varying the paint color and the placement of each house on its lot the builder avoided excessive sameness. With built-in refrigerator, washing machine, and oven Levittown homes cost as little as $7,000. By 1950 there would be over 10,000 houses in the first Levitt community, inhabited by over 40,000 people.

Levittowns soon sprang up all over the country. (See the photograph opening this chapter.) As their incomes grew, families would move to more expensive suburban development, or add on new rooms to their initially small dwellings. There had, of course, been suburbs before, but these had primarily housed the affluent. After 1950 an ever larger portion of the American population lived in single-family dwellings outside the city centers. The suburban way of life soon became the norm among middle-class, white Americans.

Intellectuals and aesthetes criticized suburbia as boring, materialistic, philistine, and above all, conformist and homogenized. As pop sociologist John Keats wrote, if you lived in the new postwar suburbs, "you can be certain all other houses will be precisely like yours, inhabited by people whose age, income, number of children, problems, habits, conversation, dress, possessions, and perhaps even blood type are also precisely like yours."

The critics were not entirely wrong; suburban life had its drawbacks. Mothers found themselves enslaved to the family car, forced to chauffeur themselves and children everywhere—to school, to lessons, to the supermarket, to the dentist. While their husbands worked in the city with adult colleagues, they sometimes found young children their only company, and often trying company by the end of the day. And undoubtedly there were fewer cultural advantages in the suburbs, although in truth it is not clear how many Americans missed live theater, museums, and concerts.

But there were also compensations. Suburban isolation was offset through various kinds of social networks. Women created informal neighbor groups among themselves. Church membership soared. In 1940 only 50 percent of American families belonged to religious denominations. By 1960 a total of 63 percent claimed formal membership in some church group, with much of the gain coming in suburban communities. Parent-teacher groups, lodges, and civic associations also compensated for the absence of the close physical contact of city life. Yet to many new residents of suburbia these were not really necessary. The trees, grass, good schools, safe streets, and order compensated for all that they had left behind in the city.

Minorities

Not all Americans shared the suburban experience. As urban middle-class and skilled blue-collar families decamped for the suburbs, they left behind the largely African-American and Hispanic poor. Soon after 1945 these people were joined by new waves of immigrants from Puerto Rico, Mexico, and other parts of Latin America, as well as further increments of rural black southerners.

The African-American and Hispanic inner-city ghettos reflected the marked inequalities and prejudices of American life. Few minority people could afford even the bargain-basement Levitt house, but even if they could, they would have been kept out by formal or informal racial and ethnic suburban exclusion practices. Increasingly, the demographic landscape would shift in the direction of white suburban rings enclosing black and brown central urban cores.

The trend had unfortunate social consequences. In 1945 the inner cities were not yet disaster areas. The presence of middle-class people helped anchor the neighborhoods and guarantee decent city services. Families remained intact; crime, although higher than elsewhere, had not yet gotten out of control; and most important of all, drugs had still not undermined the foundation of social life.

The white, middle-class exodus helped concentrate and aggravate social pathologies. More and more the inner cities became the exclusive habitat of the poor, people who needed expensive medical, social, and educational services they could not afford. The departure of the middle-class, however, inevitably eroded the cities' tax bases. At the very time that the need for social services was growing, then, the cities were becoming less able to pay for them. To compensate for a declining number of middle-class taxpayers, those who remained were taxed more heavily. This response, in turn, goaded even more people to leave the city. It was a vicious cycle that would only get worse with each passing year.

Chapter 1

The Postwar Economy

Although clearly its benefits were unequally distributed, the postwar era was a time of buoyant prosperity. To many people affluence came as a surprise.

The war, as we saw, brought immense economic improvement, wiping out Depression unemployment and adding to the capital stock of the nation. Between 1939 and 1945 per capita income doubled. But would this all change, Americans wondered, when peace returned? If prosperity had been fueled by immense government expenditures for arms, what would happen when these outlays stopped? In the closing months of the war many of the economic seers predicted that the postwar era would see a return to mass unemployment and harsh social strife.

What the prophets of doom had not reckoned with was pent-up demand. With new automobiles, houses, electrical appliances, and other expensive durables almost impossible to buy during the war, Americans were forced to save. Personal savings totaled about $2.6 billion in 1939. By 1945 it had skyrocketed to $29.6 billion. After V-J Day Americans waited eagerly for that new house with a picket fence, that new Ford or Chevrolet, that new automatic washing machine—and they had money in their bank accounts to pay for it.

It took time to "reconvert" from tanks to cars, from barracks to houses, from guns to appliances, and during the interval consumers complained bitterly—and bid against one another for still-scarce goods. Inflationary pressures quickly built up. The Office of Price Administration (OPA), the wartime price-control agency, tried to hold down prices, but with the psychological restraints of wartime patriotism gone, retailers and wholesalers refused to sell at regulated, legal prices. Scarce goods soon became available only on black markets at any price the seller could get. Inevitably OPA itself became a battleground. Many people blamed the agency for the shortages and black markets. Others, however, including most New Dealers, insisted that without continued regulation prices would shoot through the roof and precipitate another depression.

Fortunately the shortages did not last. By 1947 or 1948 American industry had converted to peacetime demand and was pouring out a flood of goods from rubber bands to limousines. By the end of 1948 the Big Three auto companies—Chrysler, Ford, and General Motors—and the half-dozen car independents then still in business were producing 5 million cars a year. In 1950 American manufacturers turned out 6.2 million refrigerators and 14.6 million radio sets. There was also an entirely new consumer durables industry. That year American electronics firms assembled 7.4 million television sets and were shipping them to consumers as fast as they came off the production line.

Rapid reconversion prevented the worst fears of the economic pessimists. Jobs appeared for over 13 million discharged GIs almost as if by magic. The number of gainfully employed Americans in 1950 was 63.5 million. Unemployment in 1946 was 2.3 million, but by 1953 it was down to 1.8 million. Gross National Product, measuring the total output of goods and services, climbed from $208 billion in 1946 to $504 billion in 1960. This increase translated into a 3.2 percent annual rate of economic growth during the 1950s. It was not spectacular measured against the long-term trend. Nor was it smooth. During the decade and a half following V-J Day there were a

Consumer durables like these washing machines poured off American assembly lines in the postwar years to satisfy pent-up demand. (UPI/Bettmann Newsphotos)

number of minor recessions when unemployment spurted. But to people used to the no-growth or even negative growth of the 1930s, the American economy's performance after 1945 seemed almost miraculous.

Pent-up civilian demand explains the postwar boom only in part. By 1945 the major industrial nations of Europe and Asia, their capital worn-out or destroyed, could no longer supply their own citizens' needs for basic items of food, clothing, and shelter. War devastation also made most of the belligerents incapable of supplying their prewar foreign customers. The United States, its mainland territory untouched by bombs or warring armies, inevitably stepped into the breech. And American industrial products were respected. American technology, after all, had produced the tools, including the atom bomb, that won the war. No country, it seemed, could make things better or cheaper. For several years following 1945 the United States would produce a third of all the world's goods. This enviable situation could not last, but for a time it enormously stimulated American production.

A longer range element in the postwar prosperity was the American investment in education and research. In the postwar era technical and scientific knowledge increasingly drove the economy.

A number of major postwar industries—electronics, pharmaceuticals, atomic energy, aircraft—benefited from the government's massive wartime investments in weapons research. After 1945 the education benefits of the GI Bill of Rights enabled thousands of young men and some young women to become scientists and engineers.

Toward the end of the 1950s Americans' confidence in their educational system faltered. Already under attack as excessively concerned with "life adjustment" rather than hard science and basic skills, it seemed even more inadequate after the Soviet Union's 1957 success in launching *Sputnik,* the first successful artificial space satellite. In response Congress passed the National Defense Education Act (1958), which provided low-cost loans to college students who promised to teach in the public schools and large matching-basis grants to colleges for laboratories and to encourage math and foreign-language teaching. The law increased the number of engineers and scientists and helped place American universities at the cutting edge of new technology and science. By 1960 it was clear that American investment in "human capital" and the "knowledge industries" had become a major source of economic growth.

Truman and the Fair Deal

The New President

Harry Truman, Roosevelt's successor, was not as sophisticated or politically skilled as his predecessor. He was a simpler, earthier man, whose strong suit was common sense and the ability to learn from experience. Despite his early connection with Kansas City machine politics he was personally incorruptible and he shared FDR's broad liberal sympathies. Americans liked the fact that he went in person to his Washington bank and that he called Bess Truman, his plain but sensible wife, "mother." But at times they deplored his profanity and his "undignified" belligerence. When a Washington music critic attacked the vocal abilities of his daughter Margaret, a would-be professional singer, the president wrote him a letter.:

> I have just seen your lousy review of Margaret's concert. . . . It seems to me that you are a frustrated old man. . . . Some day I hope to meet you. When that happens you'll need a new nose, a lot of beefsteak for black eyes, and perhaps a supporter below.

During his first few months as president, Truman seemed a bumbler. Soon after taking office, he and Congress got into a battle over extending price and rent controls. The president seemed to waffle, creating the impression that he was a confused man. His performance in dealing with labor troubles during early 1946 also seemed inconsistent. Concerned with declining overtime pay, temporary unemployment, and rising prices, labor was restless in the immediate postwar period and was determined to increase wages. Management resisted union demands and by January 1946 several million workers were on strike.

The president considered organized labor's demands excessive. Truman denounced the striking unions and brought the struck industries under his executive authority. He also asked Congress for additional authority to regulate labor and the unions. Union workers, a vital element in the Democratic coalition, resented the president's response. "Let Truman dig coal with his bayonets," declared John L. Lewis, the feisty leader of the United Mine Workers, after the president had the army seize the mines. And in the end, despite the president's vigorous intervention, the mine workers got what they wanted.

The Eightieth Congress

In November 1946 the voters elected a Republican Congress, the first since 1928. Convinced that they now had a clear conservative mandate, the Republican majority in the Eightieth Congress sought to lower taxes on upper-income recipients, reduce farm price supports, and generally speaking prevent any further liberal reform. They rejected the president's requests for a public housing bill, national health insurance, federal aid to education, a voting rights act, an antilynching measure, and a permanent Fair Employment Practices Commission. These last three measures were aimed at racial discrimination against African-Americans and offended most of the southern members of Truman's own party even more than they did the Republicans. The racial conservatives were further angered when, by executive order, Truman established a committee to investigate race segregation in the military services, setting in motion measures that soon ended the Jim Crow armed forces.

The one request the Republican Congress granted the president was a stiff labor regulation law. The Taft-Hartley Act of June 1947 expressed the conservatives' view that organized labor had grown far too powerful under the New Deal. It banned the closed shop, a practice that required employers to hire only union members; it permitted employers to sue unions for broken contracts or for damage incurred in strikes; it allowed the federal government to impose an eighty-day cooling-off period for any strike that endangered national health or safety. The act also required unions to make public their financial dealings, forbade unions to make direct contributions to political campaigns, and required union leaders to take an oath that they were not members of the Communist party.

The Taft-Hartley Act was a more stringent law than Truman wanted. "We do not need and we do not want, legislation which will take away fundamental rights from our working people," he declared in a radio message to the American people. He vetoed the measure, restoring some of his credibility with liberals and organized labor. But Congress overrode his veto and Taft-Hartley became law.

Besides Taft-Hartley the only important legislation of this Congress was the National Security Act, a measure that echoed the growing fear of Soviet power. The law unified the armed services under a single cabinet head, the secretary of defense, created the National Security Council to advise the president on national security matters, and established the Central Intelligence Agency (CIA) to gather information abroad pertaining to America's international security.

The Election of 1948

By the eve of the 1948 presidential election it looked as if Truman had alienated almost everyone. To his right were the conservative Republicans and southern

Democrats who disliked either his political or his racial policies or both. In the middle were labor leaders who resented what they considered his union-busting tactics. To his left was a contingent of liberals who compared him unfavorably with FDR as well as people who disliked his strong anti-Soviet policies.

Many of the foreign policy dissenters had begun to rally around Henry Wallace, the former vice president whom Truman had inherited as secretary of commerce from Roosevelt. In September 1946 the president fired Wallace for attacking the administration's foreign policy at a Soviet-American friendship rally in New York. Wallace become an instant hero to those who blamed the United States for the growing Soviet-American hostility.

The president had his supporters. The Democratic party regulars—voters and bosses—liked "Harry," or at least preferred him to the Republicans. He even had some organized support among the true-blue liberals, including the Americans for Democratic Action (ADA), organized in 1947 by academics, politicos, and liberal trade union leaders and dedicated simultaneously to anticommunism abroad and further social reform at home. Although many ADAers were initially skeptical of Truman, they eventually endorsed him for reelection.

In 1948 at their national convention in Philadelphia the confident Republicans turned once again to Governor Thomas E. Dewey of New York as their presidential candidate. Despite his spotty record Truman won the Democratic nomination in the same city three weeks later.

The nomination seemed an empty honor. Given his record thus far, few at the convention thought Truman could win in November. Doubt turned to near certainty when, responding to adoption of strong civil rights platform plank supported by Minneapolis Mayor Hubert Humphrey and other liberals, many southern delegates walked out of the convention and formed a separate ticket. Truman's combative acceptance speech restored some confidence. The president lambasted the Republican Congress and declared his intention to call it back into session to consider a long list of important social legislation. If the Republicans refused to pass his measures, they would prove to the voters that they were obstructionists.

The special session of Congress confirmed Truman's expectations. Presented by the president with a long "shopping list" of "must" legislation, it dithered and squabbled and enacted nothing. Truman would now be able to make the "Do-Nothing" Eightieth Congress his campaign whipping boy.

Yet as the weeks passed it seemed unlikely that Truman could win. Beside Dewey the president faced Governor J. Strom Thurmond of South Carolina on the ultraconservative States' Rights ("Dixiecrat") ticket and Henry Wallace, nominated by the Progressive party of America, an organization controlled by pro-Soviet ultra-liberals and hidden Communists. The first threatened to deprive him of the solid South, the second of left-liberal groups in the big urban-industrial states.

Yet Truman confounded the experts and the polls. (See Figure 1–2.) With little money and virtually no press support he mounted a "whistle-stop" campaign to show himself personally to as many voters as possible. Traveling 32,000 miles by train, the president made hundreds of addresses, many off the rear observation car platform to small clumps of people who appreciated the opportunity to see their president. Truman pulled out all the old populist stops, attacking the do-nothing Congress, "Wall Street reactionaries," "gluttons of privilege," "bloodsuckers with offices in Wall

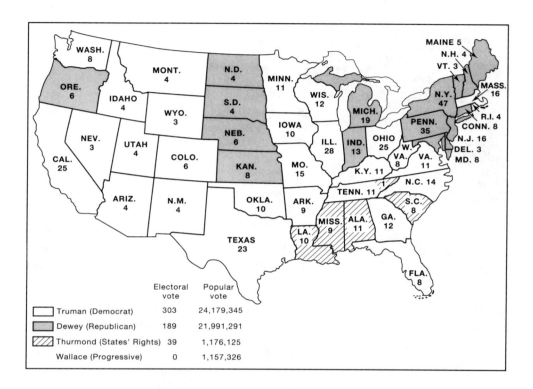

Figure 1–2   The 1948 Presidential Election

Street," and "plunderers." The pollsters continued to predict a Republican triumph, but beneath the surface Truman had awakened fears in millions of farmers, wage earners, and other voters that a Republican victory would jeopardize the gains of the New Deal. He had also projected an attractive image of a scrappy and principled man fighting "the interests."

Truman went to bed election night at 7 P.M. with the pundits still predicting a Dewey sweep. He awoke at 4:30 A.M. to find himself reelected with a plurality of twenty-four million to twenty-two million popular votes and a safe electoral majority of 303 to 189. Thurmond had taken part of the deep South as expected; Wallace had won a million votes largely in New York and California. But organized labor, African-Americans, farmers, unmovable Democrats, and the coattails of popular local Democrats had put Truman over the top.

The Fair Deal

Truman delivered his State of the Union message to the new Congress on January 5, 1949. In it he laid out a program that he called the *Fair Deal,* in obvious echo of FDR's great reform agenda. The president asked for a national health insurance plan, a tax cut for low-income people, a higher minimum wage, new federally financed

On the morning after the 1948 election, President Truman gleefully displays a Chicago newspaper whose early edition had announced his defeat. (UPI/Bettmann Newsphotos)

low-cost housing, a new farm price support system (the Brannan Plan) that would allow consumer prices to fall without penalizing growers, federal aid to schools, new civil rights legislation for African-Americans, and repeal of the Taft-Hartley Act.

The Eighty-first Congress, under nominal Democratic control, was not as obstructionist as its predecessor. It raised the minimum wage from forty cents to seventy-five cents an hour, expanded and improved social security coverage, passed a modest public-housing act, and provided federal funds for medical research and hospital construction. But it rejected all the other suggestions for domestic change the president proposed. Once more, as during Roosevelt's second term, the coalition of southern Democrats and Republicans had managed to frustrate a liberal president with a substantial public mandate.

The Cold War Erupts

Truman's place in history does not depend on his domestic accomplishments but on his handling of the major international crises of the early postwar era. Truman and his foreign policy advisers, George Marshall, and Dean Acheson, fathered the containment policy that defined the nature of Soviet-American relations for a generation.

Americans have debated endlessly the question of blame for the *Cold War*, the postwar superpower rivalry. One group of scholars, the "revisionists," is highly critical of U.S. policy. America, they say, was insensitive to valid Soviet fears of encirclement, was often the aggressor in superpower relations, frequently acted as a conservative neocolonialist world force, and was moved by arrogance, capitalist greed, or powerlust—or all three. The United States in its own way was a missionary nation determined to impose its system and its will on the world. In this view the Cold War was avoidable and it was ultimately American intransigence or drive for dominance that made it possible.

The more common perspective, at least during the 1950s, was that the Cold War confrontation derived either from traditional Russian expansionism or from Soviet zeal for the ultimate triumph of communism over capitalism. Only American might stood between the world and enslavement to Soviet tyranny. This view drew strength from the undeniable paranoia of Soviet leader Joseph Stalin in his last years and the oppressiveness of the Soviet regime under Stalin and his successors both within Soviet borders and in the East European nations that had fallen under Soviet control after 1945. In this approach too, the Cold War was avoidable—if only the Soviet Union had not provoked it time and time again.

In all likelihood neither side is entirely correct. The Soviet-American confrontation that we call the Cold War may well have been inevitable. Mutual suspicions marked Soviet-American relations from the outset. From the 1920s on many Americans saw Soviet communism as a serious threat to religion, democracy, and capitalism and the American Communist party as a subversive influence in American life. Such views had encouraged the 1920s Red Scare, delayed diplomatic recognition of the Soviet Union until 1933, and led to the creation of the House Committee on Un-American Activities in 1938 to investigate subversive groups. On the other side, fueled by the capitalist nations' efforts to suppress the Bolshevik Revolution in 1918–1920, the Soviet indictment depicted the United States as the chief exemplar of the exploitive and greedy capitalist system intent on encircling and crushing "socialism" in the Soviet Union and preventing social change in the rest of the world.

Both sides suspended their suspicions during World War II and managed to cooperate to defeat the Axis. For a time, in fact, the Soviet Union was popular with Americans for its impressive performance against Nazi Germany, and pro-Soviet enthusiasm brought new recruits for the American Communist party. But the honeymoon did not last.

The Power Vacuums

The war and Axis defeat transformed the balance of international power. Britain emerged exhausted and depleted, its industrial plant decayed, its overseas investments drained, and its empire torn by internal stresses. France, the other great prewar democracy, had been occupied by the enemy for five years and had lost any serious claim to world leadership. After 1945 it too faced strains within its overseas empire.

Germany, Italy, and Japan were, of course, the most enfeebled of the prewar great powers. Japan, after V-J Day, was a shambles, its industry destroyed, its cities ravaged, and its people frightened and uncertain of what to expect from the American conquerors and occupiers. In Germany near starvation prevailed in the months after Hitler's fall. Cities were smoking ruins, the monetary and banking systems had collapsed, factories were idle. Italy too was a ruin with its industry depleted and its people uncertain of the advantages of liberal parliamentary democracy.

Europe's decline meant that the powers, primarily Britain and France, that had long been the balance wheel of the international order had ceased to play major roles in world politics. This left the Soviet Union and the United States, the two "superpowers," facing one another around the world without intermediaries. Both were inexperienced; neither was used to world leadership. In addition, having lost 20 million citizens during the German invasion, the Soviet Union was especially sensitive to perceived threats to its security.

In 1945–46 millions of displaced persons—survivors from the concentration and death camps, prisoners of war, and people fleeing the vengeful Soviet forces—moved here and there across the European landscape seeking a permanent haven. The United States provided several billions to the United Nations Relief and Rehabilitation Administration to help these refugees. It also modified its strict immigration quotas to admit several hundred thousand displaced persons. But for many months after the Nazi collapse, Europe and its people faced extreme distress. Everything else but survival went by the board.

Misery and frustration left many Europeans susceptible to communist ideology, and in France, Italy, Greece, and other countries pro-Soviet parties attracted mass support. Fearful of Soviet encroachment into western and southern Europe, American policy-makers inevitably sought to prop up regimes that promised to resist the Soviet Union's supporters even when those governments were authoritarian and oppressive.

Closely related to the British-French decline was the emergence of a new arena for competition: the non-European, former-colonial world. Here the old Western empires were rapidly disintegrating, creating immense power vacuums that both the United States and the Soviet Union rushed to fill.

In the Far East Japan's early wartime victories had undermined the myth of the white race's invincibility. With the European nations gravely weakened, this new attitude encouraged nationalist, anticolonial movements throughout the non-European world. In August 1947, after decades of struggle led by Mohandas Gandhi, India became an independent republic. The next year Ceylon (Sri Lanka) and Burma also won their freedom from Britain. Meanwhile anticolonial wars had erupted in Indonesia against the Dutch and in Indochina between the French and the Vietnamese led by Ho Chi Minh.

Almost everywhere in the non-European world nationalism was on the rise. In Africa independence movements in the Gold Coast (Ghana), Kenya, Algeria, Madagascar, and other countries emerged to challenge the colonial powers.

In the Middle East too nationalism challenged the former European masters. In Syria, Iraq, and Lebanon resurgent Arab nationalism soon forced Britain and France to surrender the power they had exercised under old League of Nations mandates. An especially troublesome spot was Palestine, where the Jewish minority launched an uprising against the British regime for its refusal, in response to Arab opposition, to admit Jewish survivors of the Holocaust. In 1948 Britain abandoned the Palestine mandate, and the United Nations partitioned Palestine. Neither Jews nor Arabs accepted the partition and instead went to war. In the end the Jews defeated the Arabs and, with both American and Soviet encouragement, established the new state of Israel. Thousands of Arab refugees fled Palestine to Jordan and other Arab states. Thereafter Israel become an embattled nation whose existence and survival would be a major source of conflict in the region. (See Figure 5–2 in Chapter 5 for a map of the area.)

In many of these emerging "Third World" nations, nationalism was linked with communism. Ho Chi Minh in Vietnam, for example, was a disciple of Lenin. Americans found it difficult to separate the nationalist aspirations of the anticolonial movements from their Marxist component, and the United States frequently placed itself on the side of forces resisting change. The Soviet Union, on the other hand, made it difficult for the United States to avoid this choice through its enthusiastic support of anticolonial "wars of national liberation."

The Chinese Revolution

The most momentous postcolonial upheaval of all took place in China. During World War II the United Nations (Allied) powers, including the Soviet Union, had treated Nationalist China under Chiang Kai-shek as virtually an equal partner in the anti-Axis coalition. In fact China remained bitterly poor and disorganized; its ruling party, the Kuomintang (Nationalists), was corrupt and had limited popular support. Confronting Chiang and his party was Mao Tse-tung (Mao Zedong) and the Chinese Communists with their stronghold in the northern part of the country. Mao and his followers were Leninists whose dogmatism would be fully displayed in the self-destructive 1960s "Cultural Revolution." But in the immediate post-1945 era their promises of land, their dedication to fighting the Japanese invader, and their apparent incorruptibility brought them the respect and support of the vast Chinese peasantry.

Although from 1945 on Mao and Chiang were locked in a fierce combat for supremacy, China was not at first a battleground between the superpowers. At the end of 1945 Truman sent former army Chief of Staff George Marshall to China to seek a compromise between the rival groups. Marshall negotiated a truce in the fighting and then an agreement for a coalition government. But this arrangement soon broke down, and by mid-1946 the two sides were once more at one another's throats.

For the next three years the United States tried to bolster Chiang against the Communists with money, advice, and arms. Nothing helped. The Nationalists were inept and dishonest and the aid sent them was squandered or stuck to the fingers of Nationalist officials. Much of the American arms supplies were sold on the black market or allowed to fall into Communist hands. In 1949 Mao's troops defeated the Nationalists and forced them to flee to the island of Taiwan off the China coast. There Chiang and his followers established themselves as China's legitimate government, hurled defiance at the Communist People's Republic ("Red China"), and promised one day to reconquer the mainland.

China's fall to the Communist camp seemed an ominous victory for the Soviets. Even Americans who saw no way that their country could have saved Chiang from defeat agreed with Secretary of State Dean Acheson that Mao's regime would "lend itself to the aims of Soviet Russian imperialism." This fear became a loaded political issue when right-wingers insisted that China had been "lost," not by Nationalist incompetence and corruption but by the errors of the Truman administration, if not actual treason in high places in Washington.

The Bomb and the Arms Race

Hovering over the emerging superpower rivalry and making it more threatening than any previous international competition was the specter of "the Bomb."

The Soviet Union knew of America's drive to develop the atom bomb even before the war ended. After Nazi defeat the Soviet government brought captured German scientists to the Soviet Union and put them to work with their own scientists to duplicate the American effort. The Soviets would have developed their own atom bomb in any case, but they were able to accelerate the process by effective espionage in America and Britain. In 1949 the Soviet Union exploded its first atomic weapon, ending the brief American nuclear monopoly.

The atom bomb competition was only the beginning of the nuclear arms race. Both sides were soon rushing to develop the far more powerful hydrogen bomb and then competing to perfect delivery systems to ensure that the bombs hit their targets. By the 1960s both sides, using the most sophisticated technology available, had developed intercontinental ballistics missiles, giant rockets that could soar in vast arcs over continents and oceans to deliver nuclear warheads with pinpoint accuracy on enemy cities and military installations. Year after year these new weapons would grow in number and power so that they threatened the very existence of humankind. The testing needed to develop increasingly effective nuclear devices by itself released vast amounts of radiation into the atmosphere, endangering the health of millions of people, present and future.

Nor was the competition confined to nuclear weapons. Both sides poured billions into planes, ships, tanks, and guns. Both maintained enormous standing armies and navies. Some people believed these outlays stimulated economic growth and the development of new technology. Others were convinced that they starved society of the resources it needed to improve the quality of life and ultimately even slowed economic growth rates.

Early efforts to control the arms rivalry foundered on the rock of big-power mutual suspicions. The Soviets at first were behind in the nuclear race and refused to stop until they had caught up. The Americans recognized that in an open society they could not conceal violations of any arms limitation agreement while the closed Soviet society could easily do so unless it permitted on-site inspection of arms manufacturing facilities. In 1946 the United States proposed the Baruch Plan, offering to place atomic energy and weapons under UN control with unrestricted inspection of nuclear facilities. The Soviets, suspicious of the Western-dominated UN and behind in atomic development, rejected the idea. And yet the world survived, if only because neither superpower could be certain it would win a nuclear exchange. In fact, ironically, the existence of nuclear weapons served to prevent a major war between the superpowers. Mutually assured destruction (MAD), however chancy, came to be the ultimate deterrent of World War III.

Containment in Europe

Yet MAD did not prevent a succession of dangerous confrontations between the superpowers or their surrogates.

Difficulties between the Western nations and the Soviet Union go back to the war period itself and can be detected earliest in their disagreements over Poland. They also intruded at the April 1945 founding UN conference in San Francisco, where the Soviet's demand that the big powers have a veto over what issues the Security Council could discuss almost scuttled the meeting. In subsequent months the Soviet Union reneged on promises for free elections in the countries of Eastern Europe that were liberated from Nazi control by Soviet troops. By 1946 most of these—Bulgaria, Rumania, Poland, and Hungary—had become Communist-ruled satellites of the Soviet Union.

Conquered Germany too became an early bone of East-West contention. During the Big Three conference at Potsdam, Germany, in July and early August 1945 the Soviets had agreed to treat Germany as a single economic unit and accept a precise plan for German reparations. It quickly violated these promises. Thereafter the last traces of Big Three cooperation and goodwill quickly faded.

An overall American policy toward the Soviet Union soon began to gel. On February 22, 1946, an eight-thousand-word telegram arrived in Washington from George F. Kennan, an expert in Soviet affairs stationed at the U.S. Embassy in Moscow. Kennan's "long telegram" analyzed Soviet foreign policy in historical perspective and emphasized its continuity over generations. Russian expansionism predated the Bolshevik Revolution, he said. It had originated in the Russians' geographical insecurity and in the need to distract the Russian people from tyranny and poverty at home and would continue under the Soviet regime for the same reasons. The implications were clear: despite any attempt at negotiation, the Soviet Union would remain belligerent and uncooperative; it could be stopped only by strong counter-measures.

Soon after, former British Prime Minister Winston Churchill gave a name to the growing barrier between East and West. Speaking at Fulton, Missouri, on March 5, Churchill declared that "from Stettin in the Baltic to Trieste in the Adriatic, an Iron Curtain has descended across the Continent" of Europe. On the one side was democracy, on the other, "police governments." Unless the West took heed, subversive Communist groups would undermine democracy in the West as well. Britain and the United States, Churchill concluded, must continue to cooperate in the postwar period to ensure Europe's freedom.

Many Americans were not yet ready to take a strong line against the Soviet Union or help bolster the Western European democracies. Most, as we saw, had acquiesced in the rapid decline in U.S. military strength after V-J Day. In September 1945 the U.S. abruptly terminated lend-lease aid to Britain, leaving that depleted country in the economic lurch. When the administration proposed a $3.75 billion low-interest loan to replace it, Congress dragged its feet for many months and insisted on extracting many trade concessions from its former ally before granting the request.

The Truman Doctrine and the "X" Article

American policy began to stiffen when George Marshall became secretary of state in January 1947, replacing James Byrnes. Soon after accepting office, Marshall learned that the British government intended to withdraw all military and economic aid from Greece and Turkey. For a century Britain had imposed peace and order in the Near East, but now it could no longer afford this role. Both Mediterranean countries were in danger, Greece from a leftist uprising against the unpopular monarchy and Turkey from Soviet military pressure on its northeastern frontier. Clearly if the United States did not step into the breach, there was a distinct chance that both these nations would become part of the Soviet orbit.

The crisis in Greece and Turkey produced a revolution in American foreign policy. Should the United States become the guarantor of stability in distant southeastern Europe? To do so would be a major break in American foreign policy. True, the country had entered two world wars to stop a perceived aggressor in Europe, and it had finally agreed to participate in a worldwide peacekeeping organization. But should it also, on its own, seek to substitute for Britain and France around the globe as the regulator of major international change?

Marshall and Truman quickly decided that the United States must fill the vacuum in the eastern Mediterranean or see Soviet power spread over areas where Russia had never before prevailed. On March 12 the president appeared before Congress to request $400 million of economic and military aid to Greece and Turkey. The United States, he said, must "support free peoples who are resisting attempted subjugation by armed minorities or outside pressures." If America faltered in its leadership of the "free peoples of the world," it might "endanger the peace of the world." Both the political left and the right opposed this *Truman Doctrine*. Much of the left still saw the Soviet Union as a benevolent force in the world and regretted the breakup of the wartime Big Three alliance. The right was still isolationist, especially as regards Europe. Senator Robert Taft of Ohio, the leader of the Republican conservatives, condemned the Truman proposal as an "international WPA" that would drain the American economy. Walter Lippmann, the venerable political pundit, warned that it was a dangerous open-ended commitment without foreseeable limits.

Despite the opposition Congress made the appropriation. Pressure on Turkey diminished, while in Greece American aid combined with the refusal of Yugoslavia's independent Communist government under Marshal Tito to allow the leftist guerrilla forces sanctuary enabled the Greek government to survive.

But what about other soft spots in Europe? Should the Truman Doctrine be expanded beyond Greece and Turkey? In July the journal *Foreign Affairs* published an article signed "X" that spoke to this issue. It was by Kennan once again, and it represented the views of an influential circle of foreign policy experts including Kennan, Averell Harriman, Dean Acheson, and Charles Bohlen, most of whom had learned their foreign policy principles at the feet of Henry Stimson, Herbert Hoover's secretary of state. All believed that the United States must "contain" the Soviet Union if it was to avoid being overwhelmed itself. The article endorsed as the main element of U.S. policy toward Europe "a long-term, patient, but firm and vigilant containment of Russian expansive tendencies." Only such an approach could result "in either the break-up or the gradual mellowing of Soviet power." The Kennan article supplied an intellectual rationale for an open-ended *containment policy.*

The Marshall Plan

The European winter of 1946–47, one of the harshest on record, posed an immediate crisis. Subzero temperatures, heavy snowstorms, and transport break-downs added to Western Europe's immediate postwar miseries and played into the hands of the pro-Soviet left. In Italy, Germany, and France the Communists, proclaiming capitalism defunct and incapable of supplying a decent living standard for ordinary men and women, gained thousands of adherents. To the foreign policy experts in the U.S. State Department, rescuing Western Europe's economy seemed essential to preserving democratic government in a vital part of the world.

The result was the *Marshall Plan,* first presented by Secretary Marshall in a speech at Harvard in June 1947 and then, in September, submitted by Truman to Congress as a request for $17 billion in American grants and loans to help Europe recover economically. Under the plan the European countries would themselves work out a recovery program, and the United States would stand behind it. Marshall announced that all European nations, even the Soviet Union, could join the plan, but the Soviets and their satellites, suspecting an American trick, refused to attend the initial planning conference in Paris in July and later rejected the scheme drawn up by the sixteen participating nations to facilitate European recovery. Early in 1948 Congress approved the aid request, and ships were soon speeding across the Atlantic carrying American raw materials and manufactured goods to help Europe get back on its feet.

The Marshall Plan (European Recovery Program) worked magnificently well. In all the United States contributed about $13 billion to financing the scheme. The aid rescued Europe from collapse and was soon making a major contribution to reviving output and employment all over the continent west of the Iron Curtain. It also provided the impetus for further European economic cooperation in the shape of the European Economic Community, or Common Market, which soon generated additional prosperity.

The Marshall Plan evoked European gratitude. The London *Economist* called it "the most . . . generous thing that any country has ever done for others." But the goals were not solely altruistic. The United States was determined to stop the Soviet Union and in this it succeeded as well. Although the Western European Communist parties did not suddenly disappear, they ceased to grow, and Communist regimes failed to gain power through regular electoral means. In American terms Europe was "saved."

The Berlin Blockade

But the Cold War continued. In 1947 the Soviet Union revived the Communist International, the directing body of the Communist parties around the world, after having let it lapse during World War II. The following year the Soviets contrived the overthrow of the democratic government of Czechoslovakia and converted that nation into another satellite. Soon after, Stalin threatened to push the French, British, and Americans out of Berlin, an exposed salient of the West deep within the Soviet's own tightly controlled East German occupation zone. (See Figure 1–3.)

Stalin's Berlin policy was his response to British-French-American efforts to unify their three occupation zones—West Germany—and revive its economy. The Western powers hoped to save themselves from the continuing burden of keeping the Germans alive, although they were not indifferent to the value that a revived Germany could play in offsetting the Soviets. In late 1946 they merged the economies of their three zones, and then in June 1948 they reorganized the German monetary system to end the rampant inflation and restore economic confidence. The effects were dramatic.

Figure 1–3 Divided Germany

The German economy rebounded strongly, kicking off an expansion that would soon be called the "German miracle."

In late July the Soviet Union, violating wartime agreements, cut off rail and highway traffic between West Germany and Berlin. This move threatened to starve the population of the city's Western zones. But what should the Western nations do? Any attempt to break through the blockade by land promised a major military confrontation with the Soviet army and, in all likelihood, the outbreak of World War III. The solution was a massive rescue operation by hundreds of cargo planes flying around the clock to deliver daily the 4000 tons of food, fuel, clothing, and other items needed by the besieged city's 2.5 million people. By the spring of 1949 the planes were bringing in far more than the minimum amount and the Soviets were beaten. On May 12 they removed the rail and road barriers, and the trains, cars, and trucks resumed their movement to Berlin.

Soon after, under the aegis of the Western powers, West Germany became the independent Federal Republic of Germany with its capital at Bonn and a constitution modeled on that of pre-Hitler Weimar. To counter this development, the Soviets organized its own occupation zone into the German Democratic Republic (East Germany) as one of its cluster of satellites.

West Berlin children happily watch an American plane bring food and other supplies to the city during the Berlin Blockade. (The Bettmann Archive)

NATO

The culmination of the American containment policy was the creation of the North Atlantic Treaty Organization (NATO) in 1949. Originally composed of the United States, Canada, and ten European countries including France, West Germany, Britain, Italy, and the Low Countries, it was augmented by the addition of Greece and Turkey in 1952. (France ceased active participation in 1966.)

The NATO treaty was another sharp break with America's traditional foreign policy, which had always avoided "entangling alliances" with other nations. The treaty bound the signers to a mutual defense agreement. "[A]n armed attack against" any one of them in Europe or North America would be "considered an attack against all of them" and they would take collective action, "including the use of armed force," to stop it. Recognizing the special role in the alliance of the American superpower, the participating nations chose Dwight Eisenhower, the commander of the armies victorious against the Nazis, as head of NATO forces. A few years later the Soviet Union formed the Warsaw Pact with its Eastern European satellites to counterbalance NATO. (See Figure 1–4.)

Note: France ceased participating actively in NATO in 1966, and Albania withdrew from the Warsaw Pact in 1968.

Figure 1–4 The Cold War in Europe

The Korean War

Was Red China the same threat to the status quo and American interests in East Asia as the Soviet Union in Europe? Most American policymakers believed the answer was yes. By 1950 Mao and his colleagues had consolidated their hold on the mainland and were demanding control of "all of China," meaning Chiang Kai-shek's domain of Taiwan. Early in 1950 the People's Republic and the Soviet Union concluded a military pact, confirming the equivalence of the two Communist powers in the eyes of many Americans.

Far Eastern Policy

American policymakers were divided over the U.S. role in the Far East. The members of the foreign policy establishment responsible for containment were generally "Europe firsters" who believed the Soviet Union the truly dangerous enemy. As of early 1950 the Europe firsters were still skeptical of Chiang and his self-serving and corrupt officials. Another group, however, composed of assorted isolationist and "old China hands"—missionaries, diplomats, businesspeople, and teachers with personal and family connections with pre-Communist China—saw the Communist advance in the East as even more dangerous. These men and women formed a loosely defined group called the "China Lobby." They blamed the Truman administration for "losing" China to the Communists and sought to oust Mao and his regime from power and return Chiang and the Kuomintang to the mainland. They succeeded in preventing U.S. recognition of Red China and were able to exclude the People's Republic from the UN through repeated U.S. vetoes in the Security Council.

In 1950 the American presence in the Far East was still formidable politically, although not militarily. In Japan General Douglas MacArthur, head of the occupation forces, had swept away the quasifeudal political system and imposed a democratic government on the Japanese people. He had also, to a lesser degree, democratized the social system. Although they had loathed and feared the Americans during the war, the Japanese embraced the occupiers and their reforms enthusiastically. The country remained bitterly poor in 1950, but the foundation had been laid for the enormous economic surge of the 1960s.

In late June 1950 far eastern policy suddenly became a prime American concern when North Korean troops swept across the thirty-eighth parallel and invaded South Korea. The two Koreas were a product of the Allied agreements at Cairo, where the former "Hermit Kingdom" had been promised its freedom from the Japanese occupiers "in due course," and at Yalta, where the country had been divided at thirty-eight degrees north latitude into a Communist, pro-Soviet regime in the north and a pro-Western, although not democratic, administration in the south.

Each government, North and South, wished to reunify the nation under its own auspices, but that of the South, under Syngman Rhee, had been militarily starved by the United States, while that of the North had been provided with powerful arms by the Soviets. The North Korean attack may have been inspired by the Russians. Certainly American officials thought so. The connection between the Soviet Union and the regime in North Korea, according to one U.S. official was similar to the one "between Walt Disney and Donald Duck." The attack probably had been encouraged unwittingly by a January 1950 statement by Dean Acheson, Marshall's successor as secretary of state, that the United States did not consider South Korea a vital part of America's defense perimeter. Whether instigated by the Soviets or not, the attack appeared to be an opportunistic Communist attempt to change the far eastern status quo by military means.

The response in Washington was swift. Despite Acheson's earlier statement the American government perceived that the attack, if unanswered, would encourage further aggression by the Communists. Now the containment policy was to be applied to the Far East as well.

America Intervenes to Save South Korea

Truman moved fast to meet the invasion before the weak South Korean army collapsed. Taking advantage of an unexpected Soviet absence from the UN, the United States was able to secure a Security Council resolution demanding a cease-fire and withdrawal of the attacking forces. Two days later the UN also asked member nations to assist the South Koreans. UN participation sanctioned the United States calling the Korean War a "police action." Congress was never asked to declare war.

Sixteen nations sent troops and supplies to Korea, but the United States bore the brunt of the defense. On June 29 the president authorized MacArthur to use all the forces available to him in Japan to stop the invasion, thus committing the United States to a major land war in the Far East. Senator Taft and other Republicans objected to the haste of the decision; influential Democrats advised Truman to ask for a congressional vote of approval for the intervention. But the president, for all his virtues, was a hot-tempered, impetuous man, and he rejected the advice.

The war at first went badly. By the time the first American troops arrived in Korea, the invaders had easily swept aside the Korean and American defenders and captured Seoul, the South Korean capital. They advanced rapidly south, pushing the South Koreans and the inexperienced and ill-led Americans into a small pocket around the port of Pusan. Here the defenders barely held out while massive supplies and reinforcements arrived from the United States. On September 15 MacArthur, imitating his end runs against the Japanese in World War II, launched an amphibious attack at Inchon close to the thirty-eighth parallel that hit the enemy in the rear. Meanwhile, other American and Republic of Korea (ROK) troops, broke out of Pusan and swept north. The UN forces recaptured Seoul on September 26 and were soon at the thirty-eighth parallel.

With the approval of the UN, the American-ROK forces drove into North Korea and by the end of October were close to the Yalu River, at the Korean-Chinese border. (See Figure 1–5.) Their obvious purpose was to reunite the two sections of the country under Western aegis. Truman and his advisers had considered the possibility of Red Chinese intervention, but despite warnings from Beijing, had accepted MacArthur's conclusion that China was not a serious threat.

MacArthur was wrong. Mao feared a hostile, American-supported Korea on his border, and by mid-October was sending Chinese "volunteers" to bolster the North Koreans. Then in late November the Chinese struck south with thirty-three divisions,

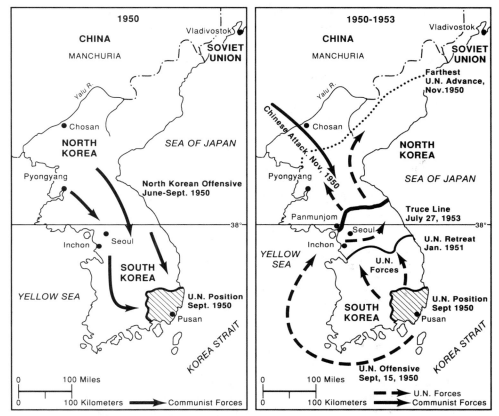

Figure 1−5 The Korean War

many composed of veterans of the long war against Chiang and the Japanese. Despite individual acts of bravery, American troops panicked and fled south the way they had come, abandoning arms, food, tents, supplies, and hundreds of prisoners to the enemy. Thousands of Chinese, facing one of the most bitterly cold winters on record, survived only by using cast-off American blankets, boots, and clothing. It was not a proud page in American military annals. To reduce the pressure, in late December MacArthur proposed that the UN forces blockade the Chinese coast, bomb Chinese war industry, and permit Chiang's military forces to create a "diversionary action" against "vulnerable areas of the Chinese mainland." Truman denied the request, fearing to bring the Soviet Union into the war. He also told the general, a vain and egocentric man who had ruled Japan as his personal fiefdom, that he must issue "no speech, press release, or public statement" on policy without clearance from Washington.

In January the UN forces finally recovered from the initial shock of the Chinese attack and resumed the offensive. They recaptured Seoul again in March and were soon once more at the thirty-eighth parallel.

At this point relations between MacArthur and the administration reached a crisis. In late March Truman told the general that the American government would seek a negotiated peace through diplomacy. MacArthur objected. Soon after this he wrote a letter, read publicly in the House of Representatives, proposing that Chiang be "unleashed" to invade mainland China and urging the United States to shift its overall strategic priority from Europe to Asia.

On April 10 Truman relieved MacArthur of command for insubordination and replaced him with General Matthew Ridgeway. The public split passionately over the MacArthur dismissal. Some approved the president's decision to limit the war and put the general in his place. Others considered the administration weak for refusing to use every means to win the war and for humiliating a great military hero. The MacArthur fans seemed more numerous than the Truman supporters. Thousands of angry and critical letters and telegrams poured into the White House, running twenty to one against the president. One particularly angry voter telegraphed, "Impeach the Judas in the White House who sold us down the river to left wingers and the UN." When the general returned to the United States, his trip across the country became a triumphal procession with ovations, banquets, and rallies in his honor. There was talk of running him for president in 1952.

Public enthusiasm quickly ebbed, however. Congress held extensive hearings on the war that revealed the general's military failings and confirmed the value of the administration's "limited war" position. Despite the shift in attitude the incident revealed a profound American dissatisfaction with any policy that did not produce quick solutions. Critics wondered if Americans were capable after all of pursuing a long-term policy of patient containment.

On July 8 cease-fire negotiations between the UN forces and the Chinese–North Koreans began at Kaesong, close to the thirty-eighth parallel. The fighting continued but was now reduced to furious small-scale firefights and bloody patrol actions, with neither side expecting a breakthrough. The negotiations continued month after month with little visible progress.

Mobilization

By this time the country was on a war footing, with thousands of reserve troops called back into service, and a full-scale draft. In all, over 1.3 million Americans would serve in the Korean theater of war; 54,000 young Americans died. Although there were no serious consumer shortages, prices rose as in World War II, despite official price controls.

Korea was a major step along the Cold War road. In 1949, at the behest of Secretary of State Acheson, the National Security Council had drafted a policy paper (NSC-68) recommending a major rearmament program to meet the growing dangers of Soviet antagonism. The paper had been accepted but it had not been implemented. In 1950 the American defense budget remained a modest $13.5 billion; the nation's total armed forces personnel about 1.4 million. Despite all the tension with the Soviet Union the country remained complacent. Korea changed this drastically. By 1955 America's military budget had soared to almost $40 billion; that year the number of U.S. military personnel reached 2.9 million.

Anticommunism at Home

The Korean War, and especially the frustrating military stalemate, intensified the anti-Communist climate in the United States and set off a campaign against supposed subversives and traitors at home.

The campaign was marked by panic and hysteria. Clearly a small number of American Communists were willing to spy for the Soviet Union. But most members of the Communist party of the United States, however sympathetic to the "Socialist Motherland," were not engaged in espionage. In fact the chief charge against them was that they were subversives. It is true that a few Communists and Soviet sympathizers occupied positions in the media, in Hollywood, in the universities, and in trade unions, and it would be naive to assume that they never used their positions to propagate their political viewpoints. Yet when this is said, it remains true that the handfull of Soviet partisans in the United States never seriously threatened American security or democracy or ever exerted a dangerous influence over American minds. By 1950, however, the United States was suffering from a full-blown anti-Communist frenzy that threatened to undermine the Bill of Rights and damage the very democratic system the crusaders professed to be defending.

It is important to distinguish between the Soviet threat on the one hand and the danger of internal subversion on the other. However valid or invalid the first, the second was clearly unreal. The United States and its capitalist system were never in danger of internal overthrow. Nor was American foreign policy secretly manipulated, as some people felt, by traitors in high places. Yet many Americans were willing to believe that Communist gains in Europe and the Third World were the work of a conspiracy by secret Communists in high Washington office to betray America's interests.

Concern over perceived Soviet expansionism and aggressiveness was the ultimate source of anti-Communism at home. But there were also self-serving gains to be made by playing on, and exaggerating, anti-Communist fears. Obscure politicians could win the limelight and keep it by unmasking hidden Communists in high places; this was the course of Senator Joseph R. McCarthy. One politician could use it against another; Richard Nixon achieved his early political victories in California by charging his opponents with pro-Communist views. It could also serve overall party purposes; some of the less scrupulous Republican leaders of the 1950s accused the Democrats of "twenty years of treason." It was a resource of right against left; conservatives would charge that liberals were "soft on communism," and label their policies "socialistic." Sometimes the gains were purely monetary; more than one former FBI agent or city police detective set himself up as an expert on communism and charged media companies or industrial firms fees to root out Communists among their employees.

Relatively few Americans could resist the anti-Communist wave that swept the country after 1945. Following the discovery in 1945–46 of major Soviet spy operations in the United States, Truman created a commission to look into the question of loyalty among federal employees. Early in 1947 the federal government began the screening of over 3.2 million federal workers, including every clerk-typist, Internal Revenue Service accountant, and postal worker in the country. By 1951 almost 300 had been dismissed and another 3000 had resigned. Meanwhile in December 1947 the attorney general issued a list of ninety organizations, later expanded, that were identified as Communist "front" groups. Membership in any group on the attorney general's list became grounds for suspicion of disloyalty and, in some cases, of dismissal from jobs.

The Hiss and Rosenberg Cases

Public anxiety was fueled by several sensational cases of actual espionage. In the summer of 1948 two witnesses before the House Committee on Un-American Activities (HUAC), Elizabeth Bentley and Whittaker Chambers, both repentant ex-Communists, revealed that a number of American Communists had spied for the Soviets during the 1930s in Washington, D.C. Chambers charged that Alger Hiss, now head of the prestigious Carnegie Foundation for International Peace and once an influential New Deal figure, had been a member of one of these secret rings. Hiss, he claimed, had stolen secret documents from the federal government and turned them over to Chambers to be passed along to Soviet agents.

Hiss appeared before the committee to answer the accusations against him. He denied every charge and made an excellent impression. Urbane, elegant, well-spoken, sincere, he convinced everyone on the committee except the young Republican congressman from California, Richard Nixon, that he was totally innocent. He had never stolen secrets; he had never known Chambers. The committee now recalled Chambers who began to supply circumstantial evidence of his association with Hiss and his family during the 1930s. Armed with this new information, the committee summoned Hiss once again and questioned him closely. Hiss might have confessed to being a Communist during the 1930s; that was not a crime. He might even have admitted that he had taken secret documents; by now the statute of limitations had run out and he could no longer be prosecuted for the offense. He did neither. He denied Chambers's charges again, although admitting he might have known the man under another name. Then he made a fatal mistake. Let Whittaker Chambers make his charges in public, he demanded; if Chambers dared to do so, he would sue him for libel.

Chambers quickly took up the challenge and on a radio program, "Meet the Press," accused Hiss of being a secret Communist and Soviet agent. He then waited for weeks for the promised libel action. When in September 1948 Hiss finally sued for defamation of character, Chambers dramatically revealed a cache of stolen govern-ment documents—originals, microfilms, and copies in Hiss's handwriting—that he claimed Hiss had given him years before for safekeeping. Some of these were trivial items, but others contained important secrets.

The Truman administration had been reluctant to prosecute Hiss. Many liberals admired the man and saw him as a symbol of all the New Deal stood for at its best. They also correctly detected in his enemies a partisan zeal to indict the liberalism of FDR and his followers. But confronted with this new, incriminating data, the Justice Department indicted him for perjuring himself before a congressional committee. The first trial resulted in a hung jury. The second trial, ending in January 1950, produced a conviction. The judge sentenced Hiss to five years in prison.

The Hiss case was important as a symbol of Cold War tensions at home. Regardless of Hiss's guilt or innocence, its outcome was a victory for those who believed that Communist gains had been made possible by men in prominent positions who had betrayed their country. If Chambers was right, some New Dealers had committed treason. To those who believed Hiss innocent, his conviction seemed either a case of mass hysteria, like the witch-hunts of the Middle Ages, or a cynical attempt to frame the political left and the New Deal.

The Rosenberg case also reinforced public fears. In 1949 British authorities arrested Klaus Fuchs, an anti-Nazi refugee and naturalized British citizen who as a theoretical physicist had helped the Americans and British develop the atom bomb. A loyal Communist, Fuchs had become a Soviet spy and had passed along secret data to the Soviet Union about atom bomb research. His apprehension in 1950 led, in turn, to David Greenglass, an enlisted man at the U.S. Los Alamos atomic laboratory who had supplied Fuchs with information on the processes for manufacturing the bomb. The trail of contacts finally led to Greenglass's sister and her husband, Ethel and Julius Rosenberg, two Soviet sympathizers. The Rosenbergs denied their guilt and claimed to be victims of Cold War hysteria, but they were both convicted and sentenced to death. Although a portion of the political left rallied to the Rosenbergs, they were executed in June 1953. To this day they remain, in some circles, martyrs of the Cold War.

Joe McCarthy

Korea and its frustrations charged all these Cold War events with special significance and created a demagogue anxious and able to take advantage of the public mood. The man was Joseph R. McCarthy, the Republican junior senator from Wisconsin.

McCarthy, a former state circuit judge, won election to the Senate in the Republican sweep of 1946. McCarthy's victory was due to the weakness of the progressive La Follette state machine and his own supposed (and false) heroic war record. The man had few ideas and little vision. Nicknamed by his colleagues "the Pepsi Cola kid" for his lobbying efforts on behalf of the soft drink manufacturer, he had impressed neither them nor his constituents. By 1950 he was, with reason, worried about reelection two years ahead and desperate for an issue to bring him favorable publicity. Early in the year he had dinner with a friend who advised him that the Communists-in-government issue might be his ticket to reelection. "That's it," McCarthy reputedly declared. "The government is full of Communists. We can hammer away at them."

On February 9, in a speech to the Women's Republican Club of Wheeling, West Virginia, McCarthy charged there were 205 "card-carrying Communists" at work in the State Department, a situation supposedly known to the Truman administration but left uncorrected. On other occasions he cited different numbers. McCarthy was bluffing; he had no idea how many, if any, Communists were in the State Department. Yet in the feverish atmosphere of the day the charge created a sensation. The senator had found his issue and was soon off and running.

McCarthy was a master of obfuscation. When the Democrats investigated the State Department claim, he managed to turn the case into an indictment of the Truman administration for "losing China." Owen Lattimore, a Johns Hopkins University

READING 1

McCarthyism

The right of free expression, even if one is wrong, is a precious part of America's heritage. As a people Americans generally prize their civil liberties, but in moments of fear and panic they sometimes push them aside. One such occasion was the immediate post–World War II era, when many citizens feared the Soviet threat abroad and linked it with subversion at home. These fears were magnified and given focus by Senator Joseph McCarthy of Wisconsin, a demagogue more interested in advancing his own and his Republican party's political interests than in making the country more secure against its enemies. The following is an excerpt from McCarthy's 1950 Lincoln Day speech, the opening shot of his campaign against the forces of "communistic atheism," domestic and foreign. Before he was brought to heel four years later, McCarthy had poisoned the country's political atmosphere and wrecked the careers of hundreds of loyal Americans.

Ladies and gentlemen, tonight as we celebrate the one hundred and forty-first birthday of one of the greatest men in American history, I would like to be able to talk about what a glorious day today is in the history of the world. As we celebrate the birth of this man who with his whole heart and soul hated war, I would like to be able to speak of peace in our time, of war being outlawed, and of worldwide disarmament. These would be truly appropriate things to be able to mention as we celebrate the birthday of Abraham Lincoln.

Five years after a world war has been won, men's hearts should anticipate a long peace, and men's minds should be free from the heavy weight that comes with war. But this is not such a period—for this is not a period of peace. This is a time of the "cold war." This is a time when all the world is split into two vast, increasingly hostile armed camps—a time of a great armaments race.

Today we are engaged in a final, all-out battle between communistic atheism and Christianity. The modern champions of communism have selected this as the time. And, ladies and gentlemen, the chips are down—they are truly down.

Six years ago, at the time of the first conference to map out the peace—Dumbarton Oaks—there was within the Soviet orbit 180 million people. Lined up on the antitotalitarian side there were in the world roughly 1,625 million people. Today, only six years later, there are 800 million people under the absolute domination of soviet Russia—an increase of over 400 percent. On our side, the figure has shrunk to around 500 million. In other words, in less than six years the odds have changed from 9 to 1 in our favor to 8 to 5 against us. This indicates the swiftness of the tempo of Communist victories and American defeats in the cold war. As one of our outstanding historical figures once said, "When a great democracy is destroyed, it will not be because of enemies from without, but rather because of enemies from within."

The truth of this statement is becoming terrifyingly clear as we see this country each day losing on every front. . . .

The reason why we find ourselves in a position of impotency is not because our only powerful potential enemy has sent men to invade our shores, but rather because of the traitorous actions of those who have been treated so well by this Nation. It has not been the less fortunate or members of minority groups who have been selling this Nation out, but rather those who have had all the benefits that the wealthiest nation on earth has had to offer—the finest homes, the finest college education, and the finest jobs in Government we can give.

This is glaringly true in the State Department. There the bright young men who are born with silver spoons in their mouths are the ones who have been worst. . . .

When Chiang Kai-shek was fighting our war, the State Department had in China a young man named John S. Service. His task, obviously, was not to work for the communization of China.* Strangely, however, he sent official reports back to the State Department urging that we torpedo our ally Chiang Kai-shek and stating, in effect, that communism was the best hope for China.

Later, this man—John Service—was picked up by the Federal Bureau of Investigation for turning over to the Communists secret State Department information. Strangely, however, he was never prosecuted. However, Joseph Grew, the Under Secretary of State, who insisted on his prosecution, was forced to resign. Two days after Grew's successor, Dean Acheson, took over as Under Secretary of State, this man—John Service—who had been picked up by the FBI and who had previously urged that communism was the best hope of China, was not only reinstated in the State Department but promoted. And finally, under Acheson, placed in charge of all placements and promotions.

Today, ladies and gentlemen, this man Service is on his way to represent the State Department and Acheson in Calcutta—by far and away the most important listening post in the Far East. . . .

This, ladies and gentlemen, gives you somewhat of a picture of the type of individuals who have been helping to shape our foreign policy. In my opinion the State Department, which is one of the most important government departments, is thoroughly infested with Communists.

I have in my hand 57 cases of individuals who would appear to be either card carrying members or certainly loyal to the Communist Party, but who nevertheless are still helping to shape our foreign policy.

One thing to remember in discussing the Communists in our Government is that we are not dealing with spies who get 30 pieces of silver to steal

---

*The following statements about Service are grossly inaccurate [Ed. note].

the blueprints of a new weapon. We are dealing with a far more sinister type of activity because it permits the enemy to guide and shape our policy. . . .

As you hear this story of high treason, I know that you are saying to yourself, "Well, why doesn't the Congress do something about it?" Actually, ladies and gentlemen, one of the important reasons for the graft, the corruption, the dishonesty, the disloyalty, the treason in high Government positions—one of the most important reasons why this continues is a lack of moral uprising on the part of the 140 million American people. In the light of history, however, this is not hard to explain.

It is the result of an emotional hangover and a temporary moral lapse which follows every war. It is the apathy to evil which people who have been subjected to the tremendous evils of war feel. As the people of the world see mass murder, the destruction of defenseless and innocent people, and all of the crime and lack of morals which go with war, they become numb and apathetic. It has always been thus after war.

However, the morals of our people have not been destroyed. They still exist. This cloak of numbness and apathy has only needed a spark to rekindle them. Happily, this spark has finally been supplied.

As you know, very recently the Secretary of State [Dean Acheson] proclaimed his loyalty to a man [Alger Hiss] guilty of what has always been considered as the most abominable of all crimes—of being a traitor to the people who gave him a position of great trust. The Secretary of State in attempting to justify his continued devotion to the man who sold out the Christian world to the atheistic world, referred to Christ's Sermon on the Mount as a justification and reason therefor, and the reaction of the American people to this would have made the heart of Abraham Lincoln happy.

When this pompous diplomat in striped pants, with a phony British accent, proclaimed to the American people that Christ on the Mount endorsed communism, high treason, and betrayal of a sacred trust, the blasphemy was so great that it awakened the dormant indignation of the American people.

He has lighted the spark which is resulting in a moral uprising and will end only when the whole sorry mess of twisted, warped thinkers are swept from the national scene so that we may have a new birth of national honesty and decency in Government.

Source: From the *Congressional Record,* 81st Congress, v. 96, part 2 (February 20, 1950).

professor who had served as a State Department adviser on East Asia, was, McCarthy said, a Soviet agent who had deceived his superiors. When Truman and Acheson attacked the senator, he called the president "a son of a bitch" and advised Acheson to seek asylum in the Kremlin.

McCarthy soon went on to attack the widely respected George Marshall, despised by the China Lobby for his refusal to support Chiang during the civil war with Mao and his forces. At Marshall's confirmation hearings as secretary of defense in 1950, the senator announced that he would expose "a conspiracy so immense and an infamy so black as to dwarf any previous venture in the history of man." Despite the attack Marshall was confirmed, but many of his friends would never forgive the senator.

Clearly McCarthy was no respecter of truth, of persons, or even of common decencies. Before long he had developed an approach guaranteed to get him headlines in the nation's papers. He would call a morning press conference and announce that he was calling an afternoon press conference. He made the news both times. He carried around a fat briefcase, supposedly full of written evidence incriminating one person, or whole groups of people, and then refused to show the documents to anyone. He produced nothing, but the performance invariably excited wide speculation.

Despite his incivility and reckless accusatory zeal the senator was a popular man. Supporters flooded his office with mail and contributions. A poll in May 1950 showed that 40 percent of Americans supported him; only 28 percent considered his charges dangerous or untrue. That year he campaigned against some of the congressional Democrats who had opposed him, and their defeat sent shivers down the spines of

Senator Joseph McCarthy, Republican of Wisconsin, and his aide Roy Cohn. (UPI/Bettmann Newsphotos)

would-be opponents. Even at the beginning and within his own party, some people despised the man and loathed his tactics. "I don't want to see the Republican Party ride to victory on . . . fear, ignorance, bigotry, and smear," declared Maine Senator Margaret Chase Smith. But for four years McCarthy managed to terrorize the nation by attacking those who crossed him or whose demise could serve his purposes.

The National Witch-Hunt

McCarthy was not the only Grand Inquisitor during these years. HUAC regularly announced investigations of major American institutions such as Hollywood, the teaching profession, trade unions, and the Protestant churches and then held highly publicized hearings where witnesses were forced to answer questions about their membership in the Communist party. The committee was especially interested in media celebrities—actors, writers, producers, and playwrights—whose presence guaranteed a flood of publicity and justified the committee's continued existence. Some of the nation's most creative people were dragged before the committee including Arthur Miller, Elia Kazan, Lillian Hellman, and Dashiell Hammett. Many of those subpoenaed had indeed flirted with the far left during the 1930s and joined some of the front organizations on the Attorney General's List. Some had been actual Communist party members. But none had spied on their nation. And in any case a democratic society accepts the right of anyone to embrace unorthodox opinions no matter how unpopular. Unfortunately in the heated atmosphere of the day admitting to membership in the Communist party or a front group could ruin a career or a reputation. And if the accused were willing to admit their own political errors, the committee then insisted that they "name names," that is, implicate other people who had shared their views and their former radical activities. Many people who were willing to confess that they had made a mistake themselves were reluctant to squeal on others. Generally the only defense against this process was to plead the Fifth Amendment, the part of the Bill of Rights that allows an accused person to be silent to avoid self-incrimination. "Taking the Fifth" enabled the accused to refuse answers to HUAC questions without prosecution. But it branded one a Communist anyway and produced the same personal stigma as an outright admission of Communist party membership.

The quest for "disloyalty" in these years permeated almost every corner of American life. Colleges, municipalities, and states demanded loyalty oaths of employees as a condition of employment. Private wage earners, especially in the media, were investigated with the help of professional red-hunters who claimed to be skilled in the job of sniffing out subversives. People usually had the right to challenge accusers, but it was often difficult and expensive to clear one's name. Hundreds of completely innocent people fell victim to the excessive zeal or malice of accusers with no effective recourse.

And the federal courts, bowing to the hysteria of the day, failed to protect civil liberties. In 1949 the federal government indicted eleven top leaders of the Communist party for violating the 1940 Smith Act, a measure making it illegal to advocate or teach the overthrow of the government by force and violence. The trial resulted in conviction and prison terms for the defendants. In 1951 in *Dennis* v. *U.S.,* the Supreme Court upheld the right of the government to try people for subversion on the basis of membership in a political party.

The 1952 Election

As the 1952 presidential election approached, the public had become disillusioned with the Truman administration. The little man from Missouri had checked Soviet expansionism in Europe and helped to restore the European economy. But in Asia the United States was hopelessly bogged down in an expensive, no-win war. At home matters seemed to be in a mess as well. Not everybody accepted the McCarthyite view of a nation riddled with disloyalty, but enough Americans believed the "where there's smoke there's fire" thesis that the administration seemed lax in its anti-Communist vigilance.

It also seemed tinged with corruption. No one seriously accused Harry Truman of personal dishonesty, but it was clear that he was surrounded by subordinates who took advantage of inside information or personal contacts to arrange lucrative federal contracts for businesspeople. Such influence peddlers usually charged a 5 percent fee for any contract successfully negotiated. The most blatant offender was General Harry Vaughan, Truman's military aide, who used his influence to get favors for businesspeople, mostly in exchange for contributions to the Democratic party but also, in one case, for a food freezer for his personal use. There was also corruption in the Reconstruction Finance Corporation (RFC), where several of the president's Missouri cronies extended large RFC loans in exchange for favors, including a $9500 mink coat. The Bureau of Internal Revenue, it came out, was also riddled with corrupt officials who took bribes to arrange lower tax bills for private citizens. These scandals produced a wave of prosecutions and convictions and reinforced the impression that Truman and the Democrats had lost their grip.

Gallup polls during 1950–52 showed an approval rating for the president at no more than 25 percent. Three out of four Americans did not believe he was doing a good job. In February 1951 the Twenty-second Amendment to the Constitution, prescribing a maximum of two terms to the president, became the law of the land. The amendment exempted Truman; nonetheless on March 29, months before the 1952 national conventions, he announced that he would not run for another full term.

With the race open on the Democratic side for the first time in twenty years, the competition became intense. Truman's withdrawal made Senator Estes Kefauver of Tennessee, whose investigations of organized crime had attracted national attention, the Democratic front-runner for a time. But the party bosses deplored Kefauver's excessive zeal in connecting racketeers with the big city Democratic machines. The president too disliked Kefauver, who had attacked him for laxity in cleaning up his administration.

Truman favored the governor of Illinois, Adlai Stevenson, the grandson and namesake of Grover Cleveland's second vice president. A thoughtful and eloquent patrician, Stevenson had been elected governor of Illinois on a reform ticket and had established a reputation as a clean-government, moderate liberal. In 1952 he was something of a hero to civil libertarians for his courageous deposition during Alger Hiss's perjury trial endorsing Hiss's reputation for integrity. But Stevenson preferred another term as Illinois governor to the Democratic nomination. His reluctance did not stop his supporters who included, besides the president, the party's ADA liberals and the southern leaders. At the Chicago convention, in something close to an authentic draft, they nominated Stevenson on the third ballot with Senator John Sparkman of Alabama as his running mate.

The Republicans had met two weeks earlier in the Windy City and nominated Dwight Eisenhower and Richard Nixon to head their ticket in November. The choice of "Ike" was a victory for the party's moderates and internationalists who opposed Robert Taft as too conservative and isolationist.

For a time both parties had considered Eisenhower, a man with no clear-cut political affiliations. As late as November 1951 Truman had asked him to consider the Democratic nomination, but Eisenhower had noted that his family affiliation had always been Republican. Yet the general, like Stevenson, was unwilling to actively seek the nomination, wanting it to come to him by acclamation. His Republican supporters took him at his word and had soon organized Citizens for Eisenhower clubs and entered his name in the primaries.

Early in April 1952 Eisenhower asked to be relieved as head of NATO forces in Europe. On June 2 he formally opened his campaign for the Republican nomination with a speech that combined conservative domestic principles with an endorsement of America's international commitments.

Ike came into the Chicago Republican convention with a hard fight on his hands. He had won most of the popular primaries, but the regular delegates from the boss-controlled states had "Taft" written on their hearts. In the end they followed their heads rather than their hearts. The polls showed Eisenhower would win in November; Taft would lose. Ike went over the top on the first ballot. It was, of course, the usual practice for the presidential nominee to chose his running mate with the delegates merely confirming it. Ike did not know this and, in a move borrowed from military staff decision-making practices, called in his supporters and asked them to make the choice. Tom Dewey thereupon named Richard Nixon, the young senator from California, who had made his reputation in the Hiss case.

We Like Ike!

The campaign held few surprises. Stevenson, as expected, proved to be an eloquent, witty, and effective campaigner. But he carried on his back the incubus of Korea, the Truman scandals, and the public's weariness with thirty years of Democratic rule. Eisenhower was a poor speaker with a talent for muddled and nebulous pronouncements. But his middle-American accent, folksy demeanor, and open, cheerful face inspired confidence. He seemed everyone's nice, competent, but undemanding grandfather. After a while, moreover, Stevenson's wit and urbanity began to seem an assertion of his intellectual superiority to his fellow citizens. The Democratic candidate was soon being sneered at as an "egghead."

For a brief period the Democrats thought they had a winning issue when they uncovered a secret "trust fund" financed by rich Californians to help pay Nixon's political expenses. The fund was not illegal, and Nixon was not the only politician who benefited from such largess. Yet it looked suspicious and threatened to cripple the Republican campaign. For a time there was serious talk among Republicans of replacing Nixon as the vice presidential candidate. Then Dewey offered a way out. Nixon should appear on national television and explain himself. If the public response was overwhelmingly favorable he would stay; if not, he would resign.

Nixon gave the speech of his life. He denied that he had received any money personally from the fund and went on to give a family financial statement. He included as his chief assets two heavily mortgaged dwellings, one a small house in California where his parents were living, the other the modest house in Washington. He also listed a two-year old Oldsmobile. His wife Pat, he noted, did not have a mink coat like some of the Democrats' wives. But she looked good in her "respectable Republican cloth coat." In a few sentences the senator had established strong rapport with millions of American wage earners.

The vice presidential candidate now waxed sentimental. It is true that he had taken one gift from a constituent. A benefactor had sent a cocker spaniel to his two little daughters, and Tricia, the six year old, had named it Checkers. "[R]egardless of what they say about it, we're going to keep it." Ever after the talk would be called Nixon's Checkers Speech.

The public loved the speech. Secretaries cried; strong men choked up. Favorable letters poured in to the Republican National Committee. Eisenhower, who had received a special tax exemption for his royalties from *Crusade in Europe,* his best-selling account of World War II, had not liked Nixon's suggestion that all the candidates reveal their personal finances. He never forgave the senator, yet he could count the letters and read the poll results. Nixon stayed on the ticket.

Thereafter the Republican campaign was back on the track. Ike clinched the race on October 24 when he promised that if elected he would go to Korea and settle the stalemate. The Democrats called it a stunt, but many Americans felt it might just do the trick. It made a difference. "For all practical purposes," commented an Associated Press reporter, "the contest ended that night." The results on election day were: Eisenhower-Nixon, 33.9 million; Stevenson-Sparkman, 27.3 million. The Republicans had carried several key southern states and gained control of both houses of Congress by narrow margins. It was a major turnover. (See Figure 1–6.) Describing his feelings, Stevenson used a Lincoln story. After losing an election, Lincoln had said he felt like a small boy who had stubbed his toe in the dark: "he was too old to cry but it hurt too much to laugh."

The Cold War's Distortions

The years immediately following World War II were a time of renewal and new found private satisfactions for many Americans. Times were good and many people felt an expansive sense of new possibilities. And yet hovering over everything was the fear and anxiety that accompanied the Cold War.

However generated, the Cold War had baleful effects on the nation's life in the 1950s. Unused to world political leadership, Americans found the frustrations of international power politics and the ambiguities of Cold War competition difficult to abide. Under unfamiliar pressures they lost their sense of proportion and their respect for dissenting opinions and descended to practices that betrayed the country's best

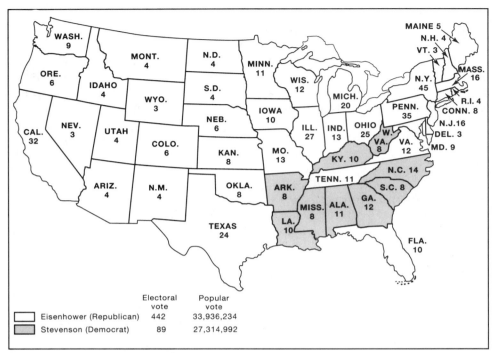

Figure 1–6 The 1952 Presidential Election

tradition of fair play. America in the fifties was a prosperous nation under a cloud. Common sense would finally take hold and the worst excesses abate, but McCarthyism had poisoned the political and intellectual atmosphere in unfortunate ways.

FOR FURTHER READING

On the readjustment of veterans the best work is R. J. Havighurst, et al., *The American Veteran Back Home: A Study of Veteran Readjustment* (1951).

The suburbanization of American life and values during the immediate post–World War II years is described critically in John Keats, *The Crack in the Picture Window* (1957) and Richard Gordon et al., *The Split Level Trap* (1960) Two more-recent works on suburbia are Landon Jones, *Great Expectations: America and the Baby Boom Generation* (1980) and Kenneth Jackson's, *Crabgrass Frontier: The Suburbanization of the United States* (1985).

Equally critical of the values of a business society are William H. Whyte, *The Organization Man* (1955) and the novel by Sloan Wilson, *The Man in the Grey Flannel Suit* (1955). A critical and highly influential view of composite American character as it had evolved by the 1950s is the work by David Reisman et al., *The Lonely Crowd* (1958). A sharp indictment of women's status after 1945, as well as a mark of change, is Betty Friedan's *The Feminine Mystique* (1963). More favorable treatments of the suburban experience are Scott Donaldson, *The Suburban Myth* (1969) and Herbert Gans, *The Levittowners: Ways of Life and Politics in a New Suburban Community* (1967). On how blacks have been excluded from the suburban experience see Michael Danielson, *The Politics of Exclusion* (1976).

The economy of the 1950s is covered in Harold Vatter, *The U.S. Economy in the 1950s: An*

Economic History (1963). Two influential contemporary works are John K. Galbraith, *The Affluent Society* (1952) and his *American Capitalism: Countervailing Power* (1956).

Much has been written on the Truman Fair Deal era. For two overall views see Alonzo Hamby, *Beyond the New Deal: Harry S. Truman and American Liberalism* (1973) and Robert Ferrell *Harry Truman and the Modern American Presidency* (1982). Specialized studies of political events during the Truman period include Allen Matusow, *Farm Policies and Politics in the Truman Administration* (1967); Arthur McClure, *The Truman Administration and the Problems of Postwar Labor* (1969); Susan Hartmann, *Truman and the 80th Congress* (1971); and Richard Davies, *Housing Reform During the Truman Administration* (1966).

On the famous election of 1948 see Irwin Ross, *The Loneliest Campaign: The Truman Victory of 1948* (1968); Norman Markowitz, *The Rise and Fall of the People's Century: Henry A. Wallace and American Liberalism, 1941–1948* (1973); and William Barnard, *Dixiecrats and Democrats: Alabama Politics, 1942–1950* (1974).

More has been written about the Cold War than about any other event of the post-1945 era. The issue divided the nation and the division is reflected in the literature. A standard mainstream liberal study of the early phase is Herbert Feis, *From Trust to Terror: The Onset of the Cold War, 1945–1950* (1970). Also see John L. Gaddis, *The United States and the Origins of the Cold War, 1941–1947* (1972) and Adam Ulam, *Containment and Co-existence* (1974). Left revisionist studies that tend to lay the blame for the Soviet-American confrontation at America's door include Joyce and Gabriel Kolko, *The Limits of Power: The World and U.S. Foreign Policy, 1945–1954* (1972) and Richard Barnett, *Intervention and Revolution* (1969). A study of the left revisionists is Robert W. Tucker's *The Radical Left and American Foreign Policy* (1978).

Specific studies of Truman period foreign policy initiatives include William H. McNeill, *Greece: American Aid in Action, 1947–1956* (1957); Hadley Arkes, *Bureaucracy, the Marshall Plan, and the National Interest* (1973); and Bruce Kuklick, *American Policy and the Division of Germany* (1972). American far eastern policy during this period is covered in Herbert Feis, *The China Tangle* (1953).

On the Korean War the best works are Glenn Paige, *The Korean Decision* (1968); David Rees, *Korea: The Limited War* (1964); John Spanier, *The Truman-MacArthur Controversy and the Korean War* (1965); and Clay Blair, Jr.'s behemoth volume, *The Forgotten War: America in Korea, 1950–1953* (1987).

The McCarthy era red scare has also spawned an immense literature. For a sharp general critique of the anti-Communist crusade see David Caute, *The Great Fear: The Anti-Communist Purge under Truman and Eisenhower* (1978). A good anti-McCarthy treatment is Richard Rovere's *Senator Joe McCarthy* (1959). Also see David Oshinsky, *A Conspiracy So Immense: The World of Joe McCarthy* (1983). For defenses of McCarthy and of the anti-Communist purges during the Truman–Eisenhower years see William F. Buckley, Jr., and L. Brent Bozell, *McCarthy and His Enemies* (1954) and Victor Lasky and Ralph de Toledano, *The Seeds of Treason* (1950). The best study of the Hiss affair is Allen Weinstein, *Perjury: The Hiss-Chambers Case* (1978). On HUAC's inquisitorial mode as directed toward Hollywood see Victor Navasky, *Naming Names* (1980). The most effective defense of the era's anti-Communism is Whittiker Chambers's *Witness* (1958). An interesting recent study of the Rosenberg case is Ronald Radosh and Joyce Milton, *The Rosenberg File: A Search for the Truth* (1983).

The 1952 election is dealt with in Heinz Elau, *Class and Party in the Eisenhower Years* (1962). For Adlai Stevenson see Kenneth Davis, *A Prophet in His Own Country* (1957). Nixon writes about his problems during the 1952 campaign in *Six Crises* (1962).

2
Culture and Public Affairs during the Eisenhower Years

Elvis Presley, "the King," elicits a typical reaction from fans during a 1956 performance.
(UPI/Bettmann Newsphotos)

Ideas and Values

Compared to the decade that followed, the years of the Eisenhower presidency seem intellectually timid and conformist. In some ways they were; but the period was also a time of needed political consolidation and of creativity in painting, literature, and the popular arts.

The intellectual climate of the 1950s was clearly more conservative than that of the 1930s. During the Depression era the country's most prestigious thinkers had criticized their society from the left of the political spectrum. After 1945 a new mood of affirmation, even self-congratulation, appeared within the American intellectual community.

Some observers have ascribed the new attitude to repression and timidity. And surely fear of McCarthyism was a element in the decline of the left critique. Equally important, however, was the disillusionment of many intellectuals with the Soviet Union and an honest rediscovery of a free society's virtues. The Soviet's paranoia and repressiveness under the cruel dictator Stalin, as confirmed by his successor Nikita Khrushchev in 1956, virtually destroyed any lingering pro-Soviet feelings among all but the most committed Communist party members. Many former supporters of the Soviet Union not only repudiated their political past but came to see the United States as the chief bulwark against Soviet expansionism. And there was also the apparent success of the American economy. Postwar America, after all, was a prosperous land where capitalism, as modified and softened by welfare state safeguards, seemed to have succeeded. What sense did the Marxist critique now make? In 1960 a former Marxist, Daniel Bell, published a collection of essays whose title, *The End of Ideology*, was the requiem for the radical intellectual mood of the immediate past.

The American Celebration

The postwar intellectuals reinforced the celebratory mood of the day in a succession of historical, sociological, and economic essays and books. John K. Galbraith's 1952 work *American Capitalism* admitted to the growth of industrial concentration, but claimed that its political and economic dangers had been offset by the "countervailing" rise of labor unions, the advent of discount retail chains, and the appearance of big government. In American history Daniel Boorstin, Louis Hartz, and Oscar Handlin sought to replace "conflict" views of the American past as formerly expounded by "progressive" historians like Charles Beard and Marxist scholars like Louis Hacker with the "consensus" position that Americans had always agreed on the fundamentals—democracy and private property—and had argued primarily over secondary matters. Political scientists like Robert Dahl meanwhile asserted that decision-making power in American society was not confined to a small elite but resided in a plurality of pressure groups.

Anticonformists

Some social thinkers, inevitably, continued to serve as dissenters and gadflies, but more and more they attacked from the elitist right rather than the proletarian left. John

Keats, in *The Crack in the Picture Window* (1957), depicted suburbia and its inhabitants as intellectually dead and culturally vacuous. William Whyte's *The Organization Man* (1956) disparaged the new, conformist executive class who had come to the top in the postwar years. A similar point was made by Sloan Wilson's novel, *The Man in the Gray Flannel Suit* (1955). The most memorable attack of all came from the sociologists David Riesman, Nathan Glazer, and Reuel Denney in *The Lonely Crowd* (1950). The book, a remarkable best-seller, described with barely disguised disapproval the advent of the new, postwar Americans who lacked any strong inner values and took their cues from the mass society around them. Their predecessors had been "inner directed," guided by internal moral and intellectual "gyroscopes"; the new breed were "other directed," their behavior governed by built-in "radar sets." The new social critics in general disliked mass society and all its tastes including television, big cars with flamboyant tailfins, shopping malls, and ranch-style houses.

Religion and Conservatism

The religious mood of the 1950s was also conservative. From the 1890s onward, although fundamentalism held sway in the hinterland, mainstream American Protestant thought had been liberal, both in theology and in its social orientation. The beliefs in progress, innate human goodness, and perfectability had been incorporated into the Social Gospel preached from the pulpits of a thousand urban Protestant churches.

All versions of religion prospered during the fifties. In 1940 less than half the population of the United States were members of churches; by the late 1950s over 63 percent belonged to some organized religious congregation. There was in this period much talk in the press about the "return to God"; Bible sales soared; politicians turned pious. In 1954 Congress added "under God" to the Pledge of Allegiance and adopted "In God We Trust" as the national motto. One important religious trend was the decline in *sectarianism* and the growth of *ecumenicism,* a unifying impulse among the major faiths. Increasingly during these years there was talk of the "Judeo-Christian tradition," a phrase that sought to embrace Protestants, Catholics, and Jews in a single religious community.

To some degree the greater religiosity of the postwar era was connected with the Cold War. The Communist enemies were atheists; Americans would be believers. It was also associated with the surge to suburbia. Joining a church or a synagogue was one way to reestablish social connections in a new community. It also represented a desire to conform by accepting part of the traditional, vaguely defined, American civic religion. For many people it did not run deep or become solidly incorporated into daily life. But for a time it seemed to confirm the nation's growing conservatism.

There was an irony here. If any serious social philosophy informed the typical churchgoer's religious outlook, it was probably vaguely liberal. People could conquer adversity and perfect themselves and society. The clergy, including Norman Vincent Peale, Monsignor Fulton J. Sheen, and Rabbi Joshua Liebman, told millions from their pulpits, through their best-selling books, and, in the case of Bishop Sheen, from the television rostrum that they could be happy and fulfilled if they used religion as their guide. Even such traditional revivalists as the popular preacher Billy Graham, although rooted in Biblical fundamentals, tended to emphasize religion's value for personal problem solving.

But after 1945 new voices began to be heard as well. The experience of the Holocaust, the threat of the atom bomb, the collapse of European world dominance—all made the optimism of the past seem increasingly fatuous and shallow. How innocent or perfectible were human beings after all, if, after five thousand years of civilization, they could destroy millions of human beings without thinking twice and threaten to do so again?

The man who restored the sense of humanity's imperfections and limitations to mainline, urban Protestantism was the theologian Reinhold Niebuhr, himself a political liberal who believed democracy valid, if only by default. Niebuhr reembraced the venerable Christian doctrine of original sin, long ignored by liberal Protestantism. Without accepting literally the account in Genesis of Adam and Eve's fall and expulsion from the Garden of Eden for defying God, he believed that people were inevitably fallible creatures who could never expect to be entirely free of hate, selfishness, greed, envy, and ambition. The "irreducible irrationality of human nature," he exclaimed, must be acknowledged. Only God was without blemish, and humankind's belief in its own perfectability represented the sin of pride. Under the circumstances there was no reason to believe that any actions of humanity would eliminate evil from the world.

It was during the fifties that, for the first time, a self-conscious conservative intelligentsia took shape. Some of these thinkers, notably Russell Kirk, drew on the conservative tradition of Edmund Burke, the eighteenth-century British political philosopher who had defended traditional society against the excesses of the French Revolution. Others, associated with William F. Buckley, Jr., of the new conservative journal *National Review,* drew from Catholic tradition. Buckley had burst on the intellectual scene in 1951 when, just out of Yale, he had attacked the liberal consensus at elite American universities in his book *God and Man at Yale* (1951). In 1955 the witty, acerbic—and rich—young man founded the *National Review* as a forum for conservative opinion.

The Arts

Painting

During the immediate postwar period the art capital of the Western world moved from Paris to New York. Until the postwar era twentieth-century American painting had been either derivative or provincial. Often trained in France, Italy, or Germany, American painters had followed the lead of the French Impressionists or, later, the Cubists. The naturalistic painters of the pre–World War I Ashcan School had produced some interesting work, but none of it was of world class. During the rebellious 1930s *social realism,* intended to make art an auxiliary of revolution, became popular in the United States. Painters in this mode—Ben Shahn, Jack Levine, William Gropper, Isabel Bishop—depicted weather-beaten farmers or workers, careworn mothers, and down-and-outers, subjects victimized by adversity or oppression. They also painted allegories of political and social injustice including race riots and the Sacco-Vanzetti case. Much of it was unsubtle and mediocre.

Then in the years immediately following the war a new group of American painters—Jackson Pollock, Willem de Kooning, Robert Motherwell, Mark Rothko, Franz Kline, Joan Mitchell, and others—broke out of the conventions of the past and created a dazzling new style that would be called by several names: *Action Painting, Abstract Expressionism,* or the *New York School.*

The action painters, like several previous generations of American artists, lived, worked, and caroused mostly in the lofts and studios of New York's Greenwich Village. But they differed from their predecessors in their conception of what a painting was. They were uninterested in representation. A painting was a visual object that should follow the flat planes of the canvas. Unlike most other artifacts of modern life that were planned and regular, it should be spontaneous. Robert Motherwell in 1950 noted that in the view of his colleagues the "process of painting . . . is conceived of as an adventure, without preconceived ideas." "The need" was for "felt experience—

Seated Woman I, a painting by Abstract Expressionist Willem de Kooning. As in this work, de Kooning did not always eliminate all representational elements. (The Bettmann Archive)

intense, immediate, direct, subtle, unified, warm, vivid, rhythmic." Action painters dripped, threw, smeared, and splattered paint on canvas to create splashes of color, lines, and shapes. Their critics claimed that the whole enterprise was a fraud; their paintings could have been done by monkeys. Their friends saw it as a creative revolution in visual art equal to any of the great aesthetic breakthroughs of the past.

Perhaps carried along by America's postwar power and prestige, the New York abstract expressionists swept the Western art world. They had intended to break out of the limited mold of American provincialism and by the mid-fifties had done so. By that time they were acclaimed throughout Europe, once the sole custodian of the Western art tradition. In 1954 the art critic Clement Greenberg, one of the discoverers of the abstract expressionists, noted that at the recent international Biennale exhibition in Venice, de Kooning's exhibition had "put to shame . . . that of every other painter his age or under."

Literature

American literary achievement during the fifties was not as surprising. For a century individual American writers had enjoyed international recognition. Yet during the 1950s American novels, poetry, and plays won unusual worldwide acclaim.

Two of the literary giants of the fifties were the novelists Ernest Hemingway and William Faulkner. Both received Nobel prizes in the decade, but both were already relics of another era. Hemingway, especially, seemed caught in a rut of monosyllabic supermasculinity. On the other hand the poets Robert Frost and Robert Lowell still had "miles to go." Much of their best work would be done during the two decades following the war.

Of the new crop of writers Norman Mailer, a young man from Brooklyn, was among the most interesting. Mailer's first work, *The Naked and the Dead* (1948), was a war novel in the adversary style of 1930s realist fiction with liberal good guys and semifascist bad guys. Mailer would remain a radical of some sort but increasingly, he become the agent for a new cultural sensibility, one permeated by the quest for sensation through sex, drugs, and violence. In his influential essay, "The White Negro" (1957), Mailer praised the "hipster," the permanent outsider of the ghetto who lived dangerously, in the total present, defying the law and seeking ever more powerful "highs." Mailer was addicted to excess. "The White Negro" praised as a courageous existentialist the ghetto hoodlum who beats in the head of a candy store owner.

Another new novelist who made the military his province was James Jones. *From Here to Eternity,* about army life just before Pearl Harbor as seen through the sensibility of an enlisted man, was the sensation of 1951 and sold four million copies.

During the 1950s the young found their inspiration and recognized their voice in Holden Caulfield, the adolescent hero of J. D. Salinger's *Catcher in the Rye* (1951). The work fits the description by Richard Ohmann of "*the* story" of the fifties novel in which "social contradictions [are] . . . easily displaced into images of personal illness." The sixteen-year-old Holden is a sensitive, rebellious young upper middle-class New Yorker who struggles for authenticity in an adult world full of insincere phonies who lie to themselves and their children. The book became a spectacular hit with the literate young because it spoke to them directly in a way they had never before been addressed and partly, no doubt, because libraries, school boards and even state legislatures, disliking its occasional obscenities and sexual words, tried to ban it. *Catcher's* popularity transformed Salinger into a figure of veneration, a reverence tinged with mystery when he shortly withdrew from the public world and became a quasi-hermit in Vermont.

Serious American theater flourished during the 1950s. Eugene O'Neill, although the twenties were his glory days, had a final burst of creativity during the postwar years with *The Iceman Cometh* (1946) and *Long Day's Journey into Night* (1956). New theatrical figures of great talent included Arthur Miller whose plays *Death of a Salesman* (1948), *The Crucible* (1953), and *A View from the Bridge* (1955) dealt with the personal and social penalties of conformity; and Tennessee Williams, a southerner, whose *The Glass Menagerie* (1945), *A Streetcar Named Desire* (1947), and *Cat on a Hot Tin Roof* (1955) depicted the interplay between illusion and reality that seemed especially vivid in the South.

Southerners and Jews, two social groups hitherto on the edges of American cultural life, came into their literary own during the fifties. Faulkner and Williams were both southern writers, but they were joined by a half-dozen others during the postwar era. Three of the most impressive were Flannery O'Connor, a young Georgia woman, whose "gothic" novels and short stories, including *Wise Blood* (1952) and *A Good Man Is Hard to Find* (1955), depict "grotesque" mountebanks, charlatans, rascals, and characters on the edge of dissolution and decay; William Styron whose *Lie Down in Darkness* (1951) concerns the tragic life and death of a southern girl; and Truman Capote whose *Other Voices, Other Rooms* (1948) dealt with a thirteen-year-old boy who finds, in a spooky, decrepit plantation house with its eccentric inhabitants, his real, although dismaying, self.

Writers who revealed in their work the special irony, skepticism, sense of paradox, and taste for gallows humor that grew out of the American Jewish experience—Bernard Malamud, Philip Roth, and Saul Bellow—also made their mark in this period. Malamud wrote about a generation of Jews still close to their Eastern European roots. *The Assistant* (1957) tells of an Italian clerk employed by a poor Jewish grocer who, when his boss dies, takes on the sorrows and burdens of his employer's life. *A New Life* (1961) is about a Jewish professor from New York in the unfamiliar environment of a far western university. Roth burst on the scene in 1959 with *Goodbye Columbus,* a collection of short works, dealing with the tensions and compromises of Jewish assimilation into prosperous postwar America. The most universalistic of the new Jewish writers was Saul Bellow, a Montreal-born Chicagoan, whose characters in *Seize the Day* (1956) and *Henderson the Rain King* (1959), whatever their ostensible ethnicity, partake of the Jewish experience of survival in the face of adversity.

There were also signs during the decade of a major African-American literary awakening in the work of Ralph Ellison, whose novel *The Invisible Man* (1952) powerfully evokes the social and psychological marginality experienced by black Americans. Another African-American novelist, whose fame would not peak until the following decade, was James Baldwin. Baldwin's *Go Tell it on the Mountain* (1953) dealt with the black migration from the South to the urban ghettos of the North.

The Beats

The *Beat generation* was the fifties' boldest departure from the existing literary tradition. The Beats were social and intellectual rebels strongly influenced, simultaneously, by the underground world of African-American musicians and by the mysticism of Eastern Buddhism. A number were homosexuals who, in the repressive fifties world, found themselves inevitably cast in the role of cultural outsider. Beats despised the "square" suburban, striving, materialist America that had emerged after the war and glorified spontaneity, free instinctual expression, and a relaxed, nonassertive approach to life. Allen Ginsberg, the outstanding Beat bard, would later say that the movement he helped to lead meant "the return to nature and the revolt against the machine."

The first Beats were young men attending Columbia University in New York or living in its environs and included Ginsberg, Jack Kerouac, Neal Cassady, and John Clellon Holmes. They soon linked up with a parallel circle of avant-garde writers in the San Francisco Bay Area. On the West Coast the new literary mood was nurtured by Kenneth Rexroth, a radical critic left over from the thirties, and a young poet, Lawrence Ferlinghetti, whose North Beach bookstore, City Lights, became a sponsor and publisher of the new literary movement.

The Beat literary movement burst onto the reading public's consciousness in 1957 with the publication of Kerouac's *On the Road*, a sprawling picaresque novel of two young men crisscrossing the country by car, experiencing the sounds, tastes, looks, and feels of fifties America like primitives from an alien culture. Although attacked as "typing, not writing," the book sold a half-million copies and put the Beat movement on the map. Ginsberg's long poem "Howl" was a powerful attack on mainstream American society, which he referred to as "Moloch" (after the fearsome god of the ancient Phoencians to whom children were sacrificed), whose "mind is pure machinery! . . . whose blood is running money! . . . whose fingers are ten armies!" Although poetry is seldom as popular as prose, "Howl" struck a resounding chord among the educated restless young and helped shift the country's cultural consciousness.

The Beats soon become role models for a portion of the rebellious young. Defiant young "Beatniks" flocked to low-rent neighborhoods in a few of the country's most cosmopolitan cities, where they lived in sparsely furnished apartments and, like other bohemians before them, challenged the values and sexual taboos of their middle-class parents. Beatniks adopted a distinctive dress style. The men wore sloppy work clothes and sneakers or sandals; the women wore black leotards, drooping peasant skirts, no lipstick, and pony tails. Both sexes smoked marijuana, practiced free love and played at being "creative," with words, or paint, or guitars.

Rock and Roll

The typical beatnik was a young person with artistic yearnings and some higher education, but the mass of adolescents and young adults found other ways to express their rebelliousness. From the beginning of this century the young have often adopted the music of outsiders, of racial minorities, and of the underclass as a way to distance themselves from their parents and their values. Before World War I ragtime played this role. During the twenties it was New Orleans style jazz. In the immediate postwar period folk music, originally cultivated by the political left to express its solidarity with "the people," attracted some of the more-literate young. So did "bebop," the new postwar "cool" or "progressive" jazz style of Dizzie Gillespie, Charlie Parker, Miles Davis, and other sophisticated black musicians. But the real music of post–World War II adolescents was *rock and roll.*

Rock music was woven of many strands. It borrowed from black music—"gospel" and "rhythm and blues." It also incorporated "country," the style of the white, rural South and Southwest. It contained elements of jazz. Rock's original base was the black urban ghettos, but it spread to the larger white community when, in 1951, Alan Freed, a Cleveland disc jockey, began to play rhythm and blues over his station. In 1954 Freed came to WINS in New York where he provided the new music with a greatly expanded showcase.

Rock remained ghetto-rooted until toned-down and prettified. Its first commercially successful practitioner was probably Bill Haley, a white disc jockey from Philadelphia. Haley's hit record of 1954, "Rock Around the Clock," derived from black musician Ike Turner's "Shake, Rattle, and Roll," brought all the strands together and gave a name to the new music. Other musicians—Buddy Holly, the Everly Brothers, "Little" Richard Penniman—quickly came out with their versions of rock and furthered the evolutionary process. Although rock rolled through the cultural world on its own merits, the process was helped immeasurably by record company promotion, the new 45 rpm record, and media showcases like the television program "American Bandstand."

The most famous, or infamous, of the early rock stars was Elvis Presley, a slender young white Mississippian with a smooth black pompadour and sideburns, "bedroom eyes," and pouting lips. Presley had merged the rhythm and blues style of black musicians with white country music and added a large dash of raw sexuality. His suggestive glissandos, heavy rhythmic beat, and swiveling hips excited his audience of young people on the edge of adulthood. (See the photograph opening this chapter.) Older Americans often hated Presley. He seemed a culturally subversive influence. At one point a Jacksonville, Florida, judge threatened to arrest him for impairing the morals of minors. The minors themselves did not seem to mind having their morals impaired; the more their parents objected the better they liked him.

The Commercial Media

Square America had its own popular music and it was not unworthy. The era of "swing" and the big bands—Benny Goodman, Tommy Dorsey, Count Basie, and Glenn Miller—was over, but the musical stage still flourished. In 1943 the musical *Oklahoma,* with scintillating songs by Richard Rogers and Oscar Hammerstein and sophisticated choreography, opened on Broadway to wide acclaim. In 1949 the same musical team created *South Pacific,* with a libretto based on the war stories of James Michener, and appealing melodies such as "Some Enchanted Evening" and "Bali Ha'i."

The nation's chief theatrical showcase was still Broadway in New York, although people elsewhere attended road-company productions of hit Broadway shows, and experimental and repertory companies performed before audiences in other large cities. Most Americans during the fifties, however, satisfied their taste for spectacle and drama through film or television.

The Movies

The years between 1920 and the end of World War II were Hollywood's golden age. This was the era when the major studios—MGM, Twentieth Century Fox, RKO, Warner Brothers, and Paramount—with their vast soundstages and glittering rosters of box-office stars turned out hundreds of movies a year to an immense weekly audience eager for romantic comedies, splashy musicals, cowboy "horse operas," and sentimental dramas. They also produced an occasion "message" film such as the antiwar *All Quiet on the Western Front,* the prison-reform–oriented *I Am a Fugitive from a Chain Gang,* and the sympathetic treatment of the Okie migration to California, *The Grapes of Wrath* .

The large companies made enormous profits not only through movie production, but also because they owned national theater chains that "block-booked" a given studio's whole film output. In 1948 the federal courts declared that the practice violated the antitrust laws and forced the studios to sell off their theater outlets. This quickly ended the studio system. The "majors" soon cut back drastically on their own production and offered their facilities to independent producers who put together "packages" (actors, directors, writers, and camera operators) for a given production.

The change in the industry's structure altered the quality of the product. The independents abandoned the narrow formula movies of the studios and, by and large, produced better, more-original films and fewer "B" efforts. Among the outstanding movies of the fifties were *The African Queen, High Noon, From Here to Eternity, Baby Doll, Shane, Sunset Boulevard, The Wild One, Rebel without a Cause,* and *Some Like It Hot.* But the change in the quality of movies owed even more to the arrival on the scene of a new medium, television, that absorbed the audience for visual potboilers.

The TV Revolution

Television—TV—had been little more than a toy before the war, although by 1939 most of the basic technology had been developed. The war itself preempted electronics production facilities and delayed manufacture of home TV sets. Not until 1946 did the first black-and-white units roll off the assembly lines.

The industry was slow to gain momentum. Television receivers at first were expensive and had small screens; broadcast technique was primitive. It was not possible, for example, to send signals beyond line-of-sight distance, so each station could transmit only to a local audience. In the absence of electronic tape, performances had to be live. And at first there was little to watch.

In May 1947 "Kraft Television Theater" began to broadcast the first live television dramas. Regularly sponsored TV news broadcasting began in the fall of 1947 with the urbane John Cameron Swayze on NBC and Douglas Edwards on CBS as "anchors." But

Television revolutionized American life. These sets, fresh from the assembly line, are being checked. (AP/Wide World Photos)

still the fare was rather thin and the audience limited. New York and Los Angeles were well provided with stations, seven in each, but even some rather large cities—Austin, Texas; Portland, Oregon; and Little Rock, Arkansas—had none as late as 1952.

By the early fifties, however, the networks had launched some of their top shows, including Milton Berle's "Texaco Star Theater" and Ed Sullivan's "Toast of the Town." Also widely popular was the sitcom "I Love Lucy" featuring Lucille Ball and her husband, Desi Arnez, and the ninety-minute-long variety program "Your Show of Shows," with the hilarious Sid Caesar and Imogene Coca.

Even before the first coast-to-coast hookup in 1951, television had begun to alter people's lives. The early owners of sets had been minor celebrities on their block and had to fend off neighbors trying to invite themselves in to see the latest marvel. By 1952 almost twenty million American homes had TV sets, about half the total number of homes. These sets often occupied the place of honor in the family living room, and meals, leisure, bedtimes, and even romance were all modified or postponed to accommodate it. Family closeness and interaction suffered, or at least underwent a major change. No family institution could stand up to the attractions of "the tube." To guarantee that family mealtimes would not interfere with favorite programs, Swanson and other food processors developed the frozen TV dinner that could be heated in the oven and eaten in front of the set.

The other media suffered from television's popularity. During the 1930s publishers had preserved their markets during a time of economic slump by developing new printing and packaging techniques. The Depression years had seen the rise of the photo magazines *Life, Look,* and their imitators. During this period book publishers had discovered how to print book pages on the high-speed presses designed for magazines and how to fasten pages firmly to paper covers with glue. These books, generally reprints of hardcover works, could be marketed from train station and drugstore racks and sold for as little as a quarter. This paperback revolution saved many publishers from bankruptcy.

After World War II the publishing industry faced new challenges. Paperback book sales expanded. But taken together the sales of books, magazines, and newspapers, forced to compete with the riveting moving images on the home screen, failed to keep up with the rising population and improving national educational levels.

The movies, already in disarray over the courts' theater divestment ruling, suffered another blow from television. Film attendance dropped sharply. Why bother to pay the money and expend the effort to get to the local movie house when you could sit in the comfort of your living room and see the "I Love Lucy" show for nothing? The movie producers countered the threat with wide-screen Cinerama and then CinemaScope, visual techniques that television could not imitate. They also reached out to a more sophisticated audience than TV, a "family" medium that had to avoid offending parents of young children. Bit by bit the old production code self-censorship forbidding nudity, sexual acts, blasphemy, and obscenity in films began to be relaxed. In 1961 the Supreme Court ruled that film was entitled to First Amendment protection as free speech and states could not impose movie licensing requirements. Not until 1968 did the present system of ratings, from G (family fare, suited to even young children), to X (frank pornography), come into effect. Yet by the end of the fifties films produced in America had attained a level of maturity and honesty at times not much below the legitimate stage.

TV and Politics

Television also affected the political process. The first national conventions to be televised were those of 1948. Both were held in Philadelphia because that city was now connected by cable to New York, Washington, and other eastern and midwestern cities, and millions would be able to see the proceedings. The campaign itself suggested that TV was not, or not yet, a potent political force. Dewey took to the airwaves; Truman, in part to save money, whistle-stopped from the back of trains. And, as we saw, Truman won.

In 1952, however, television made a difference. This time the networks were able to find sponsors for the proceedings. Westinghouse bought the whole convention coverage package on NBC, and millions of older Americans probably remember Westinghouse announcer Betty Furness opening and closing refrigerator doors better than they do the convention itself.

Whether television was responsible or not, Eisenhower's victory in 1952 made the new medium a vital, even governing element, in the political equation. Thereafter, critics would charge, American politics became a contest of competing spectacles and images rather than of competing ideas. The critics exaggerated the importance of issues in pretelevision elections, but there can be no doubt that at times following 1952 the public seemed to judge candidates more for their telegenic qualities than for their intelligence.

There was another side of the coin, however. At times TV could be a remarkable dissector of character and personality, and a brilliant illuminator of events. In 1954 its power to deflate demagogues was demonstrated by the Army-McCarthy hearings (discussed later in this chapter). In later years, too, it would, more than once, serve the republic's citizens well.

The Eisenhower Administration

The party and the people who came to office in January 1953 were not experienced in the art of government. For twenty years the Republicans had been on the outside looking in, playing the relatively easy role of naysayer and critic. Republicanism had come to mean opposition to an active, interventionist federal government, "fiscal responsibility" (balanced federal budgets), and sympathy for the needs of business and the successful middle class. These positions could be maintained in all their purity when the Democrats occupied the White House. It would not be so easy when they, the Republicans themselves, controlled the executive branch. Making matters all the more difficult from 1954 on, the Democrats would control both houses of Congress, with power to veto any major changes their opponents proposed.

Recent scholars, dismayed by the turmoil of the 1960s and by the costly entanglement in Vietnam, have praised the Eisenhower administration effusively. Ike, they say, was personally warm, reassuring, and effective. He accomplished what had to be done, avoiding war, preserving the essentials of the welfare state, and quietly disposing of McCarthy. His was a "hidden-hand presidency," says Princeton political scientist Fred Greenstein. Even Ike's public inarticulateness now seems a virtue to some. His broken syntax and obscurity when he talked to reporters, they say, avoided unnecessary confrontations and papered over difficulties.

In truth Eisenhower presided over the sort of administration that suited the American people in the 1950s. His cabinet, except for Labor Secretary Martin Durkin, a union leader who soon resigned, was drawn from the ranks of business. Critics said it consisted of "eight millionaires and a plumber." Inexperienced in the pieties of democratic politics, they often seemed to confuse the interests of business with those of the American people at large. Charles E. Wilson, the former president of General Motors, aroused a populist storm, even before he was confirmed as secretary of defense when he declared, "What was good for our country was good for General Motors and vice versa." Yet it is probably true that not since the 1920s were Americans as willing to accept the values of the business community as during the 1950s.

For good or ill, the president relied more on his cabinet and other subordinates than most of his predecessors. Ike as president used the same staff system he had employed in the army. He seldom made decisions without reports on the issues from bureaucrats and high officials. These were coordinated by the president's chief aide, former New Hampshire Governor Sherman Adams. Adams also screened the president's many visitors and was often called "Sherm the Firm" or the "Abominable No-Man." But the overall outcome seemed to be indecision. According to participants, cabinet discussions meandered and wandered from the point to a maddening degree; no conclusions ever seemed to be reached.

Legislative Accomplishments

Still many things were accomplished, although liberals did not always like the results. The administration eliminated several outmoded programs that had lasted since New Deal days, including the Reconstruction Finance Corporation, and reduced the number of federal employees by 200,000 during its first term. Adopting the policies of Secretary of Agriculture Ezra Taft Benson, it tried, although unsuccessfully, to whittle down the government's commitment to farm price supports. It cut the federal government's involvement in electric power production and sought to restore a business presence to the Tennessee Valley Authority through a contract with the Dixon-Yates syndicate. This scheme failed when the Democrats uncovered a conflict of interest violation in the key contract negotiation.

Despite the administration's conservative orientation it sponsored some liberal measures. Eisenhower often got along better with the Democratic leadership in Congress than with the right wing of his own party, perhaps in part because like himself, House Speaker Sam Rayburn and Senate Majority Leader (after 1954) Lyndon Johnson, were Texans. With their help he was able to get enacted laws broadening social security coverage to an additional 7.5 million people and improving its benefits, establishing a new Cabinet-level department—Health, Education and Welfare (HEW)—to administer federal welfare and education programs, creating a modest federal housing program for people displaced by urban renewal or slum clearance, and establishing a federal system of grants to states to improve educational facilities. The year after the Soviet Union's successful launching of *Sputnik* in 1957, Congress established the administration-sponsored National Aeronautics and Space Administration (NASA) to coordinate U.S. space efforts and enacted the National Defense Education Act to encourage science and foreign-language training in the nations' schools and colleges.

The Eisenhower era legislation with the most far-reaching effects was the Highway Act of 1956. This bill, strongly supported by the trucking firms, the automobile companies, and the construction industry, authorized the outlay of $32 billion for a forty-one-thousand-mile system of four-lane, limited-access interstate roads to connect every big city in the nation. The program was to be financed by new gasoline taxes the proceeds of which would be placed in a trust fund and reserved for road construction and repair.

The new interstate highway system undoubtedly benefited the nation. It improved highway safety, lowered transportation costs, and stimulated the automobile, trucking, motel, and tourist industries. But it also had its debit side. Railroad passenger traffic plummeted, making Americans increasingly dependent on the private car. Trucks also hurt rail freight revenues. By the mid-1960s the nation's railroad companies were in serious financial straits and passenger service was being drastically curtailed. The new highway system also helped hollow out the city centers. They encouraged suburban development and middle-class flight. By making enormous new shopping centers accessible, the new roads and superhighways cut into downtown business. Before long the business cores of many American cities were a blight of boarded-up stores and empty offices; the customers and the clients had all departed for the outlying suburban shopping malls.

The End of McCarthy

Eisenhower's 1952 victory brought McCarthyism (see the previous chapter) down. But not immediately.

Everyone expected McCarthy to soften his attacks on subversives and "security risks" in government now that his own party was in power. But the senator thrived on publicity and, unwilling to slip back into the shadows, refused to slow his pace.

During the first Eisenhower Congress McCarthy attacked the administration's list of new appointees as riddled with people of suspect loyalty. He and ultraconservative Senate Republicans tried to prevent the appointment of Charles Bohlen as ambassador to the Soviet Union, accusing that long-term public servant of possible disloyalty. When Secretary of State John Foster Dulles came to Bohlen's defense, McCarthy called him a liar and demanded that he testify before the Senate under oath. In the end Bohlen was confirmed, but the clash so bruised the administration that it was reluctant to challenge the senator again.

McCarthy was soon on the rampage once more. His next target was the Voice of America, a federal agency which broadcast news of American positions on issues and events to listeners around the world. In late November 1953 McCarthy attacked the record of the Republican administration in purging Communists from government. It was "infinitely" better than the Democrats', he stated, but it was far from perfect. He also went out of his way to criticize the administration's support of financial aid to Britain when that country continued to trade with our avowed enemy, the People's Republic of China.

Eisenhower abhorred McCarthy. He had never forgiven the Wisconsin senator for his attacks on the president's old army boss George Marshall, and he was infuriated by his criticism of the administration's foreign policy and its record on security risks. But Ike had little taste for slinging mud with the Senator. He also feared the man. By this time McCarthy had thoroughly intimidated virtually everyone in public life. Rather than taking him on directly, the president bided his time waiting for McCarthy's own excesses to bring him down.

These were not long in coming. In early 1954 the senator tangled with the army over its alleged laxity in ferreting out disloyalty. In response the army claimed that McCarthy and his aide Roy Cohn had sought special favors for G. David Schine, a former McCarthy assistant who had recently been drafted. Congress decided to investigate, and authorized hearings before McCarthy's own subcommittee, with the senator replaced temporarily as chairman by Senator Karl Mundt of South Dakota.

The televised Army-McCarthy hearings began in the Senate Caucus Room on April 22, 1954. Eight weeks later McCarthy's shadow over the nation's life had lifted.

McCarthy's nominal adversary was Army Secretary Robert Stevens and the army brass. But his real opponent—and nemesis—was Joseph Welch, the army's puckish, civilian counsel, a shrewd Boston lawyer with a carefully cultivated low-key style. The proceedings were telecast and millions of American tuned in to see the hearings or saw excerpts on the evening news.

The Wisconsin senator came across as a Hollywood villian. A physically unattractive man, his head was too large for his body, his features were coarse, and under the glaring television lights, he could not disguise his permanent five o'clock shadow. He was incapable of obeying the traditional rules of parliamentary order and ordinary civility. He bullied witnesses, interrupted the proceedings with invalid points of order, and frequently contradicted himself without seeming to care. Welch at first bided his time, getting the measure of the man, a type not familiar to Boston's elite. Then gradually he began to reveal how McCarthy had subverted government officials in his pursuit of dirt and how he had falsified evidence regarding the army's relations with Schine.

The hearings concluded with a 7400-page report that blamed both McCarthy and the army. But it soon became clear that the senator had been mortally wounded. McCarthy's approval rating in the polls had dropped 22 percent by August. Even conservative Republicans now concluded that he had outlived his political usefulness.

Even before the hearings ended, Republican Senator Ralph Flanders of Vermont, had introduced a resolution to censure McCarthy on the grounds that his behavior was "contrary to senatorial traditions and tend[ed] to bring the Senate into disrepute." After the hearings the resolution was debated fully. The vote, taken on December 2, condemned McCarthy. His spell was broken. Eisenhower greeted his Cabinet soon after with the joke: "McCarthyism is now McCarthywasm."

And in fact the senator's reign was over. He continued to have followers and he continued to make charges. But the media ceased to take him seriously and often failed to report his latest claims. Worst of all his Senate colleagues now chose to ignore him, and increasingly he became a lonely, isolated man. He died in May 1957 of liver disease brought on by heavy drinking.

The anti-Communist crusade McCarthy had profited from and fostered was by no means over. The far-right John Birch Society, founded by a Boston candy manufacturer in 1959, continued to beat the Communist conspiracy drums and to accuse people of secret subversion. The Birch Society, with chapters in scores of cities, attacked President Eisenhower for communist leanings and mounted a campaign to impeach Chief Justice Earl Warren. A number of organizations, including Billy James Hargis's Christian Crusade and Fred Schwarz's Christian Anti-Communism Crusade, combined religious fundamentalism with a passionate zeal for detecting and rooting out Communist influence in American life. And yet with McCarthy himself gone, the frenzy receded and Americans were able to bring the internal Communist threat into reasonable perspective.

The 1956 Election

Despite President Eisenhower's personal popularity, the Republicans remained the minority party. In 1954 the Democrats recaptured control of both houses of Congress. Nineteen fifty-six, however, promised to be better for the GOP because Ike would head the ticket again. But then in September 1955 the president suffered a

The Eisenhowers (right) and the Nixons at the 1956 Republican National Convention.
(UPI/Bettmann Newsphotos)

heart attack while on vacation in Denver. He sprang back quickly and by early 1956 had resumed his full duties. In March he announced that he would accept renomination. Then in June he suffered another medical mishap and had to be operated on for an intestinal obstruction. He recovered quickly from this affliction too and was renominated, with Nixon again, at the Republican National Convention in San Francisco.

The Democrats turned a second time to Adlai Stevenson, pairing him with Senator Estes Kefauver of Tennessee. Stevenson had thrown the choice of vice presidential candidate to the convention itself, and in the contest Kefauver narrowly defeated the young senator from Massachusetts, John F. Kennedy.

The campaign was uninspiring. Stevenson seemed less sparkling than the first time. He tried to capitalize on fears of the president's mortality and on Ike's penchant for "golfing and goofing." But no matter how ominous Ike's medical record, he now seemed in radiant good health and most Americans did not believe the country had suffered from his inattention. In the end, it was an Eisenhower-Nixon landslide, with the Republican candidates winning 457 electoral votes to 73 and a popular vote majority of 35.6 million to 26 million. But again it was a personal not a party victory. Stevenson's biographer has written that Ike's triumph "expressed the dominant mood of the country and . . . the warm affection he personally inspired." The Democrats actually increased their majorities in both houses of Congress.

The Civil Rights Movement

No group in America benefited as little from social change in the immediate postwar era as African-Americans. By the Eisenhower years there had been some progress on the racial front. During the Truman administration segregation in the armed forces had ended. In 1947 the brave move of Brooklyn Dodgers' manager Branch Rickey to hire Jackie Robinson as second baseman had finally broken the disgraceful Jim Crow barrier in the all-American pastime. There had been, moreover, a slow evolution of antiracist ideas among liberal and better-educated white people influenced by the sociological and anthropological studies of Gunnar Myrdal (*The American Dilemma*) and Melville Herskovits (*Patterns of Negro Segregation*). Yet through the mid-1950s the racial regime that had taken shape after Reconstruction remained in place almost everywhere.

In the North there was no legal basis for segregation or race discrimination. African-Americans could run for office and exercise their right to vote. Government services were, by and large, fairly apportioned. Yet private schools, hotels, employers, landlords, realtors, and restauranteurs excluded blacks or discriminated against them through unspoken agreement. Inevitably bigotry adversely affected the housing, income, education, and health of black people in the northern cities.

The situation in the South was far worse. There segregation by Jim Crow law was still alive and thriving. In almost every aspect of daily life state or local law prescribed separate facilities for black and white citizens. African-American and white children went to separate schools from kindergarten through university graduate and professional programs. Blacks were kept separate from whites on buses, streetcars, trains, and in terminal waiting rooms. African-Americans were not allowed to eat in most restaurants and were excluded from hotels as well as many parks and swimming pools. Churches were either black or white, almost never both. There had been legal challenges to the local and state segregation laws under the "equal protection of the laws" provision of the Fourteenth Amendment of the Constitution, but most of these had been denied. In the landmark case of *Plessy* v. *Ferguson* (1896) the Supreme Court had declared that equal protection could be satisfied if the governments in question guaranteed that the separate facilities were kept roughly equal in quality. But in fact little was done to enforce even this weak protection until well past World War II. Almost everywhere, as the fifties began, the black schools, swimming pools, waiting rooms, and bus facilities were shockingly inferior to their white equivalents.

There was also the crucial issue of voting rights. No one could deny that the Fifteenth Amendment made exclusion from the ballot because of race illegal. Yet in most places in the South African-Americans were kept from voting by rigged registration rules, intimidation, and a flock of subterfuges. The net result of Jim Crow and the absence of basic civil rights was a de facto caste system in the South that made a mockery of American democracy.

The Jim Crow system in the South, begun in the late nineteenth century, meant discrimination and humiliation for African-Americans. (Library of Congress)

The Attack on Jim Crow

During the Eisenhower years came the major breakthroughs that in a decade, would wipe out the Jim Crow system and elevate African-Americans to full citizenship if not full economic and social equality. The change was launched by the National Association for the Advancement of Colored People (NAACP), the African-American defense organization formed before World War I.

The attack began at the educational summit. During the late 1940s the NAACP instituted a series of suits against southern governments for excluding black students from all-white state university graduate and professional programs. The federal courts agreed that the alternatives offered African-American applicants did not meet even the semblance of equality and thus the students could not be excluded.

But these judicial victories only affected a tiny portion of Jim Crow. Then in 1951 Thurgood Marshall, attorney for the NAACP, commenced suit against the segregated public school system of Topeka, Kansas, a northern community with southern principles. Drawing on the work of sociologists and psychologists, Marshall and the other NAACP lawyers charged that separate facilities imposed a damaging psychological and social stigma on African-American children and hence were inherently unequal. On May 17, 1954, in an unanimous decision that ranks with *Marbury* v. *Madison* and *Dred Scott* v. *Sandford* as historic events, the Court accepted this position in *Brown* v. *Board of Education of Topeka*. In "the field of public education," declared Chief Justice Earl Warren, "the doctrine of 'separate but equal' has no place." (See Reading 11.) Soon after this, the Supreme Court directed lower federal courts to require admission of black students to formerly white schools "with all deliberate speed."

The *Brown* decision began the painful destruction of Jim Crow. But it was one thing for the federal courts to rule; it was another to get the relevant authorities to comply. School desegregation, in part or in whole, came quickly in the upper South and neighboring areas, especially Oklahoma, Kentucky, West Virginia, Maryland, Delaware, and Washington, D.C. But in the deep South many officials, with the powerful support of the Ku Klux Klan and a new group, the White Citizens' Councils, vowed to resist.

The next five years were full of fierce contention between African-Americans and their supporters and the conservative intransigents and outright bigots who cried "never" to desegregation. When a twenty-six-year-old African-American woman, Autherine Lucy, attempted to enroll in the University of Alabama in 1956, the Regents resisted, and she was attacked by shouting, stone-throwing mobs. In Clinton, Tennessee, a thousand whites, egged on by John Kasper, a racist zealot from Washington, D.C., rioted when the courts ordered twelve black students admitted to the local high school. The mob overwhelmed the town's small police force and was stopped only when state troopers and National Guardsmen arrived.

In 1957 the federal government itself had to intervene in Little Rock, Arkansas, to enforce the *Brown* decision. Eisenhower had spent most of his professional life in a segregated army and, like many conservatives, believed that you could not force people to be virtuous. "You cannot change the hearts of people by law," he said. Moreover he was skeptical of the *Brown* decision and later announced in private that his most foolish decision had been to appoint Earl Warren to the Supreme Court. But the president also would not allow federal law to be flouted, and at Little Rock when Governor Orval Faubus of Arkansas called up the state National Guard to prevent the admission of African-American students to all-white Central High, Eisenhower ordered in a portion of the 101st Airborne Division to escort the children through the mob of jeering whites who were screaming "Two, four, six, eight, we ain't gone to integrate." The troops' presence infuriated the white supremacists, but they yielded to fixed bayonets. In a few weeks passions had cooled and the escorts ceased. Central High had been desegregated and the law of the land upheld.

There were few other Little Rocks. Most communities acquiesced in the *Brown* decision at least to the point of admitting a token number of African-American students. Many northern cities were for a time spared the problems of integrating the schools by a housing pattern that was itself segregated. Black children could be excluded from white schools simply because they lived in different school districts. Where this process failed to work, white parents sometimes withdrew their children from the public schools entirely and paid tuition to enroll them in private schools. More and more big city schools became all black. However accomplished, school segregation survived as a practical fact. As of the 1962–63 school year less than one-half of one percent of African-American school children in the deep South were attending integrated schools. Yet an immensely important principle had been established: segregation was unconstitutional.

READING 2

The Supreme Court Rules on Public School Segregation

No decision of the United States Supreme Court has had such momentous social consequences as Brown v. Board of Education of Topeka, *delivered on May 17, 1954. The unanimous decision, written by Chief Justice Warren, reversed the ruling of the Court in* Plessy v. Ferguson *(1896) that separate facilities in public accommodations for whites and blacks did not violate the Fourteenth Amendment's equal protection clause as long as they were equal facilities.* Plessy *had allowed fifty years of Jim Crow in the South and had stigmatized millions of African-Americans with the badge of inferiority. Now that the Supreme Court in* Brown *had finally invalidated the separate-but-equal doctrine in the public school systems, the rest of Jim Crow clearly was threatened. In a single brief ruling the Warren Court had broken the racial logjam and launched a social revolution in the South.*

These cases come to us from the States of Kansas, South Carolina, Virginia, and Delaware. They are premised on different facts and different local conditions, but a common legal question justifies their consideration together in this consolidated opinion.

In each of the cases, minors of the Negro race, through their legal representatives, seek the aid of the courts in obtaining admission to the public schools of their community on a nonsegregated basis. In each instance, they have been denied admission to schools attended by white children under laws requiring or permitting segregation according to race. This segregation was alleged to deprive the plaintiffs of the equal protection of the laws under the Fourteenth Amendment. In each of the cases other than the Delaware case, a three-judge federal district court denied relief to the plaintiffs on the so-called "separate but equal" doctrine announced by this Court in Plessy v. Ferguson, 163 U. S. 537. Under that doctrine, equality of treatment is accorded when the races are provided substantially equal facilities, even though these facilities be separate. In the Delaware case, the Supreme Court of Delaware adhered to that doctrine, but ordered that the plaintiffs be admitted to the white schools because of their superiority to the Negro schools.

The plaintiffs contend that segregated public schools are not "equal" and cannot be made "equal," and that hence they are deprived of the equal protection of the laws. Because of the obvious importance of the question presented, the Court took jurisdiction. Argument was heard in the 1952 Term, and reargument was heard this Term on certain questions propounded by the Court.

Reargument was largely devoted to the circumstances surrounding the adoption of the Fourteenth Amendment in 1868. It covered exhaustively consideration of the Amendment in Congress, ratification by the states, then existing practices in racial segregation, and the views of proponents and opponents of the Amendment. This discussion and our own investigation convince us that, although these sources cast some light, is not enough to resolve the problem with which we are faced. At best, they are inconclusive. The most avid proponents of the post-War Amendments undoubtedly intended them to remove all legal distinctions among "all persons born or naturalized in the United States." Their opponents, just as certainly, were antagonistic to both the letter and the spirit of the Amendments and wished them to have the most limited effect. What others in Congress and the state legislatures had in mind cannot be determined with any degree of certainty.

An additional reason for the inconclusive nature of the Amendment's history, with respect to segregated schools, is the status of public education at that time. In the South, the movement toward free common schools, supported by general taxation, had not yet taken hold. Education of white children was largely in the hands of private groups. Education of Negroes was almost nonexistent, and practically all of the race were illiterate. In fact, any education of Negroes was forbidden by law in some states. Today, in contrast, many Negroes have achieved outstanding success in the arts and sciences as well as in the business and professional world. It is true that public education had already advanced further in the North, but the effect of the Amendment on Northern States was generally ignored in the congressional debates. Even in the North, the conditions of public education did not approximate those existing today. The curriculum was usually rudimentary; ungraded schools were common in rural areas; the school term was but three months a year in many states; and compulsory school attendance was virtually unknown. As a consequence, it is not surprising that there should be so little in the history of the Fourteenth Amendment relating to its intended effect on public education.

In the first cases in this Court construing the Fourteenth Amendment, decided shortly after its adoption, the Court interpreted it as proscribing all state-imposed discriminations against the Negro race. The doctrine of "separate but equal" did not make its appearance in this Court until 1896 in the case of Plessy v. Ferguson, supra, involving not education but transportation. American courts have since labored with the doctrine for over half a century. In this court, there have been six cases involving the "separate but equal" doctrine in the field of public education.

In approaching this problem, we cannot turn the clock back to 1868 when the Amendment was adopted, or even to 1896 when Plessy v. Ferguson was written. We must consider public education in the light of its full development and its present place in American life throughout the Nation.

Only in this way can it be determined if segregation in public schools deprives these plaintiffs of the equal protection of the laws.

Today, education is perhaps the most important function of state and local governments. Compulsory school attendance laws and the great expenditures for education both demonstrate our democratic society. It is required in the performance of our most basic public responsibilities, even service in the armed forces. It is the very foundation of good citizenship. Today it is a principal instrument in awakening the child to cultural values, in preparing him for later professional training, and in helping him to adjust normally to his environment. In these days, it is doubtful that any child may reasonably be expected to succeed in life if he is denied the opportunity of an education. Such an opportunity, where the state has undertaken to provide it, is a right which must be made available to all on equal terms.

We come then to the question presented: Does segregation of children in public schools solely on the basis of race, even though the physical facilities and other "tangible" factors may be equal, deprive the children of the minority group of equal educational opportunities? We believe that it does. . . .

To separate them from others of similar age and qualifications solely because of their race generates a feeling of inferiority as to their status in the community that may affect their hearts and minds in a way unlikely ever to be undone. The effect of this separation on their educational opportunities was well stated by a finding in the Kansas case by a court which nevertheless felt compelled to rule against the Negro plaintiffs:

> Segregation of white and colored children in public schools has a detrimental effect upon the colored children. The impact is greater when it has the sanction of the law; for the policy of separating the races is usually interpreted as denoting the inferiority of the Negro group. A sense of inferiority affects the motivation of a child to learn. Segregation with the sanction of law, therefore, has a tendency to retard the educational and mental development of Negro children and to deprive them of some of the benefits they would receive in a racially integrated school system.

Whatever may have been the extent of psychological knowledge at the time of Plessy v. Ferguson, this finding is amply supported by modern authority. Any language in Plessy v. Ferguson contrary to this finding is rejected.

We conclude that in the field of public education the doctrine of "separate but equal" has no place. Separate educational facilities are inherently unequal. Therefore, we hold that the plaintiffs and others similarly situated for whom the actions have been brought are, by reason of the segregation complained of, deprived of the equal protection of the laws guaranteed by the Fourteenth Amendment. This disposition makes unnecessary any discussion whether such segregation also violates the Due Process Clause of the Fourteenth Amendment. . . .

Source: Brown v. Board of Education of Topeka, 347 U.S. 483 (1954).

Martin Luther King, Jr.

Obviously an enormous battle still remained before the anti–Jim Crow decisions of the courts and federal agencies could meaningfully affect the daily lives of African-American southerners. The courts would have to deal with each instance of Jim Crow legislation and then local people would have to challenge racist diehards who sought to keep the practice even after the law was gone. And there still remained the critical problem of voting rights, and beyond that the fundamental issues of job discrimination and black working-class poverty. The federal government, clearly, could help, but it also could not be counted on to send troops to ferret out every violation of federal law and enforce every court order. Black southerners would have to force the issue themselves. The task required new leadership and new tactics, and both suddenly appeared in Montgomery, Alabama, in late 1955.

Montgomery, the capital of Alabama and "Cradle of the Confederacy," was a thoroughly segregated city. Jim Crow was everywhere, but it was encountered in its most humiliating form on the local bus line where, as in other southern cities, African-American passengers were expected to sit at the back of the vehicle and surrender their seats to white passengers whenever the "whites only" section was fully occupied. On December 1, 1955, Rosa Parks, a middle-aged black seamstress returning from a hard day's work in a downtown Montgomery department store, refused to give up her seat to a white passenger who had just gotten on. Mrs. Parks was arrested and fined ten dollars for violating a Montgomery ordinance.

Montgomery African-American leaders, many of them clergymen, had long brooded over the degrading bus system, and they now seized on the occasion to take action. Meeting at the Mt. Zion African Methodist Episcopal Church, they decided to call a boycott of the bus company to last until it had agreed to seat black passengers on a first-come, first-serve basis and hire black bus drivers for runs in black neighborhoods. The company refused, and the boycott began.

The boycott organizers called on the young pastor of the Dexter Avenue Baptist Church, the Reverend Martin Luther King, Jr., to lead the campaign. Although he was still new to the community, King accepted. It was an event that would ring loudly through the decade and beyond.

King was the son of a successful Baptist minister in Atlanta, Georgia, a southern city where racism seldom showed itself brazenly. He had taken his B.A. at all-black Morehouse College and then escaped Jim Crow for a time by going north to study theology at Crosier Seminary in Pennsylvania and take a Ph.D. in philosophy at Boston University. In 1954 he accepted the call to become minister at the Dexter Avenue Church at $4200 a year, the highest salary paid any Montgomery African-American minister.

King's philosophical studies had exposed him to the egalitarian Social Gospel views of Walter Rauschenbusch; the pacifism of the Reverend A. J. Muste; and the nonviolent protest philosophy of Mohandas Gandhi, the anticolonial political leader of India. He was intrigued by nonviolence as a protest tactic, but he was not yet a full believer in Gandhi's *satyagraha,* civil disobedience against the oppressor as a way to defeat oppression.

The fiery, year-long Montgomery bus strike in 1955–56 tempered and matured King. African-American Montgomeryans organized car pools or walked to work to avoid patronizing the Jim Crow bus line. They accepted the sacrifice with good humor. An elderly black woman en route to her job refused an offer of a ride from a white reporter, "My feet is tired, but my soul is rested," she remarked. Most white Montgomeryans feared change. The Ku Klux Klan bombed King's and other boycott leaders' houses and burned black churches. Hotheads in the African-American community were ready to riot, but King knew that counterviolence would only hurt the civil rights cause and restrained them. "We are not advocating violence," he told his followers. "We must love our white brothers no matter what they do to us." King's leadership and Christian message made him a figure of international reputation.

Although badly hurt by the boycott, the bus company held out stubbornly, and defeat only came through a Supreme Court decision on December 20, 1956, declaring Alabama's Jim Crow transportation laws unconstitutional. Shortly before 6 A.M. the following morning, King and his associates boarded a Montgomery city bus, paid their fares, and sat down in front seats.

King's Montgomery success led to the formation in Atlanta early in 1957 of the Southern Christian Leadership Conference (SCLC). Dedicated at first to ending Jim Crow in public transportation, SCLC soon took on all segregation and the denial of voting rights as well. At SCLC King collected a roster of unusually able aides and allies, including Bayard Rustin, Ralph Abernathy, Fred Shuttlesworth, Wyatt Tee Walker, Andrew Young, and Ella Baker. Some of these people were relatively new to the struggle, others—like Rustin and Baker—were battered veterans of the civil rights wars. In the next few years King and SCLC led the effort to dismantle the century-old edifice of legal segregation and restore African-American voting rights. They would win amazing victories, but the road would be rough and, despite satyagraha, marked with disorder and violence.

The Cold War Continues

The Eisenhower years also saw a modest easing of international tensions. In late November 1952, soon after his election, Ike had kept his promise and gone to Korea to try to end the stalemate in the armistice negotiations. The seventy-two-hour visit, mostly spent looking at situation maps and greeting service personnel, accomplished little. Then in March 1953 Soviet leader Joseph Stalin died, and suddenly new doors opened. On April 16 Eisenhower gave a major foreign policy speech calling for an end to international tensions and a serious effort at world disarmament. At the same time the Americans let it be known that if the stalemate in Korea did not end soon, the United States might resort to dropping an atom bomb on a North Korean target.

These developments were felt in the Far East. On July 26, 1954, despite the efforts of South Korean President Syngman Rhee to sabotage an agreement, the two sides signed the armistice document. Neither the Communists nor the United Nations forces had won. Prisoners were to be exchanged, although many of the captured Chinese and North Koreans did not want to return to their Communist nations. But the two sides would remain in place, almost exactly where they had been in June 1950. Korea would continue to be a nation divided into two hostile parts. But for most Americans the important thing was that the war was over.

Eisenhower continued the containment policy of his predecessor in a general way. But his foreign policy had its own special features.

It was a strange mixture of the pacific and the belligerent. At times the president and his chief foreign policy adviser, Secretary of State John Foster Dulles, sought to avoid entanglements that promised to stretch American commitments too far. Vietnam (discussed in Chapter 4) was an example of judicious limitation, at least at first. In Iran, an oil-rich Islamic country bordering the Soviet Union, however, Eisenhower showed no such restraint. In 1953 the United States, acting through the CIA, arranged a coup to overthrow Mohammad Mussadegh, a left-wing Iranian leader suspected of pro-Soviet goals. Four years before Mussadegh had evicted Shah Mohammed Reza Pahlavi from power and nationalized the Iranian oil industry. The coup returned the shah to power; Iran became an important American friend in the Middle East, although beneath the surface anti-shah, anti-American forces, from both the left and right, continued to seethe.

In Europe American policy was activist. Secretary Dulles, although he had spent his life studying the complexities of foreign policy-making, was given to simplistic saber rattling to frighten the Soviets. In a radio talk in January 1953 he promised the "captive peoples" of the Soviet satellite nations that they could "count on" the United States for support against their Soviet oppressor. In February the administration introduced a resolution in Congress, written by Dulles, denouncing the Soviet occupation of Poland, the Baltic states, Hungary, Czechoslovakia, and the other "captive nations."

Americans generally deplored the Soviet occupation of the small nations on its western border, but many sensible people believed the captive peoples position to be essentially foolish and dangerous propaganda. The United States, they noted, might well encourage hopes among the Eastern Europeans that it could not satisfy. When in 1956 the Hungarians rose against their Soviet occupiers, the United States indeed sat back and did nothing. Soviet troops and tanks soon crushed the brave revolt. The Hungarian "freedom fighters," critics said, were in part victims of unrealistic expectations inspired by Dulles three years before.

Massive Retaliation and a Summit Conference

Dulles's "massive retaliation" policy, announced in early 1954, was another risky foreign policy position. The president deplored the enormous expenditures for armaments but at the same time, of course, had no intention of leaving the West defenseless against Soviet expansionism. What he sought was "a bigger bang for the buck." He recognized that conventional mass armies with their millions of men and thousands of tanks were enormously expensive to maintain and sought to cut the ground forces budget. Between 1953 and 1960, helped by the end of fighting in Korea, Eisenhower reduced the army from 1.5 million to 873,000 men.

But how could deterrence be preserved without large, well-equipped American military forces? The answer seemed simple: by building up our nuclear weapons arsenal to the point where any aggressor would face total annihilation if it persisted. The United States had already detonated its first hydrogen bomb in late 1952. Thereafter the Defense Department concentrated on refining nuclear weapons through prolonged atmospheric testing in Nevada and in Bikini Atoll in the Marshall Islands and on developing improved delivery systems, especially intercontinental ballistics missiles (ICBMs). Not until early 1960 did the ICBMs become truly reliable, but on January 12, 1954, Dulles felt free to declare that in the future the United States would use massive nuclear retaliation against any hostile act "at times and places of our own choosing."

The nuclear arms race was profoundly disturbing to many Americans. Many feared the danger to health and life from the radiation fallout that accompanied the weapons-testing program. An all-out nuclear war itself seemed too horrible to contemplate. In 1957 *On the Beach,* a popular novel (and subsequently a successful movie) set in Australia, depicted what presumably would happen following a nuclear war among the great powers. The war had wiped out all human beings in the Northern Hemisphere, and as the story opens, Australians await the arrival of the deadly radiation cloud, their own deaths, and the end of the human race.

To some people massive retaliation was a seriously flawed strategy. A small number of critics believed that nuclear weapons were inadmissible under all circumstances, even to stop a full-scale Soviet attack on NATO or the United States itself. They often advocated unilateral disarmament, the abandonment by the United States of its nuclear armaments even without an equal response by the Soviet Union. This position was sometimes condensed to the slogan, "better red than dead." At the other extreme were advocates of a nuclear preemptive first strike against the Soviet Union to catch it by surprise and destroy its power before it could retaliate. But most Americans accepted a middle position: while nuclear war must be avoided at all cost, it could not be precluded in the event of a Soviet attack either on the United States itself or on our NATO allies.

What seemed wrong with massive retaliation was that it threatened to start a nuclear war over even marginal concerns. Having reduced its capacity for responding to danger with conventional forces, America would have either to respond to every Communist challenge with a nuclear holocaust or accept certain defeat. Unfortunately as events would soon show, the other alternative—of engaging the enemy at the periphery with conventional military forces—had its dangers too.

During Eisenhower's eight years as president, America's foreign policy fortunes gyrated wildly. Stalin's death led to a notable softening of Soviet policy. In 1955 the Soviets finally agreed to leave their occupied zone in Austria, permitting that country to become a united, independent, neutral nation. After 1953 more and more was heard of "peaceful coexistence" between the superpowers.

But a temporary easing of Cold War tensions did not keep both sides from maneuvering for improved military positions. In 1952 the European members of NATO established the European Defense Community to coordinate their response to a Soviet military threat. But then France, overconscious of its past glories, had second thoughts and, despite Dulles's threat that the United States would engage in an "agonizing reappraisal" of its commitment to European defense if France did not follow through, decided not to join. In 1955 the Soviet Union, fearful of NATO's military revival, arranged the Warsaw Pact, which bound the Eastern European satellites to it in a tight military alliance.

Despite this jockeying for military advantage, efforts at reconciling East-West differences continued. In the summer of 1955 Eisenhower and British and French leaders met at Geneva with Soviet leaders Nikolai Bulganin and Nikita Khrushchev to discuss problems between NATO and the Warsaw Pact nations. This was the first of the postwar summit conferences, and many people had high hopes for its success. But little was accomplished.

A major issue was the fate of Germany, divided since the war into two competing halves. The Americans proposed a unified German nation with the right to join NATO if it wished. The Soviets, not surprisingly, rejected this proposal and countered with a unification plan that required withdrawal of all foreign troops from Germany and a general European security agreement. Eisenhower also proposed a sweeping "open skies" disarmament agreement that would have allowed each nation almost complete access to the other's military installations to verify any arms reduction arrangement. Barely out of the paranoid Stalin era and rulers of a still-repressive, authoritarian state, the Soviets did not take this seriously, and it probably was not taken very seriously by the Americans either.

The Suez Crisis

Despite the absence of significant results the world hailed the "spirit of Geneva," as sign of a new, cordial attitude between the superpowers. The optimistic mood lasted for a scant few months. In 1956 events in the Middle East demonstrated that the superpower rivalry could be played out through surrogates in the Third World as well as directly.

Egypt and Israel were the focus of the new clash. Although Israel had established its independence in 1948, its neighbors were pledged to destroy it, claiming that it was an alien intrusion into the Muslim world and a state occupying what was by right the territory of the predominantly Muslim Palestinians. Israel's most formidable enemy was neighboring Egypt, a country that had recently thrown off British rule, and under its aggressive new ruler, Gamal Abdel Nasser, was intent on establishing its leadership of the Arab world. Nasser launched continuous guerrilla attacks across the Egyptian-Israeli border and promised to destroy the Jewish state.

As part of his ambitious plans Nasser sought control of the Suez Canal, the man-made waterway through Egypt connecting the Mediterranean and Red seas that provided a vital commercial and strategic shortcut to sailing around Africa. Built with British money during the previous century, it had at one time been a critical link between Britain and its Asian empire. In the postwar period it remained a major route of international trade and its tolls continued to be an important revenue earner for Britain and France.

Several nations were willing to underwrite Nasser's ambitions. The Soviet Union supplied him with large quantities of arms. For a time the United States promised to lend him money to build a vital dam at Aswan on the Nile River but then withdrew the offer when Dulles decided that Nasser was getting too close to the Soviets. Meanwhile the Israelis, fearing growing Egyptian power, had asked America for arms. Eisenhower refused, claiming it would only lead to a middle eastern weapons race.

In July 1956 Nasser seized control of the Suez Canal and declared he would use its revenues to build a dam at Aswan. He also closed the international waterway to all

Israeli shipping contrary to long-established international agreement mandating an open canal. After months of fruitless negotiation Israel invaded Egypt and advanced to within 10 miles of the canal. Meanwhile the French and British, in secret collusion with Israel, had dropped paratroopers and seized control of the waterway.

The French-British-Israeli collaboration created an international crisis. The Soviets threatened to send troops to protect its new Egyptian ally. Eisenhower, who had been kept in the dark by the French and British, became angry and sharply reprimanded the invaders. U.S. pressure forced Egypt's opponents to withdraw, leaving Nasser in possession of the canal. Bowing to Israel's concerns over the constant raids across the Egyptian border, the United Nations agreed to establish a peacekeeping military force in the Sinai region that marked the Egyptian-Israeli boundary. Eisenhower had prevented a major war, but he had also humbled America's allies and encouraged Nasser in his aggressive posture. The Middle East remained a tinder box. (See Figure 5–2 in Chapter 5.)

Berlin

Several major international crises marked Eisenhower's second term. One was the old perennial, Berlin, that detached piece of the new West German republic deep within the East German Soviet satellite.

To both the Soviets and the East Germans the Western presence in Berlin was a serious affront. The West German Federal Republic was now a democratic and prosperous country while East Germany remained poor and authoritarian. From the late 1940s on many thousands of East Germans each year fled across the border to the Federal Republic. The migration not only hurt the East German economy; it also highlighted the serious deficiencies of Communist society relative to the West. Gradually the Communists were able to stem the leak along most of the East-West border, but Berlin remained a serious hemorrhage point for refugees from behind the Iron Curtain.

During this period the Western powers refused to deal with the East Germans on Berlin or any other matter. The Soviet Union, they said, was the legal occupying power and it alone had the right to speak for the Soviet zone of Germany. In November 1958 Khrushchev, now sole leader in Moscow, announced that if an agreement on Berlin satisfactory to the Russians was not reached in six months, the Soviet Union would sign a separate peace treaty with East Germany and turn over to it control of the Soviet zone in Berlin. The implication was that unless the Allies dealt with East Germany, they would face a blockade of Berlin similar to the one of 1948–49.

Khrushchev's ultimatum created an instant crisis. But then it eased. In September 1959 Khrushchev visited the United States and conferred with Eisenhower at Camp David, the presidential retreat in the Maryland mountains. Once again the American and Soviet leaders got along personally, leading a worried world now to hail the "Spirit of Camp David." The two men agreed to hold a four-power summit meeting in May 1960 to discuss Germany and Berlin. Soon after, Khrushchev canceled the ultimatum.

The Soviet leader, however, had second thoughts about relaxing the Berlin pressure. But how could he explain changing his mind? Then just before the scheduled Paris summit, Khrushchev found the out he needed.

On May 1 a high-flying American U-2 spy plane, equipped with radiation detectors and high-tech cameras, was shot down over Soviet territory and its pilot, Francis Gary Powers, taken prisoner. Both nations, of course, regularly spied on one another through conventional human agents and through advanced technology, and each knew of the others' activities. But never before did the Soviets have such dramatic proof of American spying, and on May 5 Khrushchev announced that the United States had been caught engaging in "aggressive acts" against the Soviet Union.

The purpose, he said, was to wreck the summit conference, but he blamed American underlings, not the president. In fact Eisenhower did know about the spy plane operations and had approved them. At first the American government tried to pass the U-2 off as a weather plane, but when it became clear that the Soviets had the evidence, Eisenhower admitted the purpose of the flights and his own knowledge of them.

The leaders of France, Britain, the United States, and the Soviet Union met in Paris despite the U-2 incident. But the Soviets quickly made it clear that they had changed their mind. At the preliminary meeting on May 16 Khrushchev was blunt, accusing the president of "treachery" and of "bandit" acts against the Soviet Union. He then stalked out of the Elysée Palace. The summit collapsed and with it all immediate chance to reduce Cold War tensions.

Cuba and Castro

By the last months of Eisenhower's administration the United States confronted a problem nearer to home as well—in Cuba, just ninety miles off the Florida coast.

For years Cuba had been an informal American dependency, functioning under the shadow of the American colossus. Many Cubans despised Uncle Sam as a colonial power that impeded their country's full independence and upheld Cuban regimes that preserved political and social inequality. And at times the United States *had* clearly used its power to frustrate social change in Latin America. In 1953, for example, the CIA sponsored a coup against Jacob Arbenz Guzmán, the leftist Guatemalan president suspected of pro-Soviet sympathies. The Arbenz government was replaced by a conservative one favorable to the United States.

During the early fifties Cuba was ruled by Fulgencio Batista, a notorious despot who used brutal methods to repress opposition and lined his pockets from the proceeds of gambling and prostituion. Almost everyone in Cuba, including the prosperous, pro-American middle class, opposed the Batista regime. American public opinion too was hostile to the tyrant.

From 1956 on the anti-Batista opposition was led by a bearded young lawyer, Fidel Castro, a former University of Havana student. Castro and his small rebel band established headquarters in the rugged Cuban mountains and from there launched guerrilla attacks against the Batista forces. With the support of the majority of the Cuban people they soon made spectacular gains. On New Year's Day 1959 Batista saw the inevitable and fled into exile.

For a time Americans hailed Castro's victory. He initially denied Communist sympathies, promised democracy, and stated that American property was safe under his regime. The American left would later say that Castro need not have been an enemy of the United States; that the United States itself was responsible for turning the Cuban Revolution in a pro-Soviet direction. Perhaps so but it is clear that Castro was also never the democrat that he claimed. Once in power he established revolutionary tribunals that condemned to death or prison hundreds of accused Batista supporters without benefit of elementary legal protection and imposed censorship on Cuban writers, academics, and journalists. He was soon praising Red China and the Soviet Union and calling the United States "a vulture . . . feeding on humanity." In a matter of months he had lost the support of much of the Cuban middle class, many of whom fled their homeland for Florida.

If American liberals and conservatives deplored Castro's behavior on moral or ethical grounds, the American government saw Castro as a beachhead for Soviet influence in the Americas and resolved to bring him down as it had Guzmán in Guatemala. By the last months of the Eisenhower administration, the CIA was training cadres of Cuban exiles in Florida and Guatemala for an invasion to topple Castro's government and establish in its place one more friendly to the United States.

Ike's Farewell and the 1960 Election

Three days before Eisenhower's second term ended, the president made a farewell speech to the American people containing one of his more interesting statements. Disarmament, he declared, must be one of the nation's highest priorities. Unfortunately over the years there had developed an alliance between American military men and arms manufacturers to build up the nation's arsenal beyond legitimate need. This "military-industrial complex" posed a threat to American democracy. "The potential for the disastrous rise of misplaced power exists and will persist," he pronounced. The statement was surprising from a man who had himself been a career officer in the army, and many Americans took it to heart.

The Candidates

Ike's successor would be the handsome young Democratic senator from Massachusetts, John F. Kennedy, the man who had almost won the Democratic vice presidential nomination four years before.

Kennedy was the second son of Joseph P. Kennedy, a conservative and abrasive millionaire banker, moviemaker, industrialist, and Wall Street speculator from Boston. The Kennedys were an Irish-Catholic family that exhibited in its own history the journey of nineteenth-century Irish immigrants from poverty to affluence. Joseph's father was a successful, self-made man; he himself was a Harvard graduate who made millions in business. Yet he never felt that he had been fully accepted by the Yankee Protestant elite who ruled in Boston and his fierce desire to show the world that the Kennedys took second place to no one was a controlling motive in his behavior. Joseph Kennedy was determined to make one of his sons president and was willing to put his wide connections, his large fortune, and his enormous energy behind this goal. His first choice for high office was his oldest son, Joseph, Jr., but when Joe Jr. was tragically killed in World War II, he turned to John.

In 1946 John Fitzgerald Kennedy was a skinny Harvard graduate who had just returned to civilian life after serving as a naval officer in the Pacific. A war hero who had barely escaped death when a Japanese destroyer sank his PT boat, he ran for Congress in a Boston district and won. In 1952 he unseated Boston Brahmin Senator Henry Cabot Lodge.

As a senator, Kennedy had chalked up a mediocre record. Out of deference to his anti-Communist Catholic constituents, he had tolerated Joe McCarthy, who was a friend of his father. He also had, at times, accepted the positions of southern colleagues on racial issues. Kennedy was a pragmatist rather than an idealist, and it was not clear that he held any clear, uplifting vision beyond "success" for its own sake. In 1960 some members of the liberal intelligentsia supported him but many considered him just another rich young man driven by intense ambition and backed by immense wealth. One liberal would call him the "Democratic Nixon."

With the electorate at large Kennedy's chief handicap was his religion. He was not an especially pious Catholic, but many Protestant Americans, as in the days of Al Smith, considered the Catholic Church an alien and dangerous institution, and felt that a Catholic president might put his religion ahead of his country. Even Democratic leaders who personally dismissed such fears wondered if a Catholic could overcome the bigotry that had helped defeat Smith in 1928.

Kennedy's chief rival for the nomination was Hubert Humphrey, the exuberant senator from Minnesota. Humphrey was a certified liberal, a founder of Americans for Democratic Action, a loyal champion of labor, and a determined advocate of civil rights. But he not only lacked the personal magnetism of Kennedy but also his money and skilled staff. Another Kennedy rival was the Senate majority leader, Lyndon B. Johnson of Texas. The most effective parliamentarian since Henry Clay, Johnson suffered from his identification with the South and his reputation as a wheeler-dealer.

The key primary contest was in West Virginia, an overwhelmingly Protestant state. There Kennedy money and organization helped to overcome Humphrey's pro-labor reputation and anti-Catholic feeling to give the Massachusetts senator a whopping 61 percent majority.

The Kennedy forces came to the Los Angeles Democratic convention in early July with victory in the bag and won on the first ballot. In a move to attract the southern and southwestern vote in November, Kennedy asked Johnson to join the ticket.

The Republicans turned to Richard Nixon, the vice president, as their candidate. Although few Americans loved Nixon and some believed him unscrupulous, he had acquired a new stature since 1952, especially in the foreign affairs realm. Some of this was pure hype. In 1958 he had taken a tour through South America to express U.S. interest in, and goodwill toward, its Latin neighbors. In Peru and Venezuela he had been attacked by screaming mobs and had narrowly escaped personal injury. The press depicted him as a hero. The following year, while attending the Soviet Exhibition of Science, Technology, and Culture in Moscow, the vice president had had an encounter with Premier Khrushchev in the kitchen of a model six-room American ranch house. The two engaged in a debate on the relative consumer merits of their two societies and Americans felt that Nixon had "won." Somehow these two events had been transformed by the media into profound learning experiences for the vice president.

Nixon's only serious potential competitor was Nelson Rockefeller, New York's Republican Governor. Rockefeller represented the party's Eastern liberal wing dominated by "old" families and "old" money, and was an attractive, effective man with a famous name. Fortunately for Nixon, he seemed more interested in influencing the party's ideology than getting its nomination. Rather than challenging Nixon for the nomination, in June 1960, while the Republican Platform Committee was deliberating, he threatened a major platform fight if the vice president did not endorse his liberal domestic policies and acknowledge the need for a larger defense budget. The governor's ultimatum forced Nixon to come to his New York apartment and agree to changes in the platform. Republican conservatives like Senator Barry Goldwater of Arizona attacked the "Compact of Fifth Avenue" as the "Munich of the Republican Party."

With Rockefeller out of the way Nixon's nomination was without serious opposition. As a further sop to the Republican liberals, Nixon chose Henry Cabot Lodge, now ambassador to the UN, as his running mate.

The Campaign

The election contest that followed was one of the most exciting in thirty years. Neither man seemed to have a clear-cut advantage. Kennedy had looks, money, and a beautiful, style-setting wife. He was not above using his sex appeal as a campaign weapon. As reporter Murray Kempton wrote at one point, Kennedy had "treated southern Ohio yesterday as Don Giovanni used to treat Seville." Charisma notwithstanding Kennedy had his liabilities: inexperience, the reputation of a rich playboy, and Catholicism. By contrast Nixon was a veteran politician, came from a solid middle-class background, and had the support of most of the nation's big-business leaders. He was also the heir, or so it seemed, of the beloved Ike. In fact Eisenhower was surprisingly cool to his vice president. At one point when asked what ideas Nixon had contributed to his administration, he replied, "If you give me a week, I might think of one. I can't remember." Still Ike was willing to "do anything to avoid turning [his] chair and the country over to Kennedy" and actively supported the Republican candidate.

The Democrats campaigned on a "missile gap" that some experts thought the Eisenhower administration had allowed to open between the United States and the Soviet Union. (Subsequent intelligence revealed that in fact there was none.) Kennedy promised to close the gap and in general win the competition with the Soviets for the world's favor. He also promised to get a sluggish economy moving again and devote more of the nation's wealth to improving education, helping the poor, and upgrading the country's public facilities. Nixon, predictably, emphasized his experience, especially in foreign affairs, and the accomplishments of the Eisenhower years.

Kennedy's religion could not be avoided as an issue, although the Republican candidate to his credit did not mention it. The Democratic nominee met the Catholic issue head on by an appearance before the Greater Houston Ministerial Association in September. "I believe in an America," he told the Protestant leaders, "where the separation of church and state is absolute—where no Catholic prelate would tell the President (should he be Catholic) how to act, and no Protestant minister would tell his parishioners for whom to vote." The speech undoubtedly helped, although it did not convince the most anti-Catholic voters.

Kennedy also succeeded in overcoming much of the public's concern about his inexperience as an executive. A series of television debates with Nixon from September 25 through October 21 was crucial. The first was in Chicago and was a clear-cut Kennedy victory. The Democratic candidate seemed poised and articulate and he looked good on camera. Suffering from an infected knee, Nixon seemed nervous and tired. He perspired and appeared unshaven. After this first debate many who had doubted Kennedy's maturity concluded that he had handled himself better than the older, more experienced vice president.

Civil rights inevitably became a major campaign issue. A large majority of African-American voters by now were Democrats. But many were disturbed by the power within the party of the southern segregationists; many were also suspicious of the Catholic Church. Kennedy was in a delicate position. He feared the complete defection of the white South, Lyndon Johnson notwithstanding. But he also knew he could not afford to lose the big industrial states with millions of black voters. To his credit he chose to champion the civil rights cause even to the point of obliquely endorsing the use of civil disobedience.

John F. Kennedy and Richard Nixon hold their first 1960 campaign debate. In the center is the moderator, Howard K. Smith of ABC. (UPI/Bettmann Newsphotos)

The real breakthrough in winning black support, however, came late in the campaign when a Georgia judge sentenced Martin Luther King, Jr., to four months at hard labor for attempting to desegregate an Atlanta department store lunch counter. Given the nature of southern jails, there was an excellent chance that King would never leave prison alive. Nixon privately tried to get Attorney General William Rogers to intervene, but Eisenhower vetoed the move. Kennedy called Coretta King, expressing his sympathy and desire to help her husband; Kennedy's brother Robert, his campaign manager, contacted the Georgia judge. The next day King was out on bail. Mrs. King spread the news of Kennedy's intervention, guaranteeing a massive African-American turnout in November for the Democrats.

Kennedy won, but the victory was one of the closest in history. (See Figure 2–1.) The Massachusetts senator received only about 100,000 more popular votes than Nixon out of the 68.8 million cast and carried fewer, although larger, states for an electoral majority of 303 to 219. Even these figures may not be a true measure of Kennedy's electoral weakness. Some scholars believe, as did Nixon himself, that in both Texas and Illinois the Democratic tally had been falsified by the local Democratic machines. Many Republican leaders urged the vice president to challenge the results, but Nixon, recognizing the legal difficulties and not wishing to taint the presidential election process, refused.

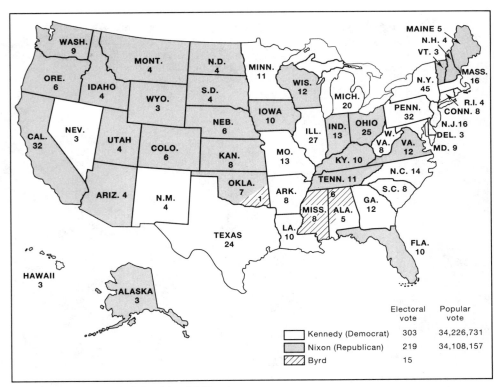

	Electoral vote	Popular vote
Kennedy (Democrat)	303	34,226,731
Nixon (Republican)	219	34,108,157
Byrd	15	

Figure 2–1 The 1960 Presidential Election

An analysis of the returns suggests that, in the end, the religious issue hurt the Democratic candidate after all. Some Republican Catholics no doubt switched to vote for him. Kennedy also got some normally nonvoting Catholics to come to the polls. But on the whole the religious issue had the effect of shifting thousands of Democratic Protestant voters, especially in the South and rural Midwest, into the Republic column. It was Kennedy's good fortune that his gains came in the large industrial states, his losses in places where he either had no chance of winning anyway (the rural Midwest) or where Democratic loyalty was still so ingrained or Johnson's appeal so strong (the South) that the defections were not enough to transfer many whole states to Nixon.

Transition and Balance Sheet

Despite the shadow over the election results, as the country awaited the new administration, many people looked forward to a new political era, one marked by youth, by style, and by bold new initiatives. In more ways than just by the calendar, the fifties were over.

A majority of the nation's most alert and active citizens were probably glad to see the era end. Yet a decade later some would look back to the 1950s with nostalgia. In part their response would reflect the excesses of the 1960s. But it would also derive from the realization that, despite their outward timidity and caution, the fifties had been a creative era when the nation made significant cultural breakthroughs in painting, popular music, literature, and philosophy. Nor was that all. The 1950s had been prosperous years for many Americans and, after the harsh years of depression and war, they had confirmed the promise of American life. Furthermore they had witnessed the start of a social revolution in the South that would not end until the promise of civic equality for all races, first made during Reconstruction, had been realized. All in all, it was not too bad a record.

FOR FURTHER READING

On the intellectual climate of the 1950s see Richard Pells, *The Liberal Mind in a Conservative Age: American Intellectuals in the 1940s and 1950s* (1984). On the new conservatism see Russell Kirk, *The Conservative Mind* (1953); William F. Buckley, Jr., *God and Man at Yale* (1951); Daniel Bell, *The End of Ideology: On the Exhaustion of Political Ideas in the Fifties* (1960); and Hans Hoffmann, *The Theology of Reinhold Niebuhr* (1956).

American painting is covered in Andrew C. Ritchie, *Abstract Painting and Sculpture in America* (1951). Serge Guibaut's *How New York Stole the Idea of Modern Art* (1983) claims that the rise of the abstract expressionists to prominence was related to American political hegemony in the postwar era. On rock and roll see Nik Cohn, *Rock: From the Beginning* (1969) and Charlie Gillett, *The Sound of the City: The Rise of Rock and Roll* (1970). Albert Goldman's *Elvis* (1981) retells the scandal of Elvis Presley's life as well as his contribution to popular music.

Bruce Cook's *The Beat Generation* (1971) and Lawrence Lipton's *The Holy Barbarians* (1959) discuss the Beat dissenters. The movies are discussed in Michael Wood, *America in Movies* (1975). The best discussion of television is Erik Barnouw's *A History of Broadcasting in the United States, Vol. III, The Image Empire* (1970).

Eisenhower and his presidency come under attack in Marquis Childs, *Eisenhower: Captive Hero* (1958) and Emmet John Hughes, *The Ordeal of Power* (1963). More positive are Merlo J. Pusey, *Eisenhower, the President* (1956) and Arthur Larson, *Eisenhower: The President Nobody*

Knew (1968). A recent work that emphasizes how effective Ike was behind the scenes while often seeming to bumble in public is Fred Greenstein, *The Hidden-Hand Presidency: Eisenhower as Leader* (1982). On the Dixon-Yates fiasco see Aaron Wildavsky, *Dixon-Yates* (1962).

The civil rights movement of the 1950s begins essentially with the 1954 *Brown* decision. For the *Brown* case see Richard Kluger, *Simple Justice* (1976). For the conservative response to it see Numan Bartley, *The Rise of Massive Resistance: Race and Politics in the South during the 1950s* (1959). For the early years of Martin Luther King, Jr.'s leadership see the recent book by Taylor Branch, *Parting the Waters: America in the King Years, 1954–63* (1988). Another, much briefer, work that covers the later years of the civil rights movement as well is Harvard Sitkoff, *The Struggle for Black Equality, 1954–1980* (1983). Also see Stephen Oates's eloquent *Let the Trumpet Sound: The Life of Martin Luther King, Jr.* (1982). David Garrow's *Bearing the Cross: Martin Luther King, Jr. and the Southern Christian Leadership Conference* (1986) is more scholarly that Oates's work, but less readable.

The Eisenhower phase of the Cold War is covered in Robert Divine, *Eisenhower and the Cold War* (1981); Townsend Hoopes, *The Devil and John Foster Dulles* (1973); and Roscoe Drummond and Gaston Coblentz, *Duel at the Brink: John Foster Dulles' Command of American Power* (1960). Also see David Wise and Thomas B. Ross, *The U-2 Affair* (1962).

The election of 1960 is skillfully evoked in Theodore White's *The Making of the President, 1960* (1961).

3
The Sixties

Members of the 1960s radical counterculture. (Gene Anthony/Black Star)

Kennedy's New Frontier

Every Democratic administration since 1932 has adopted, or been assigned, a label to describe its program for change. Republican administrations have scorned the practice and for good reason: generally, they have come to office dedicated not so much to new programs as to undoing those of their Democratic predecessors. Franklin Roosevelt's program, of course, was the New Deal, Truman's, the Fair Deal. John F. Kennedy (JFK) called his the *New Frontier*.

Kennedy first used the term in his acceptance speech at the 1960 Democratic convention. His nomination had ushered in a "New Frontier," he declared, "the frontier of the 1960s." It is hard to tell what Kennedy meant, but a certain amount of mystery is appropriate for an acceptance speech; the candidate must not give his opponent in the grueling battle ahead too many targets to shoot at. Yet the New Frontier was not explained much better in Kennedy's Inaugural Address from the Capitol the following January 20. Here was the opportunity to define the New Frontier, but instead once again Kennedy took refuge in eloquent generalities. "Let the word go forth from this time and place, to friend and foe alike, that the torch has been passed to a new generation of Americans . . . tempered by war, disciplined by a hard and bitter peace, proud of our ancient heritage." The speech echoed with uplifting phrases: "the trumpet summon us again," "ask not what your country can do for you; ask what you can do for your country," "we shall pay any price, bear any burden, meet any hardship," and "the common enemies of man: tyranny, poverty, disease and war itself." The public heard the beautiful music and ignored the empty libretto. But one thing was clear: the message was "March." After eight years of consolidation, the nation would be moving again.

The next weeks were a blur of motion. Within two months Kennedy had dashed off thirty-two official messages and recommendations for new legislation, delivered twelve speeches, announced twenty-two executive orders, and held seven press conferences. "He did everything . . . except shinny up the Washington Monument," the journalist James Reston wrote of one of JFK's early days. The public liked the vigor.

They also liked the images. Eisenhower had been the oldest president the nation ever had. Kennedy was the youngest and possibly the handsomest. He was also a cultivated man who seemed to read widely and appreciate the arts. Many intellectuals would be flattered by his interests. But it was more than just the president himself. His wife, the former Jacqueline Bouvier, was beautiful and elegant; his young daughter, Caroline, radiated delicate charm. His cabinet and close circle of advisers were sharp, articulate, and bumptious young men, many from Harvard, who worked hard and played hard and seemed to relish running the greatest nation on earth. Arthur Schlesinger, Jr., the Harvard historian who served Kennedy as a White House aide, would exult, "Never had girls seemed so pretty, tunes so melodious, and evenings so blithe and unconstrained." In later years people compared the "thousand days" of the Kennedy presidency to Camelot, the mythical court of brave knights and beautiful ladies presided over by King Arthur.

Inevitably, the image was not entirely true; this administration like all others had

President Kennedy, his wife,
Jacqueline, and his children,
Caroline and John, Jr.
(UPI/Bettmann Newsphotos)

its share of imperfect people. Many of Kennedy's advisers had more drive than discernment. Some have been described as juiceless technocrats, enamored of the quick-fix solution. The president himself was a flawed man who, as later became widely known, let others write his books and jeopardized his public reputation and the integrity of his office by his womanizing activities. Yet there can be no doubt that the public found the energy and the exuberance of the new administration a tonic for its tired blood. The young, especially, felt the thrill of new possibilities and new directions.

New Proposals

Some of the president's earliest initiatives confirmed the image of the new beginnings. On March 1 he announced the formation of a Peace Corps of young American volunteers who would go abroad to help less-developed nations improve their economies, their people's health, and their educational facilities. The new scheme to help the Third World instantly appealed to the idealism of the young, and even before Congress had passed the necessary legislation, thousands had offered to join. Another early proposal that engaged the public's imagination was the Alliance for Progress, a scheme to help Latin America achieve democracy, economic growth, and social equity through joint U.S. and Latin American cooperation.

At the end of May Kennedy asked Congress for a massive appropriation for an American space program. "I believe," he told the audience, "that this nation should commit itself to achieving the goal, before this decade is out, of landing a man on the moon and returning him safely to earth." The administration was goaded, in part, by the space successes of the Soviet Union since Sputnik in 1957. After several embarrassing failures the United States finally launched its own satellite in late January 1958. But then in April 1961 the Soviet Union announced that it had sent a man into space and recovered him successfully. Kennedy was undoubtedly playing catch-up with America's chief international rival and his space program was part of the continuing Cold War. But it was more. It was also a commitment to a bold human adventure resembling those momentous explorations of early modern times that had brought the European and non-European worlds into contact.

These early, flashy proposals were more successful in winning congressional support than Kennedy's other domestic programs. The new president was not a flaming liberal; at most he belonged among the moderates of his party. To reassure the business community, suspicious of Democrats since the New Deal, he appointed as defense secretary Robert McNamara, former Ford Motor Company executive, and as treasury secretary Douglas Dillon, a conservative Republican with Wall Street connections, although Kennedy offset the latter choice by appointing Walter Heller, a liberal economics professor, as head of the Council of Economic Advisers. But even if JFK had been a radical, the continuing informal coalition of northern Republicans and southern Democrats would have kept bold reform legislation from passing. Time and again liberal measures sent to "the Hill" encountered an impenetrable wall of resistance.

Despite this formidable opposition the president did secure an increase in the minimum wage, a modest federal housing act, and an area redevelopment measure to aid urban and rural depressed areas. In late 1961 under pressure from influential Democratic women he established the President's Commission on the Status of Women with Eleanor Roosevelt as chairperson. The commission's report in 1963 urged an end to job discrimination against women and endorsed day care centers and paid maternity leaves for married working women, but it also pronounced that "the fundamental responsibility" of women was to be "mothers and housewives." This was scarcely revolutionary, yet the commission did bring together a network of women—and some men—alert to feminist issues and helped launch the modern feminist movement.

More than this proved impossible, however. Congress defeated bills establishing a Department of Urban Affairs, a system of medical insurance for the elderly, and federal grants for school construction and teachers' salaries. The administration also found it difficult to get through a substantial federal tax cut that Heller and other Keynesians in and out of the administration believed essential to get the sluggish economy moving briskly again.

Moderate though he was, the president found it difficult to avoid offending business anyway. In April 1962 U.S. Steel, the country's steel-producing giant, announced a sharp price increase. Because steel entered into the manufacture of so many other things, this move promised to accelerate inflation, still modest in the early sixties. At a press conference soon after the company's price hike announcement, Kennedy denounced the company's president Roger Blough for his "public-be-damned" attitude. At the same time Secretary McNamara threatened not to buy steel for defense needs from any company that raised its prices. Blough retreated and rescinded the increases, but neither he nor many of his big-business colleagues ever forgave the president.

Civil Rights Crises

Kennedy came to power at a time when the civil rights movement was entering a more militant, turbulent phase. The change began in February 1960 when four young African-American students at North Carolina Agricultural and Technical College in Greensboro decided to sit down at the whites-only lunch counter of Woolworth and ask to be served. They were refused. The students came back with reinforcements the next day and for many days after, demanding that they be allowed to buy a cup of coffee. Bystanders cursed, spat at, and pummeled the students, but inspired by Martin Luther King's nonviolent philosophy, they refused to retreat or be provoked into counterviolence. The sit-in tactic soon spread to other segregated southern communities where African-American people had long accepted humiliating second-class treatment at local stores.

The brave example of the black students in Dixie acted like a massive electrical shock. Northern white students quickly formed support groups to raise money for their African-American comrades and organized boycotts of northern branches of Woolworth and other five-and-ten chains that had refused service to southern black students. Adult civil rights groups including Martin Luther King's Southern Christian Leadership Conference (SCLC) and the Congress of Racial Equality (CORE) also rushed to help. In April 1960 at a meeting in Raleigh called by Ella Baker of SCLC, the student sit-in leaders organized the Student Nonviolent Coordinating Committee (SNCC), dedicated to achieving an end to racial discrimination through black and white cooperation and the use of nonviolent means. Soon after this SNCC opened its national office in Atlanta in a corner of SCLC's national headquarters.

Early the next year CORE began the first of the "Freedom Rides" to force the desegregation of bus station facilities in southern cities. The riders refused to use segregated terminal rest rooms and coffee shops; they insisted that the recent Supreme Court decision prohibiting segregation in terminals (*Boynton* v. *Virginia*) be obeyed. Like SNCC, CORE was interracial. In these years all the major civil rights groups had a vision of "black and white together" both in the civil rights movement and in the future "color-blind" society it would help forge. When the first two CORE buses left Washington on May 4, half the riders were whites, many of them older members of pacifist groups.

At Rock Hill, South Carolina, a mob of angry whites blocked the entrance to the white waiting room and beat John Lewis, a member of the Nashville SCLC, and Albert Bigelow, a white pacifist, when they tried to enter. As the buses moved south the mobs of white racists, alerted by the media, grew larger and more savage. Attorney General Robert Kennedy, the president's brother, tried to intervene to protect the riders, calling on the governors of Alabama and Mississippi to guarantee order and the safety of the civil rights workers. They were uncooperative.

The administration was in a bind. On the one hand it sympathized with African-American aspirations and in any event needed black votes. On the other hand it also counted on the support of white southern Democrats. Hoping to prevent a showdown, the president called for a cooling off period by both sides, a move that offended many civil rights activists who noted that African-Americans had "cooled it" for several centuries with little to show for it.

Eventually the attorney general dispatched several hundred federal marshals to stop the mayhem and secured a federal injunction forbidding the Ku Klux Klan from interfering with interstate bus travel. On September 22 the Interstate Commerce Commission officially ordered the end to segregation at all bus and train stations.

If the Kennedys hoped that this would end the racial turmoil in the South, they were mistaken. In the fall of 1962 the attorney general was forced to use federal troops and marshals to force Governor Ross Barnett of Mississippi to desist from blocking James Meredith, an African-American applicant, from registering at the University of Mississippi. Many of the soldiers and marshals were injured by taunting, stone-throwing crowds of segregationists; several people were killed in the melees. Meredith was finally registered, but there was a similar confrontation at the University of Alabama during the late spring of 1963 with Governor George Wallace cast in the role of Ross Barnett. Wallace promised to "bar the entrance" of two African-American students to the state university and only backed down when the president ordered the federalized Alabama National Guard to guarantee their admission.

Meanwhile civil rights leaders had launched several major new drives. In 1961–62 they tried to desegregate public facilities in Albany, Georgia, and by early 1962 the small Georgia city had become the arena for a major battle with the segregationists. Faced with a wily police chief who avoided blatant brutality, King and SCLC suffered a defeat. The drive in 1963 to desegregate Birmingham, Alabama's largest city, was more successful. King believed Birmingham a test case. If the city's wall of public and private segregation could be cracked it would "break the back of segregation all over the nation." SCLC's weapons were nonviolent sit-ins and marches designed to advertise the city's racial failings. King understood that the authorities, led by the coarse and brutal police commissioner, Eugene ("Bull") Connor, might well be tempted to use violence against the protestors. Although he did not specifically connive at such a result, he recognized that such behavior would shock the conscience of the nation and help defeat the racists.

The outcome was as expected. Connor used attack dogs and fire hoses against peaceful marchers including women and children. He arrested hundreds. The newspapers and television networks carried pictures and film clips showing the savage confrontations; they profoundly shook the public. President Kennedy said that one picture of a ferocious dog attacking a terrified African-American woman had made him "sick," and he could "well understand why the Negroes of Birmingham are tired of being asked to be patient."

Birmingham was the regional headquarters of many important national business firms. Executives of these companies were disturbed by the turmoil and outrages as were many of the city's local merchants. They were bad for business. Under pressure from the administration and from business leaders elsewhere, on May 10 the city's business and political leaders accepted a settlement that guaranteed desegregation of the city's parks, libraries, and transport action facilities and promised the hiring of African-American workers in the city's downtown department stores. King left Birmingham satisfied that nonviolent civil disobedience could work.

New Civil Rights Legislation

The reverberations from Birmingham went beyond the city. During the Eisenhower years Congress had passed several civil rights bills. The Civil Rights Act of

1957 had established a six-person Civil Rights Commission and a Civil Rights Division in the Department of Justice to protect the voting rights of African-Americans and other minorities. The Civil Rights Act of 1960 had strengthened the voting rights provisions of the earlier measure.

These were weak laws and accomplished little. Now, in the wake of the Birmingham upheaval, Kennedy decided to push for a stronger federal civil rights bill. On June 19, 1963, he sent Congress a proposal giving the attorney general power to initiate school desegregation suits and outlawing discrimination in theaters, hotels and motels, stores, gas stations, restaurants, and ballparks and stadiums. Civil rights militants wanted strong provisions for ending job discrimination included in the bill, but the president knew that he would have a hard time getting the measure through Congress as it was and refused.

Although disappointed, the heads of the major civil rights groups decided to organize a massive summer demonstration in Washington to kindle support for the bill. This gathering would bring together thousands of black and white Americans in a vast outpouring of sympathy for the goal of an integrated society. The administration feared that the demonstration might offend some of the middle-of-the-roaders in Congress whose votes it needed, and only when the civil rights leaders refused to yield did the president give his blessing.

The Reverend Martin Luther King, Jr., (just left of center foreground) leads the 1963 March on Washington for civil rights. (UPI/Bettmann Newsphotos)

The August 28, 1963, March on Washington was the high point of the 1960s civil rights movement. As many as 200,000 demonstrators, including thousands of white people, came to the Mall in Washington to sing "We Shall Overcome" and other civil rights hymns, listen to folksingers including Bob Dylan and Joan Baez, and carry placards announcing "Decent Housing—Now!," "Integrated Schools—Now!," "Effective Civil Rights Laws—Now!" There were a dozen speeches climaxed by King's "I Have a Dream," in which the African-American leader displayed the power of his eloquence and the soaring moral authority of his cause. In sonorous periods that repeated the theme "I have a dream," King told of his vision of the future when "sons of former slaves and sons of former slaveowners" would "sit down together at the table of brotherhood," and when his four children would "not be judged by the color of their skin but by the content of their character." His listeners knew that they had witnessed a historic event and heard a legendary speech. The speech and march transformed King into a world historical figure. In October 1964 he received the Nobel Peace Prize.

Foreign Policy Crises

The Kennedy team brought to the White House a determination to avoid the foreign policy mistakes, as they saw it, of the previous administration. The nation must be prepared to stop the spread of communism around the world even if that entailed risks. The United States must rearm with conventional weapons to provide the "flexible response" required by "wars of national liberation" sponsored by the Soviet Union and China. To ensure the capacity to deal with such events it must further develop its "counterinsurgency" capacity. The troops trained to suppress guerrilla warfare were officially called the "Special Forces Group," and they were fitted with jaunty green berets.

The Bay of Pigs   Kennedy inherited his first foreign policy crisis from his predecessor. For months the Cuban-exile force Eisenhower had authorized had been training in Florida and Guatemala to invade the Cuban mainland. (See Chapter 2.) The CIA and the Joint Chiefs of Staff assured the new president that even a small force of emigrés, landed at the Bay of Pigs on Cuba's south coast, could ignite the anti-Castro opposition and quickly bring the Cuban tyrant down. Although he had his doubts, the president gave the operation the green light in April 1961.

Everything went wrong. To knock out Castro's small air force, old World War II bombers manned by anti-Castro Cubans attacked the Cuban airfields. They did little damage, although the CIA told the president that the Cuban planes had been destroyed. Soon after, five old cargo vessels carrying the invasion force arrived along the Cuban coast with several supply ships. The still-intact Cuban air force quickly sank the vessel carrying most of the invaders' munitions and communications equipment. Nevertheless 1500 Cuban exiles landed on the swampy beach and proclaimed the end of the Castro regime.

The Cuban people did not rise at the announcement, and the invaders were quickly pinned down by thousands of Castro's militia, supported by tanks. The exiles called pitifully for American help; so did the CIA. But Kennedy had already disclaimed any intention of invading Cuba and refused to send reinforcements. After three days the invaders had all surrendered to Castro's forces; they were ransomed by the United States eighteen months later. Cuban-Americans would never forgive the Democrats for the fiasco.

The Bay of Pigs defeat was a humiliation for the president. As one journalist said, the event made Americans look "like fools to our friends, rascals to our enemies, and incompetents to the rest." Kennedy winced as America's enemies chortled at his discomfiture. He would never trust the CIA again, although that did not keep him from condoning its efforts to destroy the Cuban economy by clandestine operations and, possibly, its often fantastic schemes to topple or assassinate Castro.

Encounters with the Soviets   Kennedy was to pay a high price for the Bay of Pigs disaster in his dealings with Nikita Khrushchev. In January 1961 the Soviet premier had declared his country's "unlimited support" to "peoples fighting for their liberation." In this same speech he once more threatened to force the Western powers to abandon Berlin. After the Bay of Pigs Khrushchev apparently concluded that the American president was an inexperienced, insecure, and weak young man who could be easily intimidated.

When the rulers of both superpowers met at Vienna in June, Khrushchev tried to bully the president. The Soviet premier was rude, coarse, contemptuous, and angry. Blaming UN General Secretary Dag Hammarskjöld for the death of Patrice Lumumba, the Soviet's friend in the African nation of the Congo, he demanded that the single UN head be replaced by a "troika" representing the West, the Soviet bloc, and the neutral countries. More important something must be done about Berlin. It was, he said, a bone in the Soviet Union's throat. With or without American consent, the Soviet Union would sign a treaty with East Germany that would end the right of free communication with Berlin. If the United States wanted to go to war over this, so be it.

The president returned to Washington shaken but resolute. On June 26 he told the American public that "if war breaks out it will have been started in Moscow." Kennedy asked for an additional $3.5 billion for defense, issued a call-up of army reserves, and ordered mothballed military planes and ships to be readied for combat. He also urged people to build bomb shelters, a move that set off a wave of half-funny, half-hysterical discussion of the best kind of personal shelters to build, how they should be stocked, and whether they should contain arms to fight off panicky, but improvident, neighbors when apocalypse arrived.

Meanwhile the Soviets had their own plans. For years the exodus of refugees from East to West Germany had been a humiliation for the Communists, underscoring the failings of society behind the Iron Curtain. By 1961 the flood had been lessened by guards and barbed wire along most of the East-West border, but Berlin remained a serious leak. Just after midnight on August 13 the East German army and police descended on the East-West city border; unloaded trucks carrying sawhorses, concrete blocks, and barbed wire; and began to erect a twenty-five-mile wall to separate the city's sections. Four days later the Berlin Wall was completed. All of Germany was now divided by a physical barrier guarded by searchlights and soldiers with rifles and guard dogs.

The Berlin Wall was followed by Soviet resumption of nuclear bomb testing in the atmosphere. For years scientists and medical people had warned of the health dangers of radioactive fallout from nuclear bomb tests. The United States had proposed a scheme to ban atmospheric tests, and although no formal agreement had been reached, both superpowers had suspended them. Now the Soviets set off over thirty new, more powerful bombs that, all told, released more radioactive poisons into the air than all the previous Western tests combined. Kennedy responded by authorizing resumption of U.S. testing.

For a few months in mid-1961 it looked as if the world was on the verge of war. Then in late September Khrushchev began to back off, telling a visiting Western diplomat in Moscow that "Berlin is not such a big problem for me. What are two million people among a billion communists?" In mid October he told a Communist party congress that the Western powers were acting reasonably and there was no need to press the Berlin issue to a showdown. The crisis in Europe was over.

The Cuban Missile Crisis

But not in the Americas. After the Bay of Pigs incident the Cubans, fearful of further United States–inspired attacks, had tightened their ties to the Soviet Union. By 1962 they were importing vast amounts of Soviet arms, sending Cuban technicians and pilots for training in either the Soviet Union or Czechoslovakia, and trading predominantly with the Soviet bloc countries behind the Iron Curtain.

Then in the summer of 1962 Khrushchev recklessly decided to challenge the United States on its home ground by placing in Cuba intermediate-range missiles that were aimed at the United States, ninety miles away. This was the first time the Soviet Union had ever placed nuclear weapons on foreign soil, and they were clearly intended to weaken America's position in the world.

From the beginning the Americans had observed the flow of ships, men, and supplies into Cuba, but not until mid October did U-2 overflights reveal that the Soviets were building missile launch sites in the island and had already delivered thirty or more missiles with nuclear warheads. Something would have to be done quickly if the United States was not to be faced with a nuclear-armed enemy on its doorstep. Suspicious by now of the regular national security apparatus, Kennedy quickly formed an Executive Committee (Ex Comm) of top aides and military officials to advise him on how to meet the challenge.

The Ex Comm group proffered conflicting options. The military men favored an air strike to destroy the launch sites before they could be made operational. A few even advocated an invasion of Cuba. Secretary of Defense McNamara and others urged a blockade that would prevent the installation of more missiles then approaching on Soviet ships. Robert Kennedy, who had taken charge of the group, supported the blockade option.

The president decided that it was important to make the confrontation public. On October 22 he briefed NATO representatives and the Latin American ambassadors on the crisis and that evening he addressed the American people on television. The United States, he said, was declaring a "quarantine" against any additional Soviet deliveries to Cuba and would follow this move by stronger measures if necessary. Any missile launched from Cuba would be treated as a Soviet attack on the United States and lead to full retaliation against Russia itself. It would set off World War III.

Americans, and in fact people all around the world, waited nervously to see how the Soviets would respond. Most Americans apparently believed the president was doing the right thing, but in other parts of the Western world many felt that the United States was playing "chicken" with human survival at stake. The British philosopher Bertrand Russell, an advocate of unilateral disarmament, telegraphed Kennedy, "Your action desperate. . . . No conceivable justification. . . . End this madness."

The next day the Soviets accused the United States of piracy and denied that the missiles were intended for offensive purposes. On October 24 American naval vessels arrived at their positions off Cuba and prepared to intercept twenty-five Soviet merchant vessels steaming for the Caribbean island.

The first signs of Soviet retreat came that same day when, obviously by order from Moscow, the Soviet vessels approaching Cuba stopped. Twelve then turned and headed back toward their home ports. Hearing of the withdrawal, Secretary of State Dean Rusk whispered to National Security Adviser McGeorge Bundy, "We're eyeball to eyeball and I think the other fellow just blinked."

But the crisis was not over yet. In Cuba the hasty preparations to make the missiles operative continued while the UN debated whether the American claims concerning the missiles were accurate. At 6 P.M. on October 26 a long letter from Khrushchev began to arrive by teletype in Washington. The Soviet leader admitted for the first time that Soviet missiles had been placed in Cuba. He also promised to withdraw or destroy these if the United States promised not to attack Cuba.

As Ex Comm was debating whether to accept these terms, another message arrived from Moscow. The Soviet Union would withdraw its missiles if the United States agreed to dismantle NATO missile bases in Turkey, close to the Soviet Union. The American government did not believe the bases valuable and wanted to abandon them anyway, but Washington did not want to do so under the Soviet gun. At this point Ex Comm, backed by the Joint Chiefs of Staff, came perilously close to recommending a combined airstrike and invasion of Cuba. Soviet lives would undoubtedly have been lost; war with the Soviet Union might well have followed.

The president now stepped in and reminded his advisers that the proposed attack threatened the survival of humanity. Fortunately Robert Kennedy had a bright idea. Why not reply positively to the first message and ignore the second? The attorney general and Ted Sorensen, JFK's chief domestic adviser, composed just such a response, and the president dispatched it to Khrushchev that evening, accompanying it with the public statement that he had accepted Khrushchev's proposal. How would the Soviet Union respond?

On Sunday, October 28 at 9 A.M. Washington time, Radio Moscow broadcast a reply to the American note. "In order to eliminate as rapidly as possible the conflict which endangers the cause of peace . . . the Soviet government . . . has given a new order to dismantle the arms . . . described as offensive and to crate and return them to the Soviet Union." Castro was furious; the Soviets had acted without his knowledge. But he had no choice. As for almost everyone else in the world, the sense of relief was overwhelming.

The peaceful end of the missile crisis set the stage for an improvement in Soviet-American relations. Kennedy developed a new confidence in himself and was able to deal with the Soviets less stridently and defensively. The Soviet Union, in turn, proved more conciliatory too, although the missile retreat had hurt Khrushchev and would contribute to his overthrow in October 1964. In June 1963 the United States and the Soviet Union established a "hot line" directly connecting the leaders of both nations, to be used for personal communication in case of another crisis. A month later Britain, the United States, and the Soviet Union agreed on a Limited Nuclear Test Ban pledging the three nations to cease testing nuclear weapons in the atmosphere, under water, and in space. Underground testing could continue, but the increase in atmospheric nuclear pollution would now end.

These post-missile crisis moves reduced international tensions. In Vietnam, however, Kennedy's policies were less successful. These will be considered in Chapter 4.

Destiny in Dallas

In late November 1963 Kennedy, accompanied by his wife, went to Texas to help heal a serious rift in the state's Democratic party. Despite warnings that he would encounter venomous hatred from the far right for his civil rights stand, the president and the first lady had been greeted like visiting royalty in Houston, San Antonio, and Fort Worth.

The presidential party arrived in Dallas on Friday, November 22, and Kennedy, his wife, Texas Governor John Connally, and assorted dignitaries set out by motorcade from Love Field airport to the Dallas Trade Mart where the president was scheduled to deliver a speech at noon.

The day was sunny and pleasant and the crowds lining the route through downtown Dallas were surprisingly large and enthusiastic. The president rode in the backseat of an open Lincoln convertible with Jacqueline by his side and Connally and his wife in the jump seats in front of them. At 12:30 P.M. shots rang out from the sixth floor window of the Texas School Book Depository, a textbook warehouse at the corner of Houston and Elm streets. The president fell over on his wife, hit in the head and neck; Governor Connally, sitting in front, was hit in the back, chest, right wrist, and left thigh. The presidential car sped to Parkland Memorial Hospital, but it was too late. John Kennedy was pronounced dead at 1 P.M. Vice President Lyndon Johnson had been further back in the motorcade, and later that day, while waiting to leave for Washington, he took the presidential oath of office with the stunned and still bloodstained Jacqueline Kennedy by his side.

The killer apparently was Lee Harvey Oswald, an eccentric loner who had defected to the Soviet Union and then, after returning with a Russian wife, became active in a left-wing group called Fair Play for Cuba. The killing excited the wildest speculations that were powerfully reinforced when, two days after his capture, as he was being moved from one local jail to another, Oswald himself was shot and killed by Jack Ruby, a shady Dallas nightclub owner. Oswald had never admitted anything. The left would seek to pin the assassination on the right: Oswald was paid by

Within hours of the assassination of President Kennedy on November 22,1963, Lyndon B. Johnson took the presidential oath as his successor. At Johnson's right is his wife, Lady Bird; to his left is Kennedy's widow, Jacqueline, her clothes stained by her husband's wounds. *(UPI/Bettmann Newsphotos)*

right-wing southern fanatics who hated Kennedy's civil rights stand or by the FBI or CIA with their own bizarre agendas. The right would blame the left: Oswald was an agent of either Castro or Khrushchev. President Johnson appointed a commission headed by Chief Justice Earl Warren to investigate the horrible and strange events. Despite the twenty-six-volume Warren Commission Report that found both Oswald and Ruby had acted alone, Americans' imaginations soared. Conditioned by years of conspiracy theories, CIA escapades, and spy thrillers, many people refused to accept the Warren Commission's conclusions. Some popular theories speculated that there was more than one killer, that Oswald could not have fired the gun, that he was a "Manchurian Candidate" (the name of a movie of the period), a man programmed to kill by some sinister group.

The president's assassination lacerated the nation. Although Kennedy had won by the narrowest of margins in 1960 and had made additional enemies, especially on the right, he had gained many more friends. Few people any longer feared his religion, and millions had come to admire his grace, eloquence, wit, and growing maturity in office. He seemed to millions a radiant young hero. Today it is known that there was base metal alloyed with the gold, but few people in 1963 knew of the president's personal moral lapses or the shabby plots against Castro. There was every indication that he would win big in 1964, especially if, as seemed likely, the Republicans turned to Barry Goldwater, the leader of the party's right wing.

Millions of stunned Americans watched on television the solemn funeral ceremony in Washington on November 25: the coffin resting on a gun carriage pulled by matched gray horses; the muffled drum rolls; the moving mass by Cardinal Richard Cushing of Boston, the Kennedys' old family friend; little John Jr. saluting his father outside the Washington church; and the internment at Arlington cemetary. It produced an outpouring of national grief unequaled since Lincoln's death a century before. In later months many people would say that what had kept them from panic was the firm and steady hand of the new president, Lyndon Johnson.

Johnson Takes Over

The new president was a very different man from his predecessor. Kennedy loyalists, drawing on Shakespeare, would use the phrase "Hyperion to a satyr" to compare the two. It was grossly unfair. Lyndon B. Johnson (LBJ) was not handsome; he was not young; he was not witty; he was not polished; he was not elegant. Johnson had a coarse and bullying streak. He sometimes forced subordinates to accompany him into the toilet while he dictated memos or lectured them. When he wanted political favors, he seized people by the lapels, thrust his face into theirs, and delivered long monologues on why they must do what he wanted. This was called "the treatment" and it was often effective. The new president was a virtuoso of revenge. People who crossed him risked having their political legs, if not worse, cut off. Furthermore he was "new money" rich, unlike the Kennedys whose fortune had been won a generation previously, and his methods of acquiring wealth—using political influence to gain ownership of Texas television stations, for example—were not always savory.

But great failings were accompanied by great virtues. Although now a rich man, Johnson had never forgotten his youthful poverty and the poverty of Mexican-Americans and Texas hill country farmers during the Depression. His hero was Franklin Roosevelt, for whose National Youth Administration he had worked, and he sincerely hoped to complete the New Deal program of weaving a security net for ordinary Americans and creating new opportunities for the nation's outsiders. He also commanded uncommon legislative skills. His years as Senate minority and majority leader had trained him to manipulate Congress as no other previous president. In many ways he had the parliamentary dexterity of a British prime minister. Unlike his predecessor who did not command great respect on Capitol Hill, Johnson, at least at first, had Congress securely in hand.

The Great Society Emerges

The new president, taking advantage of public grief and shame over the assassination, moved quickly to propel deadlocked Kennedy legislation through Congress. In the first months he secured passage of an important foreign aid bill, a Higher Education Facilities Act, and the long-blocked tax reduction measure to fire up the economy. Most importantly he got Congress to pass the pending civil rights legislation. The Civil Rights Act of 1964 forbade discrimination in public places; authorized federal suits to desegregate schools; outlawed job discrimination for race, religion, and sex; and swept away barriers to voter registration based on technicalities and on supposed education deficiencies.

A year before his death Kennedy had asked his aides to look into the "poverty problem." Like many other Americans he had read Michael Harrington's recently published *The Other America* showing that millions of citizens, despite overall national affluence, were still poor. Kennedy felt something should be done about it and had asked Walter Heller to come up with the facts and figures for antipoverty legislation. He died before the experts' report came in, but Johnson picked up the idea and expanded it. In January 1964 he called on Congress to declare "an unconditional war on poverty," and soon after introduced the Economic Opportunity Act.

Passed in late August, this measure established the Office of Economic Opportunity (OEO) with an initial budget of $800 million. OEO ultimately planned and administered a wide range of programs: Head Start to give young ghetto children an educational leg up; job training for the poor; a domestic peace corps (VISTA); a neighborhood youth corps to occupy inner city adolescents usefully; and a series of "community action" programs to nurture initiative and competence among the poor. Johnson chose former Peace Corps Director Sargent Shriver, a Kennedy by marriage, as its head.

Johnson also launched several legislative initiatives of his own. During these months Congress enacted the Wilderness Preservation Act to sequester nine million acres of public land for a permanent unexploitable reserve and the Urban Mass Transportation Act to help build or improve city public transportation systems.

In May 1964, speaking to the graduates of the University of Michigan in Ann Arbor, Johnson gave a name to his program. It was now time, he said, to build the *Great Society* where material abundance would provide the basis for "a richer life in mind and spirit." Such a society demanded "an end to poverty and racial injustice." It also demanded not just more, but better. "[T]he city of man [must serve] not only the needs of the body and the demands of commerce but the desire for beauty and hunger for community."

The 1964 Election

During these early months the president had been helped by the desire to memorialize the martyred Kennedy. This impulse could not be expected to last indefinitely. Fortunately for the Great Society the Republican right handed the president an enormous extension of time that he would put to good use.

Although powerful at the grass roots, especially in the Midwest and Southwest, for years the conservative wing of the Republican party had been frustrated in its quest for the presidency. Far too often the party had turned to its moderate wing at the quadrennial presidential nominating conventions. As the 1964 presidential election approached, the Republican right was determined it would not happen again. This time one of their own would carry the GOP banner.

The right had an attractive candidate in Senator Barry Goldwater of Arizona, a handsome former Phoenix department store owner and reserve air force general. Goldwater had published a book, *The Conscience of a Conservative,* urging slashes in federal spending, tough restrictions on organized labor, the end of federal involvement in racial issues, and "total victory" over the Communist effort "to capture the world and destroy the United States." He quickly became the party conservatives' standard-bearer.

The moderate and liberal Republicans led by Nelson Rockefeller and Governor William Scranton of Pennsylvania fought Goldwater and his band of "extremists" at the July national convention in San Francisco. But the Goldwater forces were too aggressive and determined. The Arizona Senator secured the nomination on the first ballot and in a defiant acceptance speech, proclaimed that "extremism in defense of liberty is no vice and . . . moderation in the pursuit of justice is no virtue." Goldwater's campaign, with vice presidential nominee William Miller, an obscure New York Congressman, used as its slogan "A Choice, Not An Echo."

Johnson won the Democratic nomination at Atlantic City by acclamation with Senator Hubert Humphrey of Minnesota as his running mate. The one flaw in what was otherwise a love feast was the challenge by the Mississippi Freedom Democratic party (MFDP) of the regular all-white state delegation, chosen in all-white primaries. Elected by an unofficial "freedom" primary during the Mississippi "Freedom Summer" civil rights drive of 1964, the MFDP delegates, mostly African-American, defended their claim before the credentials committee through the eloquent middle-aged black woman Fannie Lou Hamer, who described the systematic exclusion of black Mississippians from the ballot and argued that MFDP alone supported the president's doctrines and values in Mississippi. But the Johnson forces, fearing loss of the whole South, imposed a compromise that allowed the MFDP only a token representation, although promising to do better in 1968. In later months many young civil rights workers would remember this rebuff with anger.

The presidential campaign was a Republican disaster. Many moderate and liberal Republican leaders refused to work for Goldwater. Thousands of voters, normally Republican, deserted the party. Goldwater had left many hostages to political fortune in past ill-considered proposals and political suggestions. He had offered to sell the respected Tennessee Valley Authority to private interests for a dollar; he had speculated that it might be a good thing if the eastern seaboard were sawed off the continent and allowed to float out to sea; he had suggested the elimination of federal rural electrification programs; he had proposed making social security a voluntary system. As recently as 1963 he had made the frightening proposal that local NATO commanders be given the power to use nuclear weapons in a crisis without presidential authorization. Each of these ideas would return to haunt the candidate.

The Democrats took advantage of every opportunity their opponents gave them. They depicted Johnson as a fatherly, benevolent figure, a reasonable and moderate man compared with the "radical right" fanatic from Arizona who intended to dismantle the welfare state and blow up the world. In fact the president was not exactly a pacifist either. During these months the Johnson administration was committing the United States to an ever-expanding role in Vietnam. In August, citing an attack by North Vietnamese naval vessels on the American destroyer *Maddox,* the president secured the Gulf of Tonkin Resolution from Congress, authorizing the administration to "take all necessary measures to repel any armed attack against the forces of the United States." He would soon use the resolution as a license to expand the American commitment in Vietnam. (See Chapter 4.) Yet during the campaign Johnson pledged "no wider war" and the Democrats felt free to accuse their opponents of being trigger-happy.

The results were no surprise. The Johnson-Humphrey ticket roared to victory with 61 percent of the popular vote, an even larger proportion than FDR had won in 1936. It also took every electoral vote except fifty-two, all of these from the deep South, except Arizona, Goldwater's home state. The new eighty-ninth Congress would have overwhelming Democratic majorities: 68 to 32 in the Senate, 295 to 140 in the House.

The Great Society at High Noon

The next two years were among the most legislatively productive in American history. The president claimed an enormous public mandate, a "consensus" for change that he quickly converted into a reform tidal wave.

The first administration successes came with passage of a federal aid to education bill (the Elementary and Secondary School Act) and the Medicare Act, establishing a system of free medical care for persons over 65 under the Social Security system. Medicare did not provide the full health insurance coverage for all Americans that liberals had urged since the New Deal, but it was an important installment.

In August 1965 Congress enacted an Omnibus Housing Act providing rent supplements for low-income families; in September it established a new cabinet-level Department of Housing and Urban Development and a National Foundation of Arts and the Humanities to encourage music, dance, painting, theater, and research in the humanistic disciplines. In October it passed a Water Quality Act and an Air Quality Act mandating higher standards for the nation's waters and imposing automobile exhaust controls. That same month came a Higher Education Act providing the first federal scholarships for college students. Other measures of that remarkable eighty-ninth Congress included a teacher corps, subsidies for new mental health facilities, aid to urban mass transit, and new consumer protection legislation.

The president was even able to get another installment of civil rights legislation. The Voting Rights Act of 1965 forbade literacy tests as a requirement of voter registration and allowed the federal government to supervise voter registration where there was clear evidence that the local authorities were preventing minorities from registering.

The Tax Cut and Prosperity

Johnson owed his success in part to his legislative skill, in part to the accident of lopsided majorities in Congress. But there was another crucial factor: the nation was prosperous as never before. The tax cut of his first months as president, a measure that benefited the middle class disproportionately, had done the trick. In 1964 the GNP rose an impressive 6.3 percent; in the next year the growth rate rose even faster.

Growth rates per capita during the 1960s would exceed those for any period during this century. At the same time, in the peak years of the Great Society inflation was low, under two percent in 1965 for all consumer prices. Millions of Americans felt flush, expansive, generous. The country surely could afford to allocate some slices of its ever-expanding pie to people who were less fortunate.

An Evaluation of Great Society Programs

It is not clear how effective the Great Society was. Middle-class programs, such as the National Endowments, clearly enriched scholarship and the arts. Many professors have reason to praise Johnson. Programs to improve the environment, although obviously insufficient, were necessary early steps in the long-term campaign to avoid world ecological disaster. Education programs helped thousands of students through undergraduate, graduate, and professional programs. But what about the antipoverty measures, the crux of the Great Society?

Here the experts disagree. Conservative scholars, as we shall see, believe that many of the antipoverty programs did not work. In fact some claim that by creating a high level of dependency, they only created even more poor, people incapable of working and earning their own income. The left criticized the Great Society as too little, too late. It did not redistribute income from rich to poor. Michael Harrington, the man whose exposé of American poverty, *The Other America,* had inspired the War on Poverty, concluded, "What was supposed to be a social war turned out to be a skirmish and, in any case, poverty won."

The truth seems to be rather complex. Clearly the Great Society programs provided jobs for educated men and women, African-American and white—as administrators, office workers, social workers, and teachers of skills. Poverty programs undeniably were pork barrels, and this time new people, some of them ghetto activists with militant goals and advisers with left-liberal social agendas, were being cut in. City mayors, many good Democrats, often objected to local people, especially militants, having direct access to federal money and thereby bypassing them, and these mayors carried their objections to the president and the vice president. The media, meanwhile, gave every excess of the Community Action Programs generous attention, in the process arousing serious public doubts.

But did the programs reduce poverty and even out some of the inequalities of American life? To some extent, apparently, they did. Head Start, a program to teach poor children language and other skills at an early age, seemed to make a difference in the later performance of ghetto children in school and the job market. Job-training programs provided marketable skills for some poor people. Various "entitlements" programs—providing health, education, food, rent supplements, and other services and commodities—raised the income of those at the economic bottom. On the other hand, as Harrington says, poverty won. Its sources lay too deep to be eliminated through programs such as those supplied by the Great Society.

The Breakdown of the Civil Rights Movement

African-Americans, of course, had been major beneficiaries of the upwelling of social generosity. Americans recognized the special afflictions of the country's black people, and Great Society programs had conferred disproportionate boons on the inner-city ghettos. From 1965 on this reservoir of goodwill rapidly drained away. An important piece of the Great Society consensus would break off.

One cause was the changing mood within the civil rights community itself. As early as the Marcus Garvey movement of the 1920s a small minority of African-American leaders had attacked the idea of a nonsegregated, biracial society. Garvey had supported black separatism and urged the return of blacks to Africa. In 1931 Elijah Muhammad, born Elijah Poole, had founded the Black Muslims, a religious group that rejected Christianity as a white people's religion and turned the negative white stereotypes of African-Americans upside down. Muhammad and his disciples called whites "blue-eyed devils," the "human beast," and "liars and murderers," and advocated total separation of black people from white society.

Muhammad's most effective disciple, although later an opponent, was Malcolm X, a young street hustler converted to the Muslim faith while in prison. Malcolm advocated the use of force, although only to protect African-Americans against physical violence, and eventually abandoned antiwhite views. He broke with the main Muslim group under Elijah Muhammad in 1964 and in 1965 was assassinated, allegedly by some of his factional enemies.

The Muslims' chief following was in the northern urban ghettos. In 1966 they were joined by the Black Panthers, organized in Oakland, California by two young African-American junior-college students, Bobby Seale and Huey Newton. The Panthers favored black self-defense against police brutality. Their members wore paramilitary garb and, for a time, carried rifles openly in public. Their macho style and bravado attracted African-American inner-city youths. It provoked the police, and almost from their birth the Panthers and the cops engaged in bloody clashes for which both sides were often to blame.

The Muslims and the Panthers were the fringe. But by 1965 militancy and separatist black nationalism had begun to invade the civil rights mainstream, where a biracial, color-blind society had been the fond goal and nonviolent civil disobedience, the preferred means.

In part the change derived from the struggles of Third World peoples in Africa, Asia, and Latin America to throw off their colonial chains. In Africa by the mid-sixties there were already several independent black nations, and more were soon to follow. Their struggles and successes created a new sense of pride in young African-American men and women. They also provided a model for the African-American experience at home. Black students read *The Wretched of the Earth,* Frantz Fanon's account of the Algerian battle for freedom against the French, and identified with the revolutionists. Weren't African-Americans just a colonialized people like the Nigerians, Congolese, or Algerians who were fighting against European oppressors? This black nationalist mood emotionally bound the new militants to powerful currents sweeping the Third World.

But events at home were even more important than those abroad as a spur to militancy and separatism. In 1964 SNCC launched its "Freedom Summer" project in Mississippi, the South's poorest and most segregated state. Hundreds of northern volunteers, mostly white college students, came to Mississippi to join the SNCC workers and local African-American leaders already on the scene in a program of voter

Black Panthers on the steps of
the California Capitol. (AP/Wide
World Photos)

registration, "freedom schools" for black children, and the creation of a biracial
Democratic party.

The summer started with tragedy. While white student volunteers were training in
Oxford, Ohio, to meet the summer's trials and dangers, news arrived that three young
civil rights workers in Mississippi, including two northern whites, had disappeared.
The volunteers came anyway. They encountered ferocious hostility from white
Mississippians who saw them as an invading horde determined to upset the South's
delicate racial balance. They received little help from the federal authorities. Over
eighty SNCC volunteers were beaten, scores were shot at, and a thousand thrown into
fetid jails. One participant later wrote that Freedom Summer had been "the longest
nightmare I ever had." On August 13 the bodies of the three missing civil rights
workers were found buried in an earthen dam. Later twenty-one white men, including
several police, were arrested for the crime. The authorities judged the evidence for a
murder charge insufficient, but sixteen of the suspects were later tried for violating
the victims' civil rights.

The Mississippi Freedom Summer experience, as hoped, attracted media attention and reinforced northern liberal sympathies for the civil rights cause. Among the participants themselves it produced mixed results. Many white students returned to their northern college campuses convinced that America was an irretrievably racist society. Some of these young men and women would become leaders in the new left student movement just beginning to emerge on college campuses. African-American participants generally felt let down. Many resented the white students who had at times acted arrogantly and when the summer ended, had been able to pull up stakes and return to their safe ivy-walled campuses, leaving them to face the racists' hostility alone. These feelings further encouraged separatism. The experience also weakened SNCC's faith in nonviolence. Turning the other cheek had not protected the volunteers against attack; it had not saved the three murdered civil rights workers. Why not meet violence with violence? Before long the SNCC leaders and other young black militants would proclaim "Black Power" and challenge the nonviolence and biracialism of Martin Luther King and SCLC.

By this time SCLC had passed its peak. In early 1965 King had been able to mobilize the support of white clergy and northern white liberals to further African-American voter registration in Selma, Alabama, over the opposition of Sheriff Jim Clark and Governor George Wallace. The confrontations had been bloody; several white participants, including a Detroit homemaker and a Unitarian minister, had been shot and killed by white racists. Their martyrdom had revolted liberals and provided Johnson with the moral ammunition he needed to induce Congress to pass the 1965 Voting Rights Act.

A year later, during a march for freedom to protest the shooting of civil rights leader James Meredith, the phrase "Black Power" first surfaced. At rallies along the highway to Jackson, Mississippi, the state capital, SNCC leader Stokely Carmichael, a young black firebrand from New York, began to shout "We want black power! Black power!" The older leaders objected. Roy Wilkins of the NAACP denounced the term and the idea as "the father of hatred and the mother of violence." It meant separatism; it meant "going it alone." King, however, feared driving the young militants away and hedged. His hesitation did not help his reputation with the firebrands. By this time SNCC was ridiculing King as "de lawd" and denouncing his faith in nonviolence and "black and white together." Soon after SNCC and CORE expelled their white members to "go it alone."

Black Power frightened and offended many whites who had hitherto supported the civil rights movement. King and others tried to reassure white liberals, but increasingly white people felt hurt and excluded. Many would now stand by the sidelines; some would reconsider earlier attitudes.

King Turns North

By this time Reverend King had turned his attention to the northern inner cities, where African-American ghetto dwellers were beginning to express the new insurgent mood violently. Beginning in August 1965 with Watts in Los Angeles and then for the following three "long hot summers" in Chicago, Cleveland, Detroit, Newark, Washington, and over 100 other cities stupendous riots turned black neighborhoods into smoking ruins that resembled Berlin or Tokyo at the end of World War II. These explosions of rage were often ignited by reports of police brutality; they then fed on the enormous bottled-up resentment of black ghetto dwellers toward white storekeepers, landlords, the welfare bureaucracy, and "the man" generally.

Critics pointed to the self-serving motives of many rioters. Some African-American leaders believed they were only hurting their own cause. Yet they had their defenders. However unfocused, said black militants and white radicals, the rioters were primitive revolutionaries who were acting the only way possible against a system that would no longer yield to persuasion.

King had gone to Watts while the pall of smoke still rose over the city and had resolved to turn his attention to the problems of the northern ghettos. In a sense with Selma and the Voting Rights Act the civil rights movement of the fifties and early sixties had achieved as much as it could. Segregation was gone or going; African-Americans were beginning to vote in the South in large numbers. Yet almost everywhere African-American poverty remained, a reproach to America's promise of opportunity and economic success.

There were many causes of this continuing inferiority. Black education was substandard; blacks were excluded from trade union membership and apprenticeship programs; blacks remained segregated in urban slums where housing was expensive and dilapidated and where jobs and good shopping were limited. Soon after Watts King resolved to turn SCLC's attention to the urban ghettos, concentrating on Chicago and its harsh housing discrimination practices.

In early 1966 King set up headquarters in Chicago and launched a campaign against the North's informal discrimination. African-American ghetto housing must be improved, King announced, and African-American people must be allowed to move to any neighborhood they wished.

It was far harder to desegregate housing then King and his colleagues had anticipated. Landlords and real estate companies resisted changes in their practices. White homeowners feared that blacks would destroy the value of their property and the peace of their communities. In Chicago Mayor Richard Daley claimed that King and his associates were outsiders who were stirring up trouble for no good reason.

King and his followers were not deterred. SCLC and other local African-American organizations mounted protest marches into white neighborhoods; they held rallies downtown to demand an end to segregated housing. The protestors encountered even worse hostility in the tight-knit Chicago ethnic communities than in the South. By now a new force had appeared on the political scene in the shape of "white backlash," a formidable resistance to any further concessions to black protesters. In Chicago backlash citizens—many the white-collar and blue-collar children and grandchildren of European immigrants—felt threatened by African-American political and economic aspirations and asked why they, whose forebears had not received help from the government as had African-Americans, should be made to pay the price of black advancement. When King and his followers marched through backlash neighborhoods, they encountered jeers and violence. Many protesters, including King himself, were injured in stone-throwing incidents.

In the end King got the mayor and the city's business, real estate, and financial leaders to accept the principle of fair housing. But the pact with the city was an empty gesture, and almost everyone knew it. Chicago, like almost every place else, remained a ghet-toized city. To save face, however, King pronounced the Chicago campaign a success.

The Poor People's Campaign and Death of King

By late 1967 King had been forced to recognize that the really hard part of the struggle for racial equality remained. In December King announced that in the spring SCLC would mount a "Poor People's Campaign" to force the federal government to provide jobs, education, and housing for the poor—all the poor.

By now the full-scale war in Vietnam was causing serious problems for King and his civil rights colleagues. The antiwar movement drained off further white liberal support from the civil rights drive. The war also divided the black civil rights leadership. The conservative civil rights groups, the Urban League and the NAACP, were grateful to Johnson and the Great Society for what they had done for African-Americans and poor people and feared offending the president. The militant leaders of SNCC and CORE, on the other hand, had little use for Johnson-style liberalism in any case and saw Vietnam as a white man's neocolonial war against people of color.

By 1967 King, a man in the political middle, had become a prominent antiwar leader. He opposed the war in part because he believed in nonviolence. He also believed that ghetto youths were disproportionately sacrificing their lives while at the same time the war was starving the Great Society programs that benefited ghetto dwellers and the poor generally. Although he was reluctant to place himself in opposition to the Johnson administration, he could not keep silent. In August 1965 King began to denounce the war and demand a negotiated settlement.

The administration struck back. From 1962 on the FBI had been wiretapping King and his associates on the suspicion that SCLC was being influenced by one or more secret Communist agents. Even after these charges were laid to rest, J. Edgar Hoover and his agents continued the surveillance. Eventually they uncovered the fact that King occasionally drank too much and had committed adultery. Hoping to destroy King's reputation, Hoover leaked the information to federal officials, prominent journalists, and religious leaders and had his agents anonymously send King himself a tape of his sexual indiscretions accompanied with the advice that he commit suicide. After King's defection to the antiwar movement, President Johnson endorsed Hoover's scheme to undermine the civil rights leader's moral authority.

On April 4, 1968, Martin Luther King, Jr., was assassinated by James Earl Ray, a white man probably in the pay of southern racists, as he stood on a motel balcony in Memphis, Tennessee. King had gone to the city to help striking black sanitation workers. News of King's murder set off a wave of ghetto riots that put the long hot summers of the past to shame. Chicago, Baltimore, Detroit, and other cities previously damaged by riots exploded. Now the nation's capital joined the list of cities looted, burned, and trashed. It took 55,000 troops around the country to restore order to the nation's cities.

The Reverend Ralph Abernathy, one of King's lieutenants, now became head of SCLC. He immediately declared that the Poor People's Campaign would commence that summer on schedule.

Despite Abernathy's brave efforts, however, he could never take King's place. The campaign's centerpiece was an encampment of African-Americans, white students, and Mexican-Americans near the Mall in Washington, D.C. Called "Resurrection City," it quickly fell into disarray. Rain turned the area into a swamp; vicious elements among the poor themselves preyed on the others. When the campaign disbanded in June, little if anything had been accomplished to extract new legislation from Congress to benefit the poor.

The demise of Resurrection City ended the "Second Reconstruction." It had dismantled the edifice of legal discrimination in America, but it had failed to end the economic and social inequality of white and black in America. Time would show that these were far more perplexing and far more difficult to eradicate within the framework of liberal society than Jim Crow.

The Rise and Fall of the New Left

The militancy boiling up in the civil rights and peace movements was part of a new, radical mood sweeping the nation at large. The new attitude affected adults, but it was especially potent among the educated young.

By the mid-1960s American colleges and universities were overflowing with students. In 1966 there were over five and a half million college students in the United States, a larger number by far than ever before in its history. The educational explosion was fueled in part by the post-1945 "baby boom," a social change that had reversed the century-long trend to lower birthrates. It was also powered by the growing prestige and value of a college degree. Overall prosperity, newly available federal aid, and a strong sense that the technical and professional skills that colleges dispensed were essential to success in the new economy all combined to make B.A.s, J.D.s, and Ph.D.s the goal of an expanding percentage of young men and women. When economists were saying that the universities were the engines of national wealth and power, it was natural for the young to flock to the campuses.

But in addition to those seeking vocations, there were those seeking enlightenment. Especially in the "soft disciplines"—the humanities and the social sciences—students often displayed a less materialistic attitude than those in the career-oriented fields. By the early 1960s many young, middle-class adults were beginning to feel that material success was not enough. American society appeared to have solved most of its economic difficulties, and there was no need for college-educated people to fear joblessness and hunger. Yet having grown up in the properous postwar era when success came easy, the affluent college young took little pleasure from material abundance, a condition that had brought great satisfaction to their parents. American society was still imperfect. Racism remained; the threat of nuclear war remained. Moreover alienation, powerlessness, environmental ugliness, conformity, intellectual barrenness, and intolerance all survived to diminish life in America. The "quantity" problems had been solved; now it was time to tackle the "quality" problems.

The new mood flourished in part as a reaction to the immediate past. During the 1950s dissent and social speculation had been constrained by McCarthyism and the self-congratulatory mood that followed success in World War II and the unexpected burst of postwar prosperity. McCarthy was now gone, and young Americans had come to take prosperity for granted. It was now time for a *New Left*, detached from the old, dogmatic Communist left, to destroy complacency, end the vestiges of inequality, and create a more humane, fulfilling, and democratic society.

Campus Radicalism

Such at least were the professed attitudes and goals of the first wave of student activists. As the fifties ended, here and there on some of the more cosmopolitan campuses small groups of young men and women were beginning to place social and political change on the undergraduate agenda. Some focused on peace; many were for a time drawn into the civil rights movement, especially as support troops for SNCC. Others made civil liberties their chief concern. A sizable proportion of this early group were the children of radicals, including Communists, although most of these "red diaper babies" were not strict Marxists. They no longer glorified the industrial working-class (the proletariat). They believed they themselves were the most potent

Students occupying Columbia University, 1968. (UPI/Bettmann Newphotos)

"agents" of social change. They had abandoned their parents' one-time pro-Soviet viewpoint. If any nation won their admiration it was Cuba, whose young charismatic leader, Fidel Castro, seemed to embody the best of the radical tradition without the dogmatism. Although undogmatic they were not, even at the outset, decorous. Young people are almost invariably swept away by enthusiasms, by passions, by infatuations. From the beginning their seniors often deplored their excesses of deed and word.

The existence of a new campus left burst on the public consciousness in the fall of 1964 when student insurgents at the University of California at Berkeley challenged the university administration's decision, under conservative pressure, to restrict political advocacy on the Berkeley campus. Organized as the Free Speech Movement (FSM), the students occupied the administration building and called a strike when the police ousted them bodily. Sympathetic to free speech and appalled by the police intrusion into academe, the faculty and liberal segments of the California community supported FSM, forcing the administration to relent.

Berkeley was the precedent for a thousand student rallies, strikes, and building takeovers during the next few years. These were directed against university "complicity" in the Vietnam War, against university "racism," against campus recruitment by the military and by companies such as Dow Chemical that made war matériel; and against the impersonality and repressiveness of the campus experience, the "irrelevance" of undergraduate curricula, or some other supposed failing of college life. They would at times force administrators to adopt more "relevant" courses and curricula, abandon paternalistic rules, and exclude unpopular speakers and recruiters from campus. Many of the campus confrontations were led by Students for a Democratic Society (SDS), formed in the early 1960s as the student affiliate of the League for Industrial Democracy (LID), an anticommunist moderate socialist group dating from before World War I.

SDS

SDS's early leaders were a group of young men and women at Ann Arbor, Michigan, including Al Haber, Tom Hayden, Richard Flacks, and Sharon Jeffrey, in tune with the new post-McCarthy student mood. In 1962 the Ann Arbor activists sponsored the Port Huron Statement, which endorsed "participatory democracy" to end powerlessness in America and declared that with blue-collar labor in the rich industrial nations fat and complacent, students were the most promising agents of social change. SDS soon established chapters at other colleges, usually prestigious campuses with a large proportion of cosmopolitan, affluent students.

After 1965 SDS became a major force in the campus anti-Vietnam movement, although the SDS leadership was always curiously reluctant to make the war the organization's chief concern. By 1966 SDS had broken with its parent group, LID, over excluding Communists and opened its membership rolls to hard-line Marxists oriented either to the Soviet Union or Communist China.

SDS fell apart at its national convention in Chicago in June 1969. There the old leaders of 1962 were present, if at all, only as observers. One faction, the "national office," convinced that social change could be midwived only by "wild in the streets" rebellious youth and by Third World revolutionaries like the Black Panthers, fought the hard-line Marxists led by the Progressive Labor party. Afraid to be outvoted, the national office group marched out of the hall leaving Progressive Labor in control. Within months the national office faction was planning to go underground to fight a guerrilla war against American "imperialism." The shell of SDS, under Progressive Labor leadership, ceased to attract members and soon expired.

Before its demise SDS had helped scatter New Left seeds in all directions. College faculties, portions of the literary, artistic, and intellectual communities, journalists, and some professional groups either borrowed its views and rhetoric or actually drew part of their membership from young SDS alumni radicalized in college. By the early 1970s, moreover, several major organs of opinion—the *New York Review of Books* and *The Nation*, for example—were disseminating New Left positions widely among their readers. The journalist Tom Wolfe called the views of the adult intellectual-literary leftists "radical chic." Yet with the demise of SDS the framework of the New Left collapsed. By mid-decade it was gone.

Repression

The New Left had largely destroyed itself by its immaturity, irresponsibility, and inability to understand American realities. But its demise was helped along by its enemies. Not only had the FBI sought to undermine Martin Luther King; it had also tried to confuse and distract the student left and the Black Panthers. Under the label "COINTELPRO," the FBI had infiltrated SDS, the peace movement, and the Panthers. Its purpose was not only to gather information on possible illegal doings but also to sow confusion by dirty tricks. FBI agents, for example, tried to prevent an alliance between SDS and the Panthers by sending anonymous letters purporting to come from one group personally attacking leaders of the other organization. Hoover's agents planted stories about the sexual misconduct of radicals and peace leaders. They induced the Internal Revenue Service to examine the tax returns of left peace movement leaders to tie them up in complex audits. The FBI even established a hit list of dangerous radicals to be rounded up in event of war. All told, whatever the provocation it was not a pretty picture for a democratic society still a long way from the edge of chaos.

The Counterculture

Paralleling and often interlocking with the New Left was the counterculture. This was a movement of revolt against the moral values, the aesthetic standards, the personal behavior, and the social relations of conventional society. (See the photograph opening this chapter.) It differed from earlier bohemias and even from the fifties beatnik phenomenon by its intimate association with consciousness-altering drugs. Although the Beats smoked marijuana ("grass") and even imbibed peyote and psilocybin, they did not make these drugs central to their lives. And they did not have lysergic acid diethylamide (LSD) the most potent hallucinogen of all. So fundamental was this substance to the new bohemia that the novelist Alan Harrington has said that the counterculture was "no more than Beats plus drugs."

Psychedelia

LSD (acid) is an artificial derivative of a natural fungus, first produced by a Swiss chemist in 1943. It stimulates fantastic images and states of mind where circles whirl, solid objects liquify, and colors produce sounds or tastes. LSD "trips," when they do not turn into terrifying nightmares, create the sense in the participant that ordinary perceptions are impoverished and that the world is infinitely richer than it seems. It later became clear that the drug is also harmful genetically, can precipitate psychosis, and might destroy the mental balance of chronic users.

For a time, however, LSD promised a new world liberated from the tedium of ordinary life. In the hands of Timothy Leary, a one-time psychology professor at Harvard, and Ken Kesey, a successful West Coast novelist, along with their friends and disciples, it seemed an instrument for undermining the "square," humdrum world of competitive striving, conventional sexual relations, and "linear" thinking. Leary sought to spread his message of "turn on, tune in, drop out" through a new ecstatic religion with its headquarters in Millbrook, New York. The authorities eventually closed it down and Leary himself ran afoul of the law. Kesey, author of the best-selling *One Flew Over the Cuckoo's Nest,* a novel describing the absurd workings of a mental hospital, proselytized for the new drug-induced utopia through music. The "acid tests," a series of San Francisco area rock and roll concerts charged up with LSD and flashing strobe lights, helped popularize the use of hallucinogen.

"Psychedelic" drugs quickly merged with the rock music scene. The practitioners of "acid rock," including such groups as the Grateful Dead, the Jefferson Airplane, the Fugs, Country Joe and the Fish, and the Quicksilver Messenger Service, incorporated the blasting sounds and sights of the acid experience into their music. Their concerts were celebrations of the new psychedelia. The new hallucinogens also eventually influenced the British groups the Rolling Stones and the Beatles, the latter being four English youths from Liverpool, whose first American visit in 1964 had produced an hysterical outpouring of adulation called Beatlemania. Their song "Lucy in the Sky with Diamonds" of 1967 was a thinly disguised hymn to LSD.

Rock music was a major transmission agent for the drug culture. The concerts at San Francisco's Fillmore auditorium and its imitators in other cities enveloped young people in the words, music, and sights of the acid culture and, often, in clouds of marijuana smoke as well. Rock festivals, beginning with the 1967 outdoor concerts in Monterey, California, were two- or three-day saturnalias of music, acid, and "grass." The festivals culminated with the immense gathering at Max Yasgur's farm in Woodstock, New York, in August 1969. Woodstock brought together all the elements of the counterculture community, including a political branch led by Abbie Hoffman and Jerry Rubin, two radicals who in early 1968 had organized the Yippies, an amalgam of political and cultural dissent. Woodstock seemed to be the beginning of a new counterculture "nation." In reality it marked the beginning of the end of the counterculture as an organized (or semiorganized) movement.

Hippies

Clearly, the most committed inhabitants of psychedelia were the hippies, denizens of a new subculture that abruptly appeared in San Francisco, New York, Los Angeles, and a few other major cities and college towns in 1966–67. Mostly young dropouts from middle-class suburbia, hippies, unlike many New Left activists, totally repudiated their origins. Their parents cherished material possessions; they would cultivate holy poverty. Their parents valued emotional control and self-denial; they would cultivate free expression and hedonism. Their parents were enslaved to competitive, aggressive responses; they would be guided by "love" and "flower power."

The hippie phenomenon first came to the attention of the general public with the "Human Be-In" held in San Francisco's Golden Gate Park in January 1967. Billed as a gathering of the "tribes"—of the "new people" of the new, liberated age—the Be-In announced the appearance of a new self-conscious counterculture community in the adjacent Haight-Ashbury neighborhood.

"The Haight" had its distinctive fauna—natives wearing beards, sandals, leotards, jeans, and miniskirts. It had its distinctive economy—poster shops, coffee houses, "headshops," arts and crafts emporia, and, barely out of sight, a legion of drug pushers. It had its own media and art—underground press, "comix," and psychedelic posters. So distinctive and colorful was this latest version of bohemia that by April 1967 the Grey Line Bus Company was running tours to the Haight for curious squares. By the late spring every rebellious sixteen-year-old was talking about "making the scene" in the Haight during the summer. It would be, everyone said, a glorious "Summer of Love."

The Haight-Ashbury Summer of Love, and its equivalent in New York's East Village, was an extraordinary experience. Thousands of young people crowded the streets and the "pads," "grooving" on grass and acid and the free concerts on Hippie Hill or in Central Park. They lived on money from home, by selling dope, panhandling tourists, or by taking handouts from the Diggers, a group of political-cultural anarchists who opposed private property and made "free" their motto. Many Haight-Asbury and East Village refugees found the experience liberating. But there was another side too. Disease, bad trips, ripoffs, thefts, and rape spread among the "flower children." Several drug dealers and a number of hippies were murdered. When September came many of the visitors were glad to return home.

There would be no more summers of love, but the hippie ethic did not suddenly die. Returnees from Haight-Ashbury and the East Village brought to their college communities and home towns much of the hippie culture. Some hippies sought to make the new ethic a permanent way of life by establishing communes, utopian communities where the new values could replace the old. The public's fascination with the hippie ethic continued and helped make *Easy Rider,* a counterculture movie epic starring Peter Fonda and Dennis Hopper, a big success in 1969. The hippie viewpoint also informed *Hair,* a commercially successful "tribal rock" musical about a young, long-haired man who ends up in Vietnam. *Hair* celebrated the "Age of

Aquarius" where peace, pot, perversion, and "crystal revelation" would all prevail. "Guerrilla theater," a form of street spectacle, also drew on the counterculture style and sought to bend it to political, antiwar, and social liberation ends.

The Sexual Revolution

The counterculture proclaimed the merits of sexual freedom and placed instinctual liberation at the center of its vision. It was responding to major changes in morals and attitudes that affected American society at large.

The sixties decade marked the culmination of a sexual revolution that had been building at least since the forties. In 1948 Alfred Kinsey, a zoology professor at Indiana University, published the epoch-making *Sexual Behavior in the Human Male*. The work made sex seem a less forbidden subject by making it "scientific" and by revealing how common sex outside of marriage actually was. During the next decade Hugh Hefner's *Playboy* magazine, purveying a hedonist message and featuring young women bare above the waist, became the publishing sensation of the era. Soon the courts began to strike down local laws banning obscene books. The process of extending free speech guarantees to sexual expression culminated in the early 1960s with a series of federal court decisions allowing publication of any work so long as it contained a trace of "redeeming social value."

The courts' rulings allowed the open publication for the first time of a number of literary classics, but it also opened the floodgates for much outright pornography. A major beneficiary of this breakthrough was the underground press that appeared soon after. These publications included sexual news and "personals" offering sexual services as a staple of each issue. In 1968 the movie industry finally abandoned its dated "production code" and replaced it with a rating system—"G" (general), "M" (mature), "R" (restricted), and "X" (no one under sixteen admitted)—that allowed the showing of sexually explicit films. Soon scores of city downtowns sprouted X-rated movie houses to cater to the curious. Theater too was soon "liberated." Serious plays displayed nudity and featured dialogue formerly only heard in military barracks or locker rooms. Tom O'Horgan's *Futz* was about a man who loved his pig—physically.

By now sexual permissiveness had developed an intellectual rationale. The neo-Freudian writings of Norman O. Brown and Wilhelm Reich blamed many of society's ills on instinctual repression. Herbert Marcuse, a transplanted Middle European, labeled sexual repression a tool of capitalist domination. Marcuse, especially, became a guru to the counterculture and the spacier segment of the New Left.

The growing sexual permissiveness undoubtedly escalated sexual indulgence. Although the information is inconclusive, it seems clear that young people in the sixties had sex sooner, more often, and in more exotic ways than their parents ever dreamed possible.

The *sexual revolution* of the sixties cannot be ascribed solely to changes in cultural and moral attitudes. Even more important, probably, were two medical breakthroughs of the postwar period: mass produced antibiotics and the birth control pill. These supposedly eliminated the chief inconveniences of casual sex, disease and pregnancy. Together they created for a time a sense of security that promised to make "free love" really free. It was a brief interlude that would not last.

The New Feminism

The social restlessness and discontent and the desire for liberation that stirred African-Americans and youth during the sixties also influenced women. In 1961, as we saw, the President's Commission on the Status of Women had begun to stimulate a new response to women's concerns after the slow years of the fifties. Women, black and white, had also participated in the civil rights movement. They had become activists in the early New Left. These activities conferred new activist skills and aroused new impatience with deference and hierarchies of power. Then in 1963 Betty Friedan, a middle-aged Smith College graduate, helped crystalize a new feminist consciousness with her book *The Feminine Mystique.*

Friedan noted and deplored the decline of women's aspirations during the forties and fifties. She identified the subtle negative effects of sexism and called for a return to feminist activism to wipe out the large remaining areas of social and economic discrimination against women. In an era when all disadvantaged groups were raising the banner of equality against the white male "establishment," the book struck a resounding chord.

In 1966 Friedan and like-minded women formed the National Organization for Women (NOW). (See Reading 12.) NOW, like the NAACP, sought to work through the existing political system, using lobbying techniques and legal challenges against discrimination. In 1967 it endorsed the Equal Rights Amendment, supported by feminists since the 1920s, to insert into the Constitution a prohibition against all discrimination based on sex.

More radical than NOW were *women's liberation* groups, offshoots of the New Left. The pioneer "liberationists" were women who were former members of SNCC, SDS, and similar radical organizations. Although politically radical, these groups had often limited women to routine, unglamourous organization work while the men held the executive positions and became media celebrities. When women members of SNCC and SDS objected to their subordination, the male leaders had often resorted to ridicule and derision.

Rebuffed, the women responded by reevaluating their position in the organizations and reconsidering the place of women in society. They concluded that "sexism" pervaded even the radical movement and that women could not expect it to disappear even if the radicals triumphed and established their "classless society." There must be a separate radical women's movement that would push for women's liberation from male oppression whatever the ideology. They also concluded that the chief oppressor was not capitalism as such. Rather it was "patriarchy," the rule of men, a system that had prevailed since remote times. Patriarchy was the ultimate source of domination and oppression in the world; capitalism was only one form of this system.

The women's liberationists were more radical in their attitudes toward gender and men than other feminists. They generally held that there were no essential differences in personality or abilities between men and women. The observed disparities were the result only of early training and education designed to keep women in inferior positions. These differences were then reinforced by fashion and feminine stereotypes in later life. Some believed that marriage and the traditional

READING 3

The NOW Statement of Purpose

The chief vehicle of the 1960s feminist movement was NOW—the National Organization for Women. Founded in October 1966 as an expression of the feminist surge that followed publication of Betty Friedan's The Feminine Mystique, *NOW represented the views primarily of middle-class, well-educated white women. But despite this limited base, it quickly became the most effective voice of the new women's movement of the sixties.*

We men and women who hereby constitute ourselves as the National Organization for Women, believe that the time has come for a new movement toward true equality for all women in America, and toward a fully equal partner-ship of the sexes, as part of the world-wide revolution of human rights now taking place within and beyond our national borders.

The purpose of NOW is to take action to bring women into full participation in the mainstream of American society now, exercising all the privileges and responsibilities thereof in truly equal partnership with men. . . .

We organize to initiate or support action, nationally, or in any part of this nation, by individuals or organizations, to break through the silken curtain of prejudice and discrimination against women in government, industry, the professions, the churches, the politcal parties, the judiciary, the labor unions, in education, science, medicine, law, religion and every other field of importance in American society.

Enormous changes taking place in our society make it both possible and urgently necessary to advance the unfinished revolution of women toward true equality, now. With a life span lengthened to nearly 75 years it is no longer either necessary or possible for women to devote the greater part of their lives to child-rearing; yet childbearing and rearing which continues to be a most important part of most women's lives—still is used to justify barring women from equal professional and economic participation and advance.

Today's technology has reduced most of the productive chores which women once performed in the home and in mass-production industries based upon routine unskilled labor. This same technology has virtually eliminated the quality of muscular strength as a criterion for filling most jobs, while intensifying American industry's need for creative intelligence. In view of this new industrial revolution created by automation in the mid-twentieth century, women can and must participate in old and new fields of society in full equality—or become permanent outsiders.

Despite all the talk about the status of American women in recent years, the actual position of women in the United States has declined, and is declining, to an alarming degree throughout the 1950's and 60's. . . . Working women are becoming increasingly—not less—concentrated on the bottom of the job ladder. . . . Further, with higher education increasingly essential in today's society, too few women are entering and finishing college or going on to graduate or professional school. . . . In all the professions considered of importance to society, and in the executive ranks of industry and government, women are losing ground. Where they are present it is only a token handful. . . .

Until now, too few women's organizations and official spokesmen have been willing to speak out against these dangers facing women. Too many women have been restrained by the fear of being called "feminist." There is no civil rights movement to speak for women, as there has been for Negroes and other victims of discrimination. The National Organization for Women must therefore begin to speak.

WE BELIEVE that the power of American law, and the protection guaranteed by the U.S. Constitution to the civil rights of all individuals, must be effectively applied and enforced to isolate and remove patterns of sex discrimination, to ensure equality of opportunity in employment and education, and equality of civil and political rights and responsibilities on behalf of women as well as for Negroes and other deprived groups. . . .

WE BELIEVE that this nation has a capacity at least as great as other nations, to innovate new social institutions which will enable women to enjoy true equality of opportunity and responsibility in society, without conflict with their responsibilities as mothers and homemakers. In such innovations, America does not lead the Western world, but lags by decades behind many European countries. We do not accept the traditional assumption that a woman has to choose between marriage and motherhood, on the one hand, and serious participation in industry or the professions on the other. We question the present expectation that all normal women will retire from job or profession for 10 or 15 years, to devote their full time to raising children, only to reenter the job market at a relatively minor level. This, in itself, is a deterrent to the aspirations of women, to their acceptance into management or professional training courses, and to the very possibility of equality of opportunity or real choice, for all but a few women. Above all, we reject the assumption that these problems are the unique responsibility of each individual woman, rather than a basic social dilemma which society must solve. True equality of opportunity and freedom of choice for women requires such practical, and possible innovations as a nationwide network of child-care centers, which will make it unnecessary for women to retire completely from society until their children are grown, and national programs to provide retraining for women who have chosen to care for their own children full-time. . . .

WE REJECT the current assumptions that a man must carry the sole burden of supporting himself, his wife, and family, and that a woman is automatically entitled to lifelong support by a man upon her marriage, or that marriage, home and family are primarily women's world and responsibility—hers to dominate—his to support. We believe that a true partnership between the sexes demands a different concept of marriage, an equitable sharing of the responsibilities of home and children and of the economic burdens of their support. We believe that proper recognition should be given to the economic and social value of homemaking and child-care. To these ends, we will seek to open a reexamination of laws and mores governing marriage and divorce, for we believe that the current state of "half-equality" between the sexes discriminated against both men and women, and is the cause of much unnecessary hostility between the sexes. . . .

IN THE INTERESTS OF THE HUMAN DIGNITY OF WOMEN, we will protest, and endeavor to change, the false image of women now prevalent in the mass media, and in the texts, ceremonies, laws, and practices of our major social institutions. Such images perpetuate contempt for women by society and by women for themselves. We are similarly opposed to all policies and practices—in church, state, college, factory, or office—which, in the guise of protectiveness, not only deny opportunities but also foster in women self-denigration, dependence, and evasion of responsibility, undermine their confidence in their own abilities and foster contempt for women. . . .

We will strive to ensure that no party, candidate, president, senator, governor, congressman, or any public official who betrays or ignores the principle to full equality between the sexes is elected for appointed to office. If it is necessary to mobilize the votes of men and women who believe in our cause, in order to win for women the final right to be fully free and equal human beings, we so commit ourselves.

WE BELIEVE THAT women will do most to create a new image of women by acting now, and by speaking out in behalf of their own equality, freedom, and human dignity—not in pleas for special privilege, nor in enmity toward men, who are also victims of the current, half-equality between the sexes—but in an active, self-respecting partnership with men. By so doing, women will develop confidence in their own ability to determine actively, in partnership with men, the conditions of their life, their choices, their future and their society.

Source: National Organization for Women, Washington, D.C. October 29, 1966.

family were agencies of oppression and wished to change them drastically or even abolish them entirely.

Often in movements for social change the key precipitating element is the sudden awareness of oppression by individuals or some group. In the case of women, said the liberationists, the oppression was often deeply hidden under layers of guilt, stoicism, even love for the male oppressor. The technique for getting to these underlying feelings was "consciousness-raising" (CR), a sort of group therapy, where women gathered by themselves and discussed their problems, often their difficulties with husbands, lovers, and fathers, although with mothers and other women as well. The effect, not surprisingly, was to bring their anger against men to the surface.

Consciousness-raising spread like wildfire in the years just after 1968. For many women CR was primarily a therapeutic technique. But it also served as a recruiting device for the radical wing of the new feminism. Over the next few years a flock of radical feminist groups such as the Redstocking, Radical Feminists, and WITCH appeared to question the fundamental relations of the sexes and indict male-dominated, sexist society. Several of these small organizations produced headlines and aroused both support and antagonism by disruptive tactics. One of their biggest publicity coups came in September 1968 when a group of radical feminists from the New York area picketed the Miss America contest in Atlantic City, charging that contemporary beauty standards were designed to keep women in silken bondage.

The Great Society Ends

As Johnson's full term drew to a close it became clear that he and his programs were in serious trouble.

The president's consensus was unraveling at both ends. To his extreme left were the student rebels and their supporters among the intellectuals. But these were not numerous, and besides their hostility probably helped politically more than it hurt.

Far more serious opponents on his left flank were the anti–Vietnam War group collecting around Senator Eugene McCarthy of Minnesota. These people despised the war and opposed the administration's continued escalation. In late 1967 the antiwar liberals had convinced McCarthy to challenge the president for the Democratic nomination in 1968. Although he considered the attempt quixotic, the senator had agreed and early in the election year had entered the New Hampshire Democratic primary.

The McCarthy drive captured the imagination of thousands of college students who poured into the Granite State to ring door bells, make calls, organize rallies, and stuff envelopes. To everyone's amazement, the challenger almost beat the incumbent president in the primary. Soon after, Robert Kennedy, then U.S. Senator from New York and another antiwar "dove," also threw his hat into the ring.

By this time LBJ realized that the Vietnam War could probably not be won. In January 1968 the Vietcong–North Vietnamese Tet offensive shook the president and undermined the public's confidence that a victory was possible. After Tet Secretary of Defense Clark Clifford and Johnson's closest foreign policy advisers recommended that the United States reduce its Vietnam commitment. (See the next chapter.) Meanwhile the president was also under attack on the right where the Great Society, and indeed the whole thrust of the sixties, had raised up a host of enemies.

Backlash

Much of the problem was beyond Johnson's reach. The American middle-class public had become skeptical of the civil rights movement now that it had shifted its attention north and had entered its black power phase. Among blue-collar white citizens, especially, the mood since the ghetto riots had become frankly hostile to African-Americans. Why were they rioting and destroying property when the country had tried so hard to help them? "We build the city, not burn it down," declared one blue-collar group.

Many of these same "middle Americans"—white, middle- and working-class people of conservative, family-oriented value—deplored other social trends as well. As the central cities decayed, urban crime rates rose. Many middle Americans believed that blacks were primarily responsible for both the decay and the crime. They also deplored the disruptive tactics of the radical students; they saw the counterculture as immoral and disrespectful; they regarded the sexual revolution as dangerous; they considered the radical feminists a disgrace to women. By the late sixties many of these backlash dissenters were enlisting under the banner of Governor George Wallace of Alabama and were spoiling to challenge the reign of the "pointy-headed liberals" who had encouraged the forces of immorality and chaos.

Inflation and a Tax Rise

In the 1966 midterm elections, the Republicans had recovered from the Goldwater debacle and cut sharply into Johnson's lopsided liberal majority in Congress. Further reform might have been possible, nevertheless, if the economy, so successful through most of the Johnson administration, had not begun to falter. By late 1967 the remarkable price stability of the preceding decade came to an end. The following year the consumer price index rose almost 5 percent. At the same time foreigners began to cash in their dollars for gold, pulling the yellow metal out of Fort Knox and the vaults of the New York Federal Reserve Bank. On New Years' Day 1968 the president announced restrictions on American private investment abroad and on the amount of money American tourists could spend overseas. But these were stopgaps, and in early March there was a near panic in the world's gold exchanges.

The basic problems were the federal deficit and Johnson's reluctance to tax the American people to pay for the Vietnam War because he feared that taxes would make the war even more unpopular. Finally in late 1967 he was forced to acknowledge the gap between federal income and outgo and ask for a 10 percent surcharge on federal income taxes.

This was a major defeat for the Great Society. Wilbur Mills, a southern fiscal and social conservative who headed the all-powerful House Ways and Means Committee, refused to sanction a tax increase unless the president promised to cut back on domestic social programs. To stop inflation the president must abandon his remaining reform agenda.

In mid-1968 Johnson finally got his tax increase. But he paid the price. The administration promised Mills that it would trim the federal budget. The president would continue to urge new social legislation to help the country's poor, but he recognized that he could no longer get more money to end poverty. In later years the outlays for the poor would actually grow as cost of living increases and other escalators pushed up dollar appropriations. But after mid-1968 there would be few new initiatives; the spirit of the Great Society experiment had departed.

The 1968 Election

The Candidates

By this time too Johnson had decided to withdraw from the presidential race. Fearing further humiliation in the primaries at the hands of the McCarthy and Kennedy forces and hoping that his withdrawal might encourage a peace settlement in Vietnam, he decided to renounce a second full term. On the evening of March 31 he appeared on national television to speak on Vietnam. Just before signing off the president read an addendum to the speech. He had concluded, he said, that he should not permit the presidency to become involved in the noisy contentions of the coming presidential year. "Accordingly, I shall not seek and I will not accept the nomination of my party for another term as your President."

The 1968 presidential campaign then moved into high gear. With Johnson out of the race, the two antiwar Democratic candidates battled it out in a series of bruising primary fights in Indiana, Oregon, and California. Kennedy's followers included most of the African-American, Hispanic, and blue-collar Democratic voters; McCarthy proved strongest among students, professionals, and suburbanites. The big prize was California, the nation's largest state. In June Kennedy won a close victory there, but in Los Angeles, minutes after his victory statement, the New York senator was gunned down by Sirhan Sirhan, an Arab nationalist who disliked his support for Israel. Within three months the nation had suffered a double trauma of politics by assassination. Many Americans wondered how things had come to such a sorry pass.

Kennedy's assassination made Vice President Hubert Humphrey the front-runner. As vice president, Humphrey, of course, had waited until Johnson's withdrawal to announce his candidacy. By that time it was too late to enter the primaries, but with the support of most of the Democratic mayors and public officials, the trade union leaders, and the party's power brokers, the vice president did not need the primary delegates. He won the nomination over McCarthy easily at the Chicago convention in late August. His running mate was Senator Edmund Muskie of Maine.

Yet Chicago was scarcely a Humphrey triumph. Well before the Kennedy assassination the antiwar left, represented by the National Mobilization Committee to End the War in Vietnam (the "Mobe"), had announced plans to demonstrate for peace in Chicago during the convention. The Yippies, the Rubin-Hoffman attempt to merge radical politics with radical culture, proclaimed their intention to hold a disruptive "Festival of Life" in Chicago to offset the Democrats' "Festival of Death" and provoke the authorities to show the "naked face of power." Fearing that chaos would disgrace his city, Mayor Daley, refused permits to the Yippies or the Mobe for marches or the right to use the parks for sleeping.

McCarthy advised his followers to stay away. And in the end only a few thousand Yippies and Mobe people came. Yet for most of a week the Chicago streets near the convention hotels and convention hall witnessed club-swinging, stone-throwing violence between the police and demonstrators in which scores of innocent reporters and other bystanders were also roughed up and hurt.

An investigating committee later called what had transpired a "police riot." There is strong evidence, however, that Rubin, Hoffman, and their colleagues were intent on a confrontation. Whoever was responsible, the violence in downtown Chicago, transmitted to television viewers all over the nation, created the impression that the Democrats were incapable of keeping order. As a result Humphrey, although despised himself by the militants, suffered in the public estimate.

The Republican convention at Miami Beach was a more sedate affair. After Governor George Romney of Michigan, a naive, well-intentioned man, had destroyed his credibility by confessing to having been brainwashed on Vietnam by U.S. officials in Saigon, Richard Nixon became the clear front-runner. Most of the Republican professionals appreciated his loyal support for Goldwater and his help in restoring the party's fortunes after the 1964 debacle. Nixon's only possible challenger was Governor Ronald Reagan of California, a man who represented the party's most conservative wing. Nixon fended off the Reagan threat by promising the conservative southern Republicans that if nominated he would choose as his running mate a man the South could accept, and if elected he would do nothing to accelerate school desegregation. After nomination Nixon selected as the ticket's vice presidential candidate Spiro Agnew, the governor of Maryland, a man from a border state with a reputation for disliking African-American militants.

George Wallace was also a candidate, having been nominated in September by his own tailor-made organization, the American Independent party. His running mate was air force General Curtis LeMay, a military hard-liner who had once suggested bombing Vietnam "back to the stone age." Wallace attracted a large following in the white South. He also was popular among blue-collar middle Americans and backlash voters generally. Here was a man who would put the kooks and crazies in their place, impose "law and order," stop the campus disrupters, and conclude the war in Vietnam by tough, all-out action instead of the pussyfooting of the Johnson administration.

The Campaign

For a time the Wallace candidacy cut deeply into Democratic ranks. Thousands of blue-collar union members seriously considered deserting their traditional party for the Wallace-LeMay ticket. Nixon too appeared to draw defectors from Democratic ranks. The Republicans followed a shrewd strategy of appealing to the "silent majority." Nixon avoided the bigoted rhetoric of Wallace, although he did not disdain using "code" terms such as "law and order" that touched the same chords. Agnew, however, sounded like a country-club Wallace and had to be toned down lest he offend too many moderates.

For weeks following the Democratic convention the Humphrey-Muskie ticket limped badly. Many of the big money Democratic contributors, seeing the vice president as a loser, refused to help. Johnson had control of a large pool of funds but did not want to release it to the vice president. By the fall American–North Vietnamese preliminary peace talks were under way in Paris and LBJ hoped to prevent the vice president from promising his own independent, soft line that would encourage the enemy to stand tough.

Yet to win, Humphrey had to detach himself from the dead-end Vietnam escalation policies of LBJ. Eventually he found the moral courage to strike out on his own with a statement in Salt Lake City on September 30 that as president he would unilaterally cease all bombing of North Vietnam if the enemy promised to end infiltration of additional troops into the South. It wasn't a dramatic change from the Johnson position, but it did show some independence and brought liberal voters and their contributions back in a wave. Meanwhile the labor unions mounted a major campaign against Wallace among their members, pointing out how, during his gubernatorial administration, Alabama workers had been poorly paid and the state had lacked minimum-wage and child labor laws. As the campaign wound down, union members too began to return to the Democratic fold.

As election day approached the Democrats pulled almost even with the Republicans, while Wallace fell far behind. The results were exceptionally close. (See Figure 3–1.) Nixon got 31.8 million popular votes; Humphrey 31.3 million; Wallace 9.9 million. Less than a one percent margin separated the two major candidates. Nixon received 301 electoral votes, however, with 270 needed to win, and was elected president of the United States. He had succeeded, as his election strategy required, in carrying the traditional Republican states, several of the major industrial states, and the states of the upper South, surrendering only the deep South to Wallace. The Democrats retained control of both houses of Congress, but again the liberals could count on a conservative majority against them.

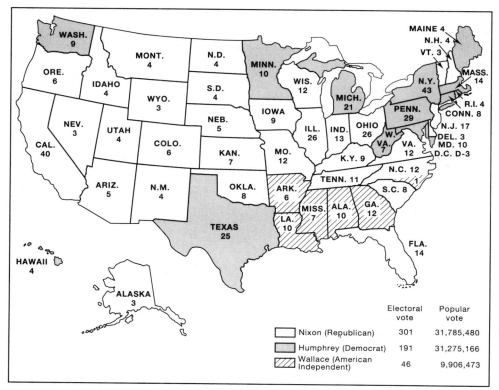

Figure 3–1 *The 1968 Presidential Election*

The Sixties End

And so the noisy, vivid, militant, confrontationist, chaotic, innovative, outrageous, and prosperous sixties ended, not chronologically, perhaps, but in most other ways. Its critics would call it "a slum of a decade," and clearly its legacy was mixed. An era that began when, briefly, influential Americans concluded that they had solved the problem of abundance and now could confront the issues of quality and equality, it allotted immense energies to flagrant excess—of rhetoric, expression, behavior, and theory. More positively it also witnessed a diminution of power inequality and status rigidities and the legitimation of views and groups once beyond the pale of respectability. Segregation ended, feminism regained its voice, and new sounds, sights, and freedoms found outlet. But it also left behind a legacy of self-indulgence, irresponsibility, and diminished personal and intellectual standards that some believe are with us yet.

FOR FURTHER READING

There are a number of works that attempt to deal with the entire sixties decade. William O'Neill's, *Coming Apart: An Informal History of America in the 1960s* (1970) is amusing as well as instructive. A work covering the same ground by a former SDS leader is Todd Gitlin's *The Sixties: Years of Hope, Days of Rage* (1987). Also see Irwin Unger and Debi Unger, *Turning Point: 1968* (1988), which, despite its title, covers much of the decade.

Two sympathetic works on the Kennedy administration that the student should consult are Arthur Schlesinger, Jr., *A Thousand Days* (1965) and Herbert Parmet's two-volume biography *Jack: The Struggles of John F. Kennedy* (1980) and *JFK: The Presidency of John F. Kennedy* (1983). Two more critical books are Garry Wills, *The Kennedy Imprisonment* (1983) and Henry Fairlie, *The Kennedy Promise* (1976). An interesting assessment of the Kennedy clan is David Burner and Thomas West, *The Torch Is Passed: The Kennedy Brothers and American Liberalism* (1984).

For an overall assessment of JFK's domestic policies see Aidi Donald (ed.), *John F. Kennedy and the New Frontier* (1966). The Peace Corps is discussed in Robert Carey, *The Peace Corps* (1970) and the Alliance for Progress in Herbert K. May, *Problems and Prospects of the Alliance for Progress* (1968). For JFK's early moves against poverty see Daniel Knapp and Kenneth Polk, *Scouting the War on Poverty: Social Reform Politics in the Kennedy Administration* (1971). The space program for the Kennedy years as well as before and after is covered in Walter A. McDougall, *The Heavens and the Earth: A Political History of the Space Age* (1985) The way the economy fared during JFK's administration is described in Seymour Harris, *The Economics of the Kennedy Years* (1964).

There are a number of books on the Kennedys and the civil rights movement. See Carl N. Brauer *John F. Kennedy and the Second Reconstruction* (1977) and Victor Navasky's critical study *Kennedy Justice* (1971).

For the civil rights movement during the sixties see, once again Harvard Sitkoff, *The Struggle for Black Equality* (1983). Also see Clayborne Carson, *In Struggle: SNCC and the Black Awakening of the 1960s* (1980); Mary King, *Freedom Song: A Personal History of the 1960s Civil Rights Movement* (1987); Cleveland Sellers, *River of No Return* (1976); and James Peck, *Freedom Ride* (1962).

Kennedy era foreign policy is discussed in Richard Walton, *Cold War and Counter-revolution* (1972). The Bay of Pigs crisis is covered by Peter Wyden, *Bay of Pigs* (1980). The Cuban Missile crisis is considered in Graham Allison, *Essence of Decision: Explaining the*

Cuban Missile Crisis (1971) and Robert Kennedy, *Thirteen Days* (1969). For the Berlin crisis see Jack M. Schick, *The Berlin Crisis, 1958–62* (1971).

The Kennedy assassination has generated a veritable deluge of studies, most advancing some pet conspiracy idea. The best narrative treatment, however, is still William Manchester, *Death of a President* (1966).

Lyndon Johnson's own defense can be found in his memoirs *The Vantage Point: Perspectives of the Presidency, 1963–1969* (1971). A scathing analysis of Johnson's character before he became president is Robert Caro's *The Path to Power* (1982). More sympathetic is Doris Kearn, *Lyndon Johnson and the American Dream* (1977). An analysis of the Johnson administration from a scholar who was the resident White House intellectual for a time is Eric Goldman, *The Tragedy of Lyndon Johnson* (1969).

The Great Society has been attacked from both the left and the right. Critics on the left include Allen Matusow, *The Unravelling of America* (1984) and Stephen Rose, *Betrayal of the Poor: Transformation of Community Action* (1972). A critic on the right is Daniel Moynihan, *Maximum Feasible Misunderstanding* (1970). For a good overview of the war on poverty see James Sundquist (ed.), *On Fighting Poverty* (1969).

The 1964 election is covered in Theodore White, *The Making of the President, 1964* (1965).

Black power and black nationalism are described in Archie Epps, *Malcom X and the American Negro Revolution* (1969) and Charles Hamilton and Stokeley Carmichael, *Black Power* (1967). Eldridge Cleaver's *Soul on Ice* is a personal memoir of a black power advocate. On the ghetto riots see Joe E. Feagin and Harlan Hahn, *Ghetto Revolts: The Politics of Violence in American Cities* (1973). A brief book on northern students and Freedom Summer is Mary Aickin Rothschild, *A Case of Black and White: Northern Volunteers and the Southern Freedom Summers, 1964–1965* (1982). On another aspect of the Freedom Summer of 1964 see William Bradford Huie, *Three Lives for Mississippi* (1965).

No one has written a history of the emerging sixties backlash, but see Marshall Frady, *Wallace* (1970). Also see Kevin Phillips, *The Emerging Republican Majority* (1969); Patricia Cayo Sexton and Brendon Sexton, *Blue Collars and Hard Hats* (1971); and Andrew Levison, *The Working Class Majority* (1974).

There are many books on the sixties student left and their activities. Among the better ones are James Miller, *Democracy Is in the Streets: From Port Huron to the Siege of Chicago* (1987); Kirkpatrick Sale, *SDS* (1974); and Irwin Unger, *The Movement: A History of the American New Left, 1959–1972* (1974). On the Berkeley Free Speech Movement see Max Heirich, *The Spiral of Conflict: Berkeley, 1964* (1971).

The counterculture is described in Theodore Roszak, *The Making of a Counter Culture: Reflections on the Technocratic Society and its Youthful Opposition* (1969); Martin Lee and Bruce Shlain, *Acid Dreams: The C.I.A. and the Sixties Rebellon* (1985); Charles Perry, *The Haight-Ashbury: A History* (1984); Morris Dickstein, *Gates of Eden: American Culture in the 60s* (1977); and Tom Wolfe's amusing *The Electric Kool-Aid Acid Test* (1969). For the acid rock scene see Ralph Gleason, *The Jefferson Airplane* (1972). There is no adequate history of the sexual revolution, but see Gay Talese, *Thy Neighbor's Wife* (1980).

The student interested in the woman's movement of the 1960s should first consult Betty Friedan, *The Feminine Mystique* (1963). Also see Judith Hole and Ellen Levine, *The Rebirth of Feminism* (1971); Sara Evans, *Personal Politics: The Roots of Woman's Liberation in the Civil Rights Movement and the New Left* (1979); and Robin Morgan (ed.), *Sisterhood Is Powerful: An Anthology of Writings from the Woman's Liberation Movement* (1970).

For the momentous 1968 election see Theodore White, *The Making of the President, 1968* (1969); Lewis Chester, Godfrey Hodgson, and Bruce Page, *An American Melodrama; The Presidential Campaign of 1968* (1969); Arthur Herzog, *McCarthy for President* (1969); and Jules Witcover, *85 Days: The Last Campaign of Robert Kennedy* (1969). Robert Kennedy's whole career is covered eulogistically in Arthur Schlesinger, Jr., *Robert F. Kennedy and His Times* (1974).

4
The Vietnam War

A 1967 anti–Vietnam War protest in Los Angeles. (AP/Wide World Photos)

The Vietnam Morass

Although the growing disunity of the civil rights movement, the radicalization of the left, and the rise of the backlash impulse all weakened the Johnson consensus, it was the Vietnam War, ultimately, that destroyed Lyndon Johnson's administration. This conflict, the longest foreign war in our history, checked the forward momentum of the Great Society and ultimately lead to the president's renunciation of a try for a second full term of office. The war ended, years later, with American goals frustrated and American morale and self-confidence depleted. The meaning of the Vietnam experience is still debated by Americans today.

The Historical Background

Vietnam is an ancient land that Europeans called Cochin China when they first encountered it in the sixteenth century. It was part of a larger cultural entity that included adjacent Laos and Cambodia and, like these other lands, had derived many of its institutions from the neighboring civilizations of India and China. (See Figure 4–1.)

Vietnam, the "lesser dragon," lived in the political shadow of China, the "greater dragon," and had long struggled to remain independent of it. Yet the Vietnamese had borrowed much from the Chinese: government by an educated class of civil servants (mandarins), rule by an emperor, rice culture, and the system of Confucian ethics that emphasized respect for authority and for ancestors.

Europeans—Portuguese, Dutch, French, and British—intent on trade, began to penetrate the region in the sixteenth century. But profits were elusive. The Vietnamese disliked foreigners and, tough and warlike, they could not be strong-armed into yielding trade concessions or other advantages. The Europeans soon lost interest. Yet one aspect of European civilization, Christianity, took deep root. By 1800, thousands of Vietnamese, especially in the northern part of the country, had become Roman Catholics.

Serious French political intrusion into the region began in the 1840s, justified by the Vietnamese emperor's persecution of French Catholic missionaries. In 1861 French forces captured the south Vietnamese city of Saigon (now Ho Chi Minh City) and soon after annexed several south Vietnamese provinces as colonies. Thereafter, bit by bit, France incorporated Vietnam, Laos, and Cambodia into its growing empire as French Indochina, although it retained local officials and even the Vietnamese emperor as intermediaries to transmit its orders and policies to the people.

The French brought their law, schools, language, and economy. Some Vietnamese eagerly assimilated French culture; some went to Paris to further their educations. Many, however, resented French cultural as well as political rule, and resisted. As early as 1859 Vietnamese irregular troops had begun to attack the French authorities and sporadic military resistance continued through the remainder of the nineteenth century.

During the opening years of the twentieth century Vietnamese resentment of French rule was amplified by increasingly exploitive economic policies. These

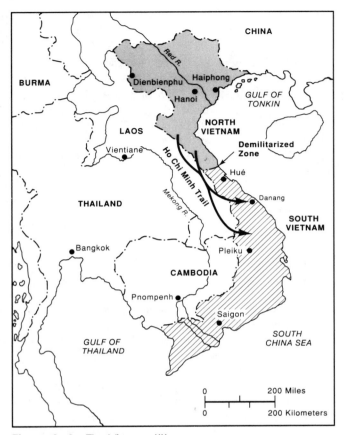

Figure 4–1   The Vietnam War

included turning over vast stretches of rice lands to French and favored Vietnamese landlords and displacing thousands of formerly landowning peasants, establishing large French-owned rubber plantations worked by disease-ridden indentured servants, and creating official monopolies of alcohol, salt, and opium production.

World War II

France's hold on its Indochinese colony weakened after its defeat by Germany in mid-1940. The expansionist Japanese soon began to demand that the French Vichy regime grant them the right to station troops on Indochinese soil. After Pearl Harbor Japanese troops occupied the whole colony, ruling through French Vichy officials. In several East Asian countries, where Japanese conquest displaced the former European rulers, the local people rallied to the new conquerors—at least they were Asian. But not in Vietnam. There the anticolonial movement was led by Ho Chi Minh, a Marxist revolutionary, and he firmly believed that the Allies would eventually defeat Japan and then grant Vietnam its independence.

Ho Chi Minh was a Communist and a nationalist simultaneously. He had left his native country in 1911 and traveled about the West, staying for a year in New York and passing some time in London before settling in Paris during World War I. There his Vietnamese nationalism was reinforced by Wilsonian self-determination doctrines and there, in 1920, Ho became a charter member of the new French Communist party.

In 1924 Ho went to Moscow where he met Soviet leaders Joseph Stalin and Leon Trotsky and studied techniques of revolution. He then returned to East Asia and, from the refugees of China, Hong Kong, and Thailand helped organize movements to overthrow the French and create a united, independent, and Communist Vietnam. In early 1941 Ho slipped across the border into Vietnam disguised as a Chinese journalist and established the Vietminh (the Vietnam Independence League) to fight the Japanese. Believing the time "not yet ripe" for open Communist leadership, the Vietminh proclaimed themselves a front of "patriots of all ages and all types, peasants, workers, merchants, and soldiers."

War against the French

After Japan's defeat the French sought to regain control in Indochina. The Americans were at first skeptical of French goals. In 1943 Roosevelt, who believed the French had "milked" their colony "for a hundred years," proposed an international trusteeship for the country. After FDR's death, however, the pro-French circles in the State Department prevailed, and in May 1945 Secretary of State Edward Stettinius assured the French foreign minister that the United States would support France's claims in the region.

But Ho Chi Minh and his Vietminh colleagues had no intention of letting the French return to power. In September 1945 in the northern city of Hanoi, before the French were able to reassert their authority, Ho and his associates announced the independence of Vietnam. Although a Communist Ho was also a pragmatist and still hoped that the United States might help him rebuff the French when they tried to return. His words from the platform at Hanoi's Ba Dinh Square included lines directly from the American Declaration of Independence.

During the next months confusion reigned in Vietnam with Ho's forces holding in the north and the French easily regaining control in the south. In 1946 Ho agreed to accept Vietnamese inclusion within the "French Union" in exchange for recognition of the "free state" status of the Democratic Republic of Vietnam. This arrangement quickly broke down and the two sides were soon engaged in a bitter war.

American Interest

Despite the early American tilt to the French, it took the Cold War to focus American attention on Vietnam. In 1949 came the North Atlantic Treaty Organization

(NATO), of which France was a key member. Soon after, the Chinese Communists defeated Chiang Kai-shek and took control in Beijing. In 1950 the North Koreans crossed the thirty-eighth parallel launching the frustrating Korean War. (See Chapter 1.) These events forced a reconsideration of the United States' Vietnam policy. France, American policymakers now concluded, must be supported—to keep the French loyal to NATO and encourage them to hold the line against Communist expansionism in Asia. This second goal would be given vivid expression by President Eisenhower at a 1954 press conference when he noted that the Southeast Asian nations were like "dominos." If "you knock over the first one . . . the last one . . . will go over very quickly."

Under President Truman the United States, after extracting promises from the French to accord some degree of autonomy to the Vietnamese under Emperor Bao Dai, had began to subsidize the French effort to defeat Ho Chi Minh and the Vietminh. By 1954 the United States was paying almost 80 percent of the cost of the bitter French-Vietminh struggle.

Dienbienphu and the Geneva Agreements

Despite American financial aid the war did not go well for the French. By the end of 1952 the Vietminh had won control of almost all of northern Vietnam and were intruding into neighboring Laos. Then in July 1953 the United States and the North Korean–Red Chinese allies signed the armistice ending the Korean War. This freed the Chinese to send supplies and heavy weapons to the Vietminh. By 1954 the desperate French were asking for American troops to stop Ho. The United States, having just extricated itself from one land war in Asia (Korea), did not relish entering another. After the British rejected a joint British-American intervention to aid their NATO ally, the Eisenhower administration turned down the French request. French defeat quickly followed. On May 7, 1954, after a fifty-five-day siege, the French surrendered their garrison at Dienbienphu to General Vo Nguyen Giap, Ho's talented military associate, a blow that virtually ended the fighting.

Fortuitously the next day nine nations met at Geneva to consider a Vietnamese settlement. What emerged was an agreement that proclaimed Vietnam free, but divided the country along the seventeenth parallel with a 5-kilometer-wide demilitarized zone (DMZ) to separate the two portions. The Vietminh would withdraw to the north, and the remaining French troops remove to the south pending their departure from the country. Vietnamese civilians would be allowed to choose freely which half of the country they wished to live in. This separation into a north and a south would not be permanent, however. In July 1956 an International Control Commission would call an election to decide what action should be taken to create a united Vietnam.

The United States was present at the conference but did not sign the Geneva Agreement, although it consented to abide by its general terms. Soon after, in an effort to prevent further Communist gains in Southeast Asia, Secretary of State John Foster Dulles induced seven nations with western Pacific interests—Great Britain, France, New Zealand, Australia, Pakistan, Thailand, and the Philippines—to join the United States in creating the Southeast Asia Treaty Organization (SEATO). SEATO, like NATO in Europe, would "act to meet the common danger" of "Communist aggression" in its region. Unlike NATO, however, it would not have a unified military command.

South versus North

Fighting would soon break out again in Vietnam, this time between Ho Chi Minh's Communist government (the Democratic Republic of Vietnam) in North Vietnam with its capital in Hanoi and a new pro-Western regime (Republic of Vietnam) in South Vietnam with its capital in Saigon. The premier of the new South Vietnamese government, under the nominal rule of Emperor Bao Dai, was Ngo Dinh Diem, a Vietnamese Catholic and a sincere Vietnamese patriot but an aloof and austere man of limited vision who easily confused the welfare of Vietnam with the well-being of his own extended family.

During the early months following Geneva several hundred thousand Catholics left North Vietnam for the more congenial south, while many Communists in the south went north to find a similar friendly environment. Diem, who hoped to establish a centralized regime based on traditional Vietnamese concepts of obedience and deference, was soon engaged in bitter struggles with competing religious sects anxious to dominate the country and with remaining Vietminh who had not followed the majority north. With massive injections of American economic aid Diem soon consolidated his power, and in October 1955, in a election managed by his brother Ngo Dinh Nhu, he eliminated Bao Dai politically and had himself elected president of South Vietnam. Fearing a Communist victory, Diem, with United States approval, ignored the Geneva Agreement call for national elections. The partition along the seventeenth parallel, which had started as a temporary expedient, became a permanent reality of Vietnamese life.

From the outset the Eisenhower administration supported Diem as a bulwark against a Communist takeover of the whole country, and the United States quickly superseded the French. Between 1954 and 1959 approximately 2.3 billion American dollars poured into South Vietnam. One-fifth of this was earmarked for Diem's military forces; the rest took the form of economic aid. American officials saw themselves as "nation-building" in Vietnam. They hoped to bring peace and prosperity to the country as an offset to Communist blandishments, but much of the aid was wasted and American demands for land reform were ignored. To make matters worse, Diem and his associates threw suspected political opponents into reeducation camps, arbitrarily abolished elected village governments, and "re-grouped' peasant villagers to prevent opposition by removing them from their accustomed homes near the graves of their ancestors. Before long Diem had stirred up a guerrilla war in the countryside against his regime.

At first the peasant opposition was spontaneous. The North Vietnamese government, although it despised the Diem regime and hoped eventually to impose its own rule over a unified nation, initially gave the anti-Diem guerrillas (soon to be called Vietcong by their opponents and the National Liberation Front by their friends) little help. By 1959, however, the North had changed its mind and was supplying the Vietcong with arms, military advisers, and strategic aid. By 1960 the North Vietnamese were calling for the "liberation" of South Vietnam.

The Kennedy Administration and Vietnam

President Kennedy feared giving his domestic opponents the opportunity to attack his foreign policy as weak. He also believed, as we have seen, that East-West confrontation in the future would take the form of small wars by Soviet and American surrogates and guerrilla disturbances, not head-on superpower collisions. Vietnam seemed an obvious example of this new form of confrontation. Kennedy felt it must be met by counterinsurgency methods and by measures to reduce grievances, including land reform and political reform. Diem must be induced to win the confidence of the Vietnamese peasants to wean them away from the Communists.

Should the Diem regime also be given further military aid? In May 1961 Vice President Lyndon Johnson went to Saigon to report on the Vietnamese situation for the president. Johnson recommended continued massive American aid to avoid a "domino effect," but advised against sending any American combat troops. Such involvement was "not only not required, it is not desirable." Johnson lavishly praised Diem, comparing him to Winston Churchill, although in fact he was privately skeptical of the South Vietnamese leader.

In October 1961, after a summer of turmoil in the Vietnamese countryside, Kennedy dispatched General Maxwell Taylor and White House aide Walter W. Rostow to Saigon to examine the ground once again. The two men recommended sending American military advisers to be attached to Army of Vietnam (ARVN) units and a force of 10,000 combat troops to backstop the South Vietnamese military. The United States should also consider military actions against North Vietnam if it continued to aid the Vietcong.

Kennedy rejected this advice. It would only lead to ever deeper involvement. "It's like taking a drink," he remarked. "The effect wears off, and you have to take another." But he could not resist. He soon increased the number of military advisers in South Vietnam. By the time of his death in late 1963 there were about 15,500 Americans attached to ARVN or the Saigon government to provide expert military and administrative help.

The Elimination of Diem

For a time the policy of help for Diem seemed to work. Under a new counterinsurgency policy, personally administered by Nhu, peasants were herded into fortified, barbed wire-surrounded "strategic hamlets." There they could, presumably, be protected against intimidation by the Vietcong, and the Communist guerrillas in turn could be deprived of supplies and recruits. In fact the program deeply offended many peasants and only helped the Vietcong, but American officials, the first of a long line of naive or self-deluded bureaucrats, reported to Washington that the Communist tide was receding. American journalists stationed in South Vietnam related a much bleaker picture, but Kennedy too was taken in. In his 1963 State of the Union message he informed the American public that the "spearpoint of aggression has been blunted in South Vietnam."

Then Diem made a major mistake. A devout Catholic, in May 1963 he forbade the

A Buddhist immolates himself on the streets of Saigon, June 1963. (UPI/Bettmann Newsphotos)

large Buddhist community in Vietnam from displaying their flags. When a Buddhist crowd at Hue refused to comply, Diem's troops fired into the crowd. A stampede ensued; nine people died. Diem now found himself with a major religious revolt on his hands.

The Buddhists proved to be skilled manipulators of the media. On June 11 a Buddhist monk sat down on the pavement in Saigon, drenched himself with gasoline, and then set himself on fire. Other Buddhist self-immolations followed soon after. In each case the media had been informed in advance and were waiting to take and send the appalling pictures to the international press, which treated the events as examples of the Diem regime's brutality. Kennedy tried to induce Diem to meet the Buddhists' legitimate demands, but Diem resisted all the way.

By the early fall the Diem regime seemed to have lost its grip entirely. The Saigon government began to jail students and to persecute Catholics as well. By now the American president had lost faith in Diem, and in late August the State Department hinted to the American ambassador in Saigon, Henry Cabot Lodge, that the United States would not be opposed to Diem's replacement. On receipt of this message, Lodge informed Diem's enemies in the South Vietnamese army that the United States would not intervene to save him. This was the signal they needed. On November 1 the insurgent generals besieged the government palace. Diem and his brother had escaped, but they were quickly caught and mowed down by a rain of bullets.

Americans hoped that now the needed reforms would be imposed and South Vietnam would be transformed into a stable country, able to defend itself against the

Vietcong guerrillas and serve as a bulwark in Southeast Asia against the spread of the Communist virus. In Saigon too there was new optimism. At news of the anti-Diem coup people danced in the streets and showered the victorious generals with confetti. They even cheered Ambassador Lodge in public. Then, three weeks later, President Kennedy was assassinated in Dallas.

Johnson and Vietnam

Johnson was not as astute an international player as his predecessor. An incomparably skilled legislator, LBJ knew the crochets and crannies of Capitol Hill as no other American. But his foreign policy comprehension did not go much beyond the conventional wisdom of Americans who had learned their lessons in World War II. The president saw Hitler's aggressive expansionism of the 1930s as the relevant precedent for Vietnam. Appeasing the Führer at Munich had only whetted his appetite and led ultimately to a larger war. He sometimes put the matter in earthy language. "If you let a bully come into your front yard one day," he said, "the next day he will be up on your porch and the day after that he will rape your wife in your own bed." Besides America was leader of the "Free World" and if it did not draw the line now, it would lose credibility everywhere, even among its European allies.

Another force that drew Johnson ever further into the Vietnam morass was the masculine need to prevail. Many Americans, certainly many American men, shared this competitiveness, but the president's personal roots in the country's southwest—a "man's country"—amplified this quality in him. To Johnson, and other Americans, losing seemed intolerable. America, he believed, had never lost a war, and he did not intend to be the first president to be at the helm when it happened.

We can now see that all this reasoning was flawed. In part American east Asian policy was based on the fallacy that China was behind the North Vietnamese. Actually the Chinese were wary of the Hanoi regime, which they saw as a potential rival in Southeast Asia. China provided far less of the North Vietnam's military support than did the Soviet Union. It is also clear that the domino effect was an illusion. South Vietnam's final fall in 1975 did not trigger a major wave of Communist takeovers. Nor did the United States' failure to fight to the bitter end convince our NATO allies that we were untrustworthy. On the other hand the administration was not wrong to see the Hanoi regime as authoritarian and repressive. The Communists would prove to be harsh conquerors and rigid ideologues whose rule over a united Vietnam, after peace, would make a shambles of the national economy. As for the "macho" factor, it seems an unconvincing basis for conducting a world power's foreign policy. Besides, even though the United States had never lost a war, it had not actually "won" in Korea, and still the heavens did not fall.

The Johnson Administration's Early Response

However certain that the Communists must be stopped, the new president, anxious to consolidate his home political base, at first soft-peddled Vietnam. In his first State of the Union message in January 1964 he virtually ignored Southeast Asia.

He had not forgotten the war, however, especially since General Nguyen Khanh, the new South Vietnamese leader, seemed no better able to consolidate the country behind him and suppress the Vietcong than Diem. Faced with the continuing danger of Communist takeover, the administration considered a major bombing campaign against North Vietnam but then thought better of it to avoid allowing Vietnam to become a partisan issue in the approaching 1964 presidential election campaign. Seeking some way to defuse the war's political danger, in August, with a dubious attack by North Vietnamese patrol boats on American destroyers as its excuse, the administration requested a congressional resolution of support for a retaliatory policy "to prevent further aggression." All indications were that the American public overwhelmingly supported the administration, and on August 7, by an almost unanimous vote, Congress passed the Tonkin Gulf resolution, granting the president power to "take all necessary measures to repel any armed attack against forces of the United States." In later months the attorney general would claim that the resolution was the "functional equivalent" of a "declaration of war."

Johnson was able to keep Vietnam from becoming a major campaign issue by denying any plan to escalate American involvement. He would "seek no wider war," he told the American people from a dozen rostrums across the country. "We do not want to get tied down in a land war in Asia," he proclaimed in late September. "We are not going to send American boys nine or ten thousand miles away from home to do what Asian boys ought to be doing for themselves," he announced a month later. His enemies later charged that LBJ was following the uncandid precedent of his hero Franklin Roosevelt during the months preceding Pearl Harbor but in a far worse cause. In reality Johnson was in a quandary. He feared he was damned if he did and damned if he didn't. He did not want to be charged with "losing" Vietnam, as Truman had "lost" China; he also did not want a land war in Asia to destroy his consensus and drain all life from the Great Society. His deceptions reflected his own confusion as well as a natural devious streak in his personality.

Rolling Thunder

After November 1964 with the victory over Goldwater behind him, Johnson faced major decisions in Vietnam. In late December Vietcong agents exploded a car bomb beneath the Brinks Hotel in Saigon, housing American military advisers, killing two and injuring fifty-eight. The new American ambassador, General Taylor, along with every other senior officer in Saigon, urged the president to retaliate against North Vietnam. When Johnson demurred, Taylor responded that the United States was "presently on a losing tack" and that to "take no positive action now is to accept defeat." He recommended a major air offensive against the source of Vietcong power, North Vietnam.

In February the president sent National Security Adviser McGeorge Bundy to Saigon to appraise the situation. Bundy had been in Saigon for just a few days when the Vietcong attacked the American base at Pleiku, killing eight American military advisers, wounding a hundred, and destroying ten U.S. planes. After consulting Taylor and General William Westmoreland, the American military commander in South Vietnam, Bundy telephoned the White House advising that the United States commence bombing attacks on North Vietnam promptly. Unless it did so American determination to "stay the course" would be in doubt.

Within hours American planes were bombing a North Vietnamese army post north of the seventeenth parallel. In early March Johnson launched a sustained bombing campaign (*Rolling Thunder*) against targets in North Vietnam to compel the North Vietnamese to desist from further attacks and force them to come to the bargaining table. On March 8 the first U.S. combat troops, sent to protect the Rolling Thunder air base at Da-nang, waded ashore at Nam O Beach. Ten pretty Vietnamese girls carrying flowers greeted them. In early April, with the air war clearly a failure, the president sent additional marines to Vietnam and authorized their use in offensive actions. Soon after this American troops participated in their first "search and destroy" mission against the Vietcong.

The War Goes On

Thus began the full participation of the United States in the longest, and least defensible, war in its history. To Johnson and his advisers the war seemed a valid effort to hold the line against communism. Let Ho Chi Minh and his North Vietnamese Communists succeed in destroying the South Vietnamese government and unifying Vietnam under their rule and what would prevent them from subverting and conquering the rest of Southeast Asia? Only the Red Chinese or the Soviets could benefit from such an outcome.

Had the war been quick and cheap, the American public might have accepted the Johnson diagnosis and prescription. Unfortunately for the administration it could not fight the way Americans preferred—with overwhelming firepower and technology that could pulverize the enemy and bring a quick decision. In Vietnam the enemy seldom appeared in force to fight a battle. Instead they used stealth, ambush, and infiltration to hit the ARVN and the Americans and then escape. Vietnam became a dirty guerrilla war where American soldiers and marines struggled against an elusive foe in an unfamiliar and atrocious environment of jagged mountains, leech-infested tropical swamps, and steaming jungles. Bombing North Vietnam, although it spared American lives, did not work. The air force dropped enormous tonnages of bombs on the Vietcong and North Vietnamese troops south of the seventeenth parallel and on North Vietnam above the line to flatten the enemy and break Communist morale. The attacks failed. The Vietcong lived on a few handfuls of rice a day and were armed primarily with knives, rifles, and light mortars. They had little heavy equipment to destroy. The North Vietnamese economy was primitive by modern standards and, although many North Vietnamese died in the bombing raids, Hanoi's ability to fight was scarcely affected and its resolve to hold out undiminished.

In the end thousands of American ground troops, many of them draftees, had to be sent to the battlefields eight thousand miles away. By early 1968 a half-million Americans were fighting and dying in Vietnam.

The Antiwar Movement

Through the first few years following Rolling Thunder a majority of Americans supported the president. Many agreed that the war was a test of American determination to stop communism around the world. At first antiwar sentiment was confined to the academic community, students, the left, pacifists, and certain portions of the country's intellectual class. Then, as the dreary months passed with mounting costs and casualties, more and more citizens began to perceive the war as a mistake. (See Figure 4–2.) Could defense of a place so remote and alien as Vietnam really be vital to the nation's safety? Democracies are formidable opponents in war when citizens feel their own safety endangered; they seldom will go the distance in a prolonged struggle when the goals are unclear and ambiguous.

The first serious organized opposition to the Vietnam War erupted in March 1965 in response to Rolling Thunder when students and faculty at the University of Michigan at Ann Arbor held the first "teach-in." This was a full day of critical lectures and seminars on Vietnam and American involvement that was quickly copied at other universities and colleges around the country.

The sudden escalation of the war also reactivated established pacifist groups such as the Fellowship of Reconciliation and the War Resisters' League and antinuclear groups like the Committee for a Sane Nuclear Policy. Before many months various "umbrella" peace groups with a wide variety of names and differing positions on how to end the war were marching and rallying to demand a major change in American policy in Southeast Asia.

Some peace advocates were moderate; they wanted the United States to begin serious negotiations with the North Vietnamese and the Vietcong to achieve an honorable settlement, and they usually endorsed petitions and peaceful demonstra-

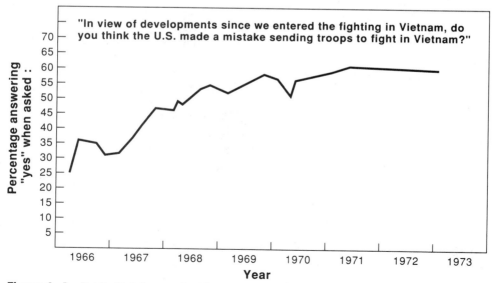

Figure 4–2   Public Opinion on the Vietnam War

Source: Gallup Poll data.

Vietnamese children fleeing a napalm attack. In the background are South Vietnamese soldiers. Scenes like these, shown on evening television, contributed to the American public's disillusion with the Vietnam War.
(UPI/Bettmann Newsphotos)

tions and rallies. Other groups were militant; they insisted that the United States leave Vietnam immediately and unconditionally, and they often supported civil disobedience and at times flaunted anti-American slogans and Vietcong and North Vietnamese flags. Beginning in mid-1965 a few determined antiwar activists began to burn their draft cards.

The most militant "peaceniks" were apt to be college students. Until late in the war college students in good standing were deferred from the draft. Even when white middle-class men could not claim an academic deferment they could often evade service through false medical exemptions or some other manipulation of the draft system. Many sought conscientious objector status. Hundreds fled to Canada where the arm of Uncle Sam could not reach them. Others simply defied the government by refusing to be inducted and accepted jail. In their place the Selective Service system inducted those too poor or too unmotivated academically to attend school. A large proportion of such young men were either black or Hispanic. A line from *Hair,* a popular rock musical of 1968, wittily described the Vietnam War as "white people sending black people to make war on yellow people to defend the land they stole from red people."

Yet white college students were under enormous pressure from the draft, and even when they themselves successfully evaded induction they often felt a heavy burden of guilt over the disproportionate sacrifice of minority young men. Fear and guilt are two potent sources of militancy.

The typical antiwar action was the march to some designated spot—often one symbolically connected with the war—such as the Pentagon outside of Washington, D.C., or the UN complex in New York. Protesters carried banners and signs with

READING 4

A Marine Reminisces about Vietnam

A large proportion of the young men who served in Vietnam came from lower- and working-class backgrounds. Jim Noonan, whose reminiscences are given below, was raised in Brooklyn, New York. A high school graduate, in early 1966 Noonan decided to join the Marine Corps, partly from patriotic considerations. In this reading he recounts his experience in Vietnam, briefly contrasting it with his work among extremely poor people in New York.

I was born in Brooklyn Hospital and educated at Brooklyn College. Still live in Brooklyn. I only left Brooklyn once in my life—that was to Vietnam. And they were shooting at me, so I decided to never leave Brooklyn again.

I got out of high school a year before I joined the Marine Corps. I was not a very promising student and didn't have any college prospects. I was working. And the normal thing for a kid in my neighborhood to do if you weren't in college, you went into the service.

I was deferred because I was the sole support of my mother. My father died when I was fourteen years old and she raised me alone. But it really seemed like it was my duty to go. So on March 2, 1966, I joined the Marine Corps. I enlisted on a buddy plan with George Hankin, who is now a cop in New York City, and Richie Radcliffe. We all went down to Parris Island together.

Richie and I wound up going to Vietnam. But George hurt his arm—he had already broken it playing football—and he didn't go. He was pretty bitter about that because his cousin had been killed in Vietnam. And it was a holy mission for George.

I went to communications school as a message center man, learning to operate teletypes and things like that. From there, I was sent to Vietnam in late September 1966. I was assigned to the 1st Shore Party Battalion in Chu Lai. I remember it was the rainy season. The truck that took us to our outfit couldn't make it in the mud. So they left me out with my seabag over my shoulder. And I hiked the last mile through mud that at times was up to my waist.

I reported to the company office in our base-camp area and they assigned me a bunk. Several months later, when the sun came out, was the next time anything was dry. Mud was just everywhere. We had no electricity. The only reason we had showers was because we found a fuel tank that had fallen off a jet.

I had contact with Vietnamese people in the villages nearby. I have this crazy theory that sanity stops at about the age of eight and begins again at sixty-five. So the children, no matter where you were in Vietnam, provided a certain buffer against insanity.

My mother, my two sisters, and my sister-in-law were always sending me "care packages." I would then hitchhike to this orphanage and give them the canned food from home and play with the kids. In Chu Lai we had Vietnamese working in our base camp. That was something not all of us were comfortable with, but we grew accustomed to it.

One thing that made a dynamic impression on me was the place where these Vietnamese lived. They would come in from the hills to work at the base. Trucks would pick them up and bring them back. They lived in places surrounded by Cyclone fences, with barbed wire on the top. Their huts were fashioned out of flattened beer cans and cardboard boxes. Each night these people would take our garbage. And they didn't take it to make compost—they took it for their dinner. They were transients, refugees. And in a difficult time, they were the ones who had the fewest rights. That made a pretty big impression on me.

Right now, I don't have to close my eyes to get a vision of the children's hospital . . . and a particular kid I probably spent twenty minutes staring at with my mouth open. The wounds on his back and the backs of his legs and buttocks were opened, festering, with flies. No mosquito netting, no bandages, he lay on a dirt floor. It was nothing more than a tent.

My last year in college I worked as a medical technician for New York City's lead poisoning program. I would take kids' blood in tenement buildings. And I had difficulties. The kids in Bedford-Stuyvesant called me "Dracula." I saw serious poverty. I remember walking up to the top floor of a four-story tenement. I wore a white clinical coat because I looked so young that nobody would believe I was able to stick a needle in a kid's arm.

When I reached the top of the stairs, my coat was drenched with sweat. I sat down in front of the kid and I thought I was going to faint. The wall across the room appeared to be moving. It was covered with cockroaches. Thousands of them! It was an ill-lit apartment and the wall was coming in and out, like breathing. But it was the cockroaches crawling all over each other, just festering on there. I saw that kind of poverty. But even still, I've never seen anything like the Vietnamese people gathering our garbage, protecting it like it was precious stones.

In the Chu Lai base camp I lived a relatively secure life. But the worst three days I had in Vietnam was when we were hit with 122-mm Russian rockets and just about everything else the North Vietnamese could throw at us. It was absolutely extraordinary. Everywhere you looked, it was tracer bullets. Every light bulb in our hootches [huts] was shot out. The air mattresses were flattened . . . bullets went through just about everything. And then the 122-mm rockets came in. There's a slight second between the banshee whistling and the explosion. During one of those slight seconds, I just about bit through my lip. It was terrifying.

I came home on Halloween 1967. I arrived at Kennedy Airport with all my nieces and nephews waiting in their Halloween costumes. It was wonderful seeing my mother, my brother, my sisters, and all the kids. My nephew Chip was standing there in a skeleton costume.

My Uncle Jim, my mother's brother, died the day before I came home. He had been sick for a long time, so my nieces and nephews didn't know that he existed. And my nephew Chip heard his mother say, "Uncle Jim died." Now the only Uncle Jim he knew was me. He was very upset. My sister asked him what was wrong. And he said I was dead. She said, "No, No."

When I came home that night, Chip handed me a note that said, "Dear Uncle Jim, I'm glad you're not dead. Love, Chip." It had little American flags, soldiers, a stickmen kind of drawing. You know, the art of a child that age. It was a wonderful note. I couldn't have agreed with him more. So I kept it, and to this day, keep it in my little area for precious things that can't ever be replaced.

Source: From *To Bear Any Burden* by Al Santoli. Copyright © 1985 by Al Santoli. Reprinted by permission of the publisher and E. P. Dutton, a division of Penguin Books USA, Inc.

slogans: "Stop the War," "Out Now!," "America out of Vietnam." (See the photograph opening this chapter.) They often chanted and sang peace songs. At their destinations the protesters listened to antiwar speeches by prominent peace activists, such as A. J. Muste, David Dellinger, and Martin Luther King. The largest and best publicized of these demonstrations took place in New York, San Francisco, and Washington and were usually conducted by antiwar coalitions that often disagreed bitterly over tactics, ideology, and leadership. Most of the demonstrations were orderly, although occasionally some radical splinter insisted on causing trouble.

Campus antiwar demonstrations were often more violent than the city marches. The campus actions frequently had a specific target, usually a campus recruiter such as the navy or a military contractor associated with the war effort. At the universities of California, Wisconsin, and Michigan campus riots broke out when demonstrators sought to stop job interviews with Dow Chemical Company, which manufactured napalm, the incendiary jelly used against guerrillas in Vietnam that produced horrible burns. At Columbia and Pennsylvania universities the targets were university-affiliated institutes that did contract work for the Defense Department.

The President's Deceptions

Anger at the president's Vietnam policies was reinforced by his failure to confide in the American public. Johnson was not a trusting man. His years in the labyrinthine politics of Texas and Washington had convinced him that deception was often wiser than truth. Besides he wanted both "guns *and* butter" and feared that revealing the full costs of the war would jeopardize his cherished Great Society programs. The administration talked constantly of "the light at the end of the tunnel," but the months dragged on without the tunnel's end. Before long critics were referring to the president's "credibility gap."

The president's most serious deception was financial. Johnson avoided asking for new taxes from Congress to pay for Vietnam's costs and instead hid the bill in the Pentagon's huge annual budget. In effect he borrowed the money, creating a federal deficit of almost $10 billion in 1966. By 1968 this figure was over $25 billion. The process only created inflationary pressures. By 1968 consumer prices were rising at almost 5 percent annually, a figure that appeared deeply disturbing after the stable prices of the previous decade.

Pro-War Attitudes

Militancy against the war was met by militancy in its favor. At times antiwar demonstrators were set on by pro-war groups who threw rocks or tomatoes or spray painted the marchers. Conservative and far-right organizations countermarched and counterrallied carrying signs reading "My Country—Right or Wrong," "No Glory Like Old Glory," and "I Wish I Had a Draft Card." Increasingly, the all-out pro-war position became the property of the political right and, along with anger against the civil rights movement, a part of the backlash position that had begun to emerge.

The administration also struck back. Soon after the first draft card burnings Congress made "willful destruction" of a draft card a crime punishable by five years in jail and a $10,000 fine. Federal agents soon arrested several violators.

Johnson believed that the antiwar movement was a powerful weapon of Hanoi and its allies which, unable to match American military might, intended to undermine the American will to fight. He was not wrong about Hanoi's plan for winning. The Communists knew they could not defeat the Americans on the battlefield and that to win they had to shake their enemy's determination. But LBJ also believed that elements in the antiwar movement were in Hanoi's pay and authorized the CIA to investigate links between the North Vietnamese government and the antiwar protesters. It is true that after 1966 a number of American antiwar leaders conferred with representatives of Hanoi behind the Iron Curtain, but no one accepted "Hanoi gold," and the agency did not discover any complicity. The FBI too got into the act as well. One purpose of the agency's clandestine COINTELPRO dirty tricks operation was the harassing of antiwar leaders and the derailing of antiwar demonstrations.

In addition to these covert measures the government took tough legal action against a flock of peace activists, culminating in the January 1968 indictment of Dr. Benjamin Spock, the famous baby doctor, and four other peace activists for conspiring to subvert the draft. None of the defendants in this case, or the others, served time in jail, but this legal offensive drained the energies and depleted the funds of the insurgents.

Tet

However prolonged the fighting and delayed the outcome, not until early 1968 did the administration and large portions of the American public cease to believe that victory was possible. Then during Tet, the Vietnamese lunar New Year, the Vietcong launched an offensive that destroyed all hope and led to a reversal of Johnson's policy.

On January 31 more than 70,000 Vietcong guerrillas and North Vietnamese regulars suddenly struck at a hundred or more South Vietnam cities and towns, including half the provincial capitals, and at a dozen American military bases. At Hue, the beautiful old capital, they took the Citadel, the ancient fortress in the city's center, and then proceeded systematically to murder people identified as "cruel tyrants and reactionary elements." Communist political agents shot, clubbed to death, or buried alive more than 3000 people. Not until late February were they rooted out in house-to-house fighting by marines. Three Vietcong battalions captured Ben Tre in the Mekong Delta and had to be blasted out by artillery and bombs at the cost of half the town's structures. In one of the more deplorable remarks of the war, an American officer explained afterward, "It became necessary to destroy the town to save it." At Khesanh, where the attack began before Tet, the Communist forces besieged a marine garrison, and until it was relieved, worried Americans feared the battle would repeat the French defeat at Dienbienphu.

Psychologically the Vietcong attack on the U.S. Embassy in Saigon was the most telling blow. There nineteen Vietcong commandos, smuggled into the South Vietnamese capital months before, broke into the embassy compound and tried to blast their way into the embassy building itself. They did not succeed. Fleet-footed guards slammed the doors and held them off until troops arrived and killed the intruders. Although the Vietcong had failed, Americans were shocked at the enemy's ability to penetrate to the very core of American power in Vietnam.

The primary purpose of the Vietcong attackers was to demonstrate their prowess and inflict a moral defeat on the Americans and South Vietnamese. They succeeded. The enemy suffered very heavy casualties, yet to a public fed a steady diet of official optimism, the Tet offensive was profoundly disillusioning. Walter Cronkite, the respected CBS anchorman, went to South Vietnam soon after Tet to see what had happened. Hitherto a "hawk" on the war, he reported to the American people that it now seemed "more certain than ever that the bloody experience of Vietnam is to end in a stalemate."

The president himself put on a brave front, but he too was shaken. Soon after Tet, General Westmoreland asked for an additional 206,000 troops. This request precipitated a crisis within the administration. To grant it would be to continue the escalation process, committing even more American resources to the prolonged struggle. To refuse it would require a major reconsideration of American goals. Johnson asked his close military and foreign policy advisers to review the whole Vietnam involvement. The advice of almost all these experienced men was stop the escalation in Vietnam and by slow stages turn the fighting over to the South Vietnamese. The United States must try to get out.

One incident connected with the Tet offensive did not come to the American public's attention until later. Guerrilla wars are dirty wars. There are no front lines or enemy troops wearing identifiable uniforms. Death comes not only from gunfire but from booby traps, ambushes, and poisoned stakes. Both sides use brutal methods and take few prisoners. In Vietnam the inhumanity was compounded by the racial and cultural differences between the antagonists. Many Americans regarded the Vietnamese, even their South Vietnamese allies, as only half-human "gooks."

At Mylai, a small community in coastal Quangngai province, a detachment of American soldiers under lieutenant William Calley was sent to oust suspected Vietcong guerrillas. When they were through they had massacred 300 civilians, many women and children. The army tried at first to cover up the atrocity but could not, and

Calley and another American soldier were eventually court-martialed. Calley was convicted, but many pro-war Americans believed him innocent of serious wrongdoing. For the other side Mylai would become the symbol of all that was evil about the Vietnam War.

The War and the 1968 Election

As we have seen (see Chapter 3), the growing public opposition to the war brought two peace candidates—senators Eugene McCarthy of Wisconsin and Robert Kennedy of New York—into the lists against Lyndon Johnson for the 1968 Democratic nomination. Johnson's moral defeat in the New Hampshire primary and the likelihood that he would also lose in Wisconsin led to his decision at the end of March not to run for another full term.

But the same speech that announced his political decision also offered to stop the bombing of North Vietnam north of the twentieth parallel, most of the country's area, in exchange for peace negotiations. At the same time the president authorized veteran American diplomat Averell Harriman to open peace talks with the Communists whenever they wished. Soon after, the North Vietnamese announced they were ready to parlay, and on May 10, 1968, in a mood of optimism peace talks began in Paris. They would drag on for five years.

The 1968 Humphrey-Nixon presidential campaign did little to advance a peace settlement in Vietnam. By the time the campaign got underway the Paris peace talks had stalled over the issue of making the bombing halt unconditional and whether the Vietcong and the Saigon government should be included in the discussions. If Johnson had agreed to the North Vietnamese conditions it would have helped Humphrey and the Democratic candidate's advisers strongly endorsed it. But the president, seeing acceptance as repudiation of his policies, at first refused. When he decided for the sake of the Democratic ticket to yield, South Vietnamese President Nguyen Van Thieu, believing Nixon a stronger Saigon partisan than Humphrey, refused to go along, and the agreement bogged down. Humphrey came so close to winning that some observers have argued that the last-minute boost of an agreement would have changed the results.

Nixon and Vietnam

By the time Richard Nixon became president in January 1969, approximately 30,000 Americans had died in Vietnam. Nearly 20,000 more would go to their deaths before the fighting stopped. In Vietnam itself American troop morale plummeted when it became clear that winning a military victory was no longer a serious option. Among the fighting troops there were increasingly frequent racial incidents between African-Americans and whites, enlisted men turned to marijuana and hard drugs as a way to face danger and fight off boredom, and discipline all but collapsed in some units where enlisted men "fragged" unpopular officers by rolling live grenades into their tents. And it would get worse. The morale of the American armed forces became one of the most serious casualties of Vietnam.

As president, Nixon pressed efforts to extricate the country from the war. Unlike

Johnson, who had led the country into the Vietnam quagmire, he had no political stake in continuing. But no more than Johnson did he wish to be tarred with defeat. As he would later say, he did not intend to be "the first president of the United States to lose a war." His plan, an elaboration of Johnson's post-Tet policy, called for the progressive withdrawal of all American combat forces from Vietnam and the gradual shift of all military responsibility to the South Vietnam government, whose forces would be built up through massive American aid. This *Vietnamization,* he apparently believed, could lead to peace between the two halves of permanently divided Vietnam, without an American presence.

His optimism was not shared by National Security Adviser (later secretary of state) Henry Kissinger, Nixon's chief agent in the negotiations with Hanoi. Kissinger was a realist who recognized that without American troops the Saigon regime would probably fall. All that could be achieved, as he later phrased it, was "a decent interval."

Whatever the administration's doubts Vietnamization proceeded apace under the new administration. In June 1969 Nixon announced a withdrawal of 25,000 American troops. In September he promised to withdraw an additional 35,000. Meanwhile a flood of American guns, planes, and munitions poured into South Vietnam to build up its forces so that they could do the job themselves.

These moves did not satisfy the antiwar activists, however. In October and again in mid-November student-organized Moratorium Days brought thousands of protesters into the nation's streets and to the nation's capital. Vice President Agnew, the administration's conservative spokesman, denounced the demonstrators and other critics as "an effete corps of impudent snobs who characterize themselves as intellectuals." The president ostentatiously ignored the Washington march by spending the day watching a Redskins football game.

The Cambodia Incursion

Meanwhile the Paris negotiations dragged on inconclusively. The North Vietnamese believed that talking did not preclude fighting and sought every advantage in positioning their forces logistically and winning ground on the battlefield while the talks proceeded. The United States responded by blows intended to raise the costs of continued delay. These began in early 1969 with a secret bombing campaign against North Vietnamese supply lines and depots in Cambodia, Vietnam's supposedly neutral neighbor, that would last for fourteen months. In April 1970 Nixon authorized a limited invasion of Cambodia to deny the North Vietnamese a sanctuary and clean out suspected pockets of Vietcong troops and supplies. Thousands of American and ARVN ground troops swept across the Cambodian border, achieving little in the end.

The incursion created a powerful shock wave at home. By now Nixon had reduced the number of American troops to about half the maximum number in 1968. But despite all the talk of Vietnamization he had now apparently expanded the war. In a matter of days half the campuses in the United States had detonated in strikes and disruptions. Thousands of students ceased attending classes to organize rallies; on many campuses that spring the activists forced cancellation of final examinations.

The Cambodia incursion produced the closest thing to a political massacre that America experienced during the turbulent era following Johnson's Vietnam escalation. Kent State University in Ohio had been only one of the hundreds of campuses that had exploded after Cambodia. But the authorities there were more clumsy and short-tempered than most. On Monday, May 4, 1970, while students were changing classes, the National Guard, untrained in crowd control but called in by Ohio Governor James Rhodes to stop disorder, responsed to taunting and stone-throwing by firing a volley of live ammunition at the students. Four were killed and thirteen wounded. None of the injured or dead was a militant; one was an ROTC member.

Many Americans, perhaps a majority, thought the students deserved what they got. But a substantial—and influential—portion of the public was horrified by the shooting. Thousands of students took to the streets in protest. It seemed the appalling culmination of all the anger, division, and ferocity of a decade.

Peace at Last

Still the war continued with no end in sight. In February 1970 serious peace negotiations had shifted from the formal talks to secret discussions in a dingy Paris suburb between Kissinger and Le Duc Tho, a senior member of the North Vietnamese politburo. Such sub-rosa parleys had the advantage in Kissinger's view of bypassing the press and also the State and Defense departments. For a time these talks made progress and then they too stalled. To force the Communists's hand, in early 1972 Nixon ordered resumption of the long-suspended bombing raids on Hanoi and other North Vietnamese cities. Soon after, he announced the mining of the harbor of North Vietnam's major port, Haiphong, and further heavy bombing raids on the North. These would stop if the enemy accepted a cease-fire. Yet at the same time American troop withdrawals continued with the last American combat units gone by August 13, 1972.

Peace talk progress resumed during the 1972 American election campaign, and on October 26 Kissinger announced a settlement agreement. It proved premature; South Vietnamese President Thieu objected to its provisions and his response scuttled the agreement. Bombing attacks on North Vietnamese targets, suspended to encourage an accord, now were resumed with special ferocity to force the Communists to make further concessions. This reaction may have been decisive. On January 27, 1973, the Americans, North Vietnamese, South Vietnamese, and Vietcong signed a final agreement in Paris ending the Vietnam War.

Peace Provisions

The terms were simple, but at many points ambiguous. The United States would remove its remaining military advisers, and within sixty days North Vietnam would return the 500 or so American prisoners of war in its custody. The fighting in Vietnam would stop, with all forces remaining in place, and the cease-fire would be supervised by an international commission. All military activities in Laos and Cambodia would also cease. To foster the prosperity and guarantee the survival of South Vietnam, the object of American concern for almost ten years, the United States would send modest replacement military aid and a large but unspecified amount of economic aid. The all-important political arrangements were left vague: there would be a National Council of National Reconciliation and Concord composed equally of Saigon government and Vietcong partisans to being together the two sides and eventually arrange free national elections. How this would be accomplished was not clear.

It is hard to believe that Nixon and Kissinger truly believed they had achieved "peace with honor"; it seems unlikely that they did not recognize they had merely constructed a rickety face-saving device. Yet the weary American public cheered the results. America's longest war was over.

The Legacy

The peace in Vietnam lasted little more than two years. It proved impossible to implement the reconciliation terms. Neither South Vietnam nor North Vietnam took them seriously and fighting shortly resumed. This time, without American troops and bombers, the South Vietnamese could not hold, and in early 1975 the North Vietnamese army finally overran the South. Thousands of refugees, many identified with the American regime, fled the country and were admitted to the United States. In late April as the Communist Army entered Saigon, American helicopters transported 1000 panicky Americans and 5000 South Vietnamese from the American Embassy compound in Saigon to U.S. navy ships offshore. It was an inglorious end to the struggle that had cost so much in lives, money, and national morale.

The Communist regime established in South Vietnam proved as repressive and rigid as its enemies anticipated. It clamped down on dissenters with an iron hand, dealt harshly with former opponents and thousands of long-term Chinese residents of Vietnam, and imposed a centralized economic order that soon destroyed the South's economy. Thousands of "boat people" were soon fleeing Vietnam and taking their chances with pirates and storms on the high seas rather than face the harsh regime.

The war left a legacy for Americans. Many, especially those who opposed it, would thereafter be extra wary of American entanglement in anticolonial uprisings. In 1973

One of the last U.S. helicopters to leave Saigon in April 1975, as North Vietnamese troops were closing in. (UPI/Bettmann Newsphotos)

such feelings induced Congress to pass the War Powers Resolution requiring the president to get congressional approval before sending American troops to a combat zone for more than ninety days. In the 1980s, as we will see, resistance to U.S. involvement in Nicaragua drew fuel from the "lesson" of Vietnam. Many of these same people opposed increased arms expenditures and favored nuclear disarmament schemes.

Yet the war's outcome also encouraged the opposite reaction. To other Americans the result seemed a humiliation. The United States had not really been defeated; it had been betrayed by its own people. This must never be allowed to happen again. American must rearm and stand tall. It was this response, this current of opinion, that the political right would tap so successfully in 1980.

FOR FURTHER READING

Students interested in the background of the Vietnam War, as well as the war itself, should consult Stanley Karnow, *Vietnam: A History* (1983). A briefer history of the whole Vietnam involvement is George Herring, *America's Longest War: The United States and Vietnam, 1950–1975* (1986). For treatments that support the Johnson administration positions see Norman Podhoretz, *Why We Were in Vietnam* (1983) and Gunther Lewy, *America in Vietnam* (1978).

The antiwar movement is covered exhaustively in Nancy Zaroulis and Gerald Sullivan, *Who Spoke Up!: American Protest against the War in Vietnam, 1963–1975* (1984) and in Fred Halstead's Trotskyist study, *Our Now!: A Participant's Account of the American Movement against the Vietnam War* (1978). Two books that deal with the country as a whole during the Vietnam era are Alexander Kendrick, *The Wound Within: America in the Vietnam Years, 1945–1974* (1974) and Thomas Powers, *The War at Home: Vietnam and the American People, 1964–1968* (1973). Specialized descriptions of the antiwar movement include Louis Menashe and Ronald Radosh (eds.), *Teach-Ins USA* (1967); Norman Mailer, *The Armies of the Night* (1968); Alice Lynd (ed.), *We Won't Go: Personal Accounts of War Objectors* (1968); and Michael Ferber and Staughton Lynd, *The Resistance* (1971).

The American government's response to the antiwar movement is dealt with in Jessica Mitford, *The Trial of Dr. Spock* (1969); Tom Hayden, *Trial* (1970); and Jason Epstein, *The Great Conspiracy Trial* (1970). A scathing denunciation of government surveillance practices is Frank Donner's *The Age of Surveillance* (1980).

For the Tet offensive and some of its accompaniments see Don Oberdorfer, *TET! The Turning Point in the Vietnam War* (1983) and Peter Braestrup, *Big Story: How the American Press and Television Reported and Interpreted the Crisis of Tet 1968 in Vietnam and Washington* (1983). For the Johnson decision to end escalation see Herbert Schandler, *The Unmaking of a President: Lyndon Johnson and Vietnam* (1977) and Townsend Hoopes, *The Limits of Intervention: An Inside Account of How the Johnson Policy of Escalation in Vietnam was Reversed* (1973). On Mylai, see Seymour Hersh, *Mylai: A Report on the Massacre and Its Aftermath* (1971).

Nixon, Kissinger, and Vietnam are covered critically in Seymour Hersh, *The Price of Power: Kissinger in the Nixon White House* (1983); David Landau, *Kissinger: The Uses of Power* (1972); and William Shawcross, *Side-Show* (1979). Kissinger has ably defended his Vietnam policy in his own *The White House Years* (1979).

Kent State is described in James Michener, *Kent State: What Happened and Why* (1971) and Peter Davies, *The Truth about Kent State* (1973).

5
The Great Malaise

Signs like this one were common in America during the OPEC oil embargo of 1973. (Alain DeJean/Sygma)

The Nixon Administration

From today's perspective the 1970s seem a time of *malaise*. The word, of French origin, was used by journalists and other observers to describe the poorly defined collective illness that seemed to beset the nation during much of the seventies. Those who used the term often meant the state of the economy in the wake of the oil price surge and the energy crisis, but they also applied it to the insecure and dissatisfied political and psychological mood of the American people after 1968.

Richard Nixon helped to create the negative public mood. Nixon was a complex and deeply flawed man. His personality was protean, taking on a bewildering range of shapes to suit the circumstances. This is true of many politicians, but few seemed so lacking in an inner core of authentic self. It was this malleability that led to the frequent assertion of his political allies that there was currently "a new Nixon" in operation who was somehow better than the old one.

As president, Nixon was not especially interested in domestic affairs. From the outset of his political career he had felt most comfortable dealing with foreign policy issues, and even his early identification with anticommunism had been a domestic echo of America's new postwar role in world affairs. Yet he claimed to have a domestic agenda. His fondest desire, he said, was to heal the nation's wounds. In his victory statement soon after the election he recalled a sign carried by a young girl in Ohio during the presidential campaign that read "Bring Us Together." That would be his purpose: bridging the gap between the generations, between the races, and between the parties.

Wooing Middle America

Perhaps the new president really believed these words, but other goals came first. He had promises to keep to the white South for helping him get elected. He also hoped to please "middle Americans," a gentler term than "backlash," for white working- and middle-class people of conservative, family-oriented values. Both constituencies abhorred the perceived cultural excesses of the 1960s and wished to slow the pace of social change that, in their view, was tearing the nation apart. Somehow the federal government must shift its weight to the other side of the scale, toward the forces of consolidation and stability and away from change. In effect the new administration must change sides in the mighty social and cultural war that had erupted during the previous decade.

The shift reflected the administration's own sincere beliefs. But it was also a move to make the Republicans the majority party. During the presidential campaign one of Nixon's advisers had been an astute young political analyst from New York, Kevin Phillips. In 1969 Phillips's book *The Emergence of a Republican Majority*, recommended a new strategy for the GOP. A major shift was underway in American politics, Phillips announced. In the sweep of territory from Virginia to California—"the Sunbelt"—white, old-stock Americans were disgusted by the social and political activism of the day and offended by radical students and intellectuals and by militant blacks. So were many urban, predominantly Catholic, ethnics. Many of those exasperated people were traditional Democrats, but they could be wooed away from their party and converted into Republicans if the GOP made clear its opposition to all forms of militancy. A consistent conservative strategy could transform the Republican party into the normal majority party, a position it had not enjoyed since the rise of the New Deal in the early 1930s.

Judging by their actions, Nixon and his advisers took the Phillips thesis seriously. Nixon had promised to slow the pace of school desegregation in the South, and after taking office, he directed the Department of Health, Education, and Welfare and the Justice Department to ease the pressure on southern school districts to end segregated practices. He later publicly attacked the policy of court-ordered busing of pupils from one school district to another for the sake of promoting racial balance. Under orders from Attorney General John Mitchell, Nixon's former law associate, the Justice Department cooperated with local police departments in cracking down on the Black Panthers and instituted indictments against a variety of antiwar and radical groups.

The president also sought to shift the ideological center of gravity of the Supreme Court. Under Chief Justice Earl Warren the nation's highest court had been a dynamic force in the drive for a more egalitarian and libertarian society. From *Brown* v. *Board of Education* onward, federal judges had pushed the pace of desegregation, had insisted on the right of accused criminals to legal counsel and to keep silent (*Gideon* v. *Wainright* and *Miranda* v. *Arizona*), had required the reapportionment of state legislatures to reflect racial and demographic shifts (*Baker* v. *Carr*), had struck down book censorship statues (*A Book Named 'Memoirs of a Woman of Pleasure'* v. *Attorney General of Massachusetts*), and had denied the right to any local government to mandate prayer or Bible reading in the public schools (*School District of Abingdon Township* v. *Schlempp*). In all these matters the Court had seemingly taken the side of people outside the mainstream or critics of American values, and it had offended the conservative middle American voter.

When Earl Warren retired as chief justice in 1969, Nixon selected Warren Burger, a man less committed to "judicial activism,"—using the federal courts to compel social or political change—to succeed him. Although Burger was a conservative, he was also a believer in the doctrine that the courts should not abruptly overthrow the decisions of their predecessors. His appointment, accordingly, was less helpful than conservatives had hoped in shifting the Court's ideological emphasis. When another vacancy occurred, Nixon determined to select a judge who could be counted on without fail to resist the judicial trends of the recent past. With his debts to Strom Thurmond and other southern Republicans in mind, such a jurist should, he believed, also be a southerner.

Unfortunately for his strategy his first nominee, Judge Clement Haynsworth of South Carolina, had a too blatantly segregationist, antilabor record and was tainted by conflict of interest charges besides. Nevertheless, the Senate's refusal to confirm him angered the president, who promptly submitted the name of G. Harrold Carswell, a Florida federal judge with a record that suggested not only flagrant racism but also legal mediocrity. When the Senate rejected this nomination too, Nixon attacked the Senate's liberal majority as unalterably opposed to giving the South a voice in the governing of the nation. It was clear, he said, that he could not "successfully nominate to the Supreme Court any . . . judge from the South who believes as I do in strict construction of the Constitution." Ultimately the Senate did confirm a conservative, Harry Blackmun, but he was from Minnesota. Although defeated in his attempt to accommodate the traditional South, Nixon had scored points with southern conservatives.

Yet Nixon was not the consistent conservative hard-liner in domestic matters that liberals had feared. Following the advice of his domestic affairs adviser, Daniel Moynihan, a Harvard professor of government who had served under Kennedy and Johnson, he did not dismantle the Johnson poverty programs. To do so, Moynihan said, would create chaos in the inner cities. For a time the president even endorsed Moynihan's plan for a federal takeover of state welfare programs and a federally "guaranteed annual income" for the poor of $1600 per family of four. Attacked by the right as too liberal and by the left as too limited, the scheme died, leaving the country with a welfare patchwork that satisfied no one.

Environmental Issues

The president also responded to the growing clamor over pollution and the general deterioration of the nation's physical environment. The public concern was a delayed response to the downside of the technological revolution of the postwar era that had provided new sources of energy, new industrial processes, new building and packaging materials, and new ways to combat insect pests and weeds that destroyed crops and reduced agricultural output. Many of these advances had unfortunate side effects: they polluted the air, food, and water supplies and in the process increased the incidence of cardiovascular disease and cancer and degraded the beauty and recreational value of the environment.

Fears of the negative effects of technology were not new, of course; they go back to medieval times. The modern *ecology,* or environmental, movement dates, however, from the 1962 publication of Rachel Carson's *Silent Spring,* a description of how DDT and other synthetic insecticides were damaging the nation's natural environment and destroying its animal and plant life. The drive to protect the environment soon merged with a broad-gauged consumer protection movement inspired by Ralph Nader, a Harvard-educated lawyer whose book *Unsafe at Any Speed* (1965) indicted the automobile industry for its excessive focus on styling, speed, and engine power to the neglect of safety. When General Motors (GM) was caught trying to discredit Nader by hiring private detectives to poke into his personal life, Nader sued and won a large financial judgment against the firm. The publicity goaded Congress into passing the first significant auto safety law (the National Traffic and Motor Vehicle Safety Act of 1966) and began the long process of improving highway safety.

Nader soon become father of a powerful new environmental and consumer protection movement. The GM money settlement enabled him to establish his Center for the Study of Responsive Law, staffed by young men and women called "Nader's Raiders" who devoted their skills to ferreting out consumer fraud and environmental wrongdoing. Other environmental groups, including the Sierra Club, the National Wildlife Federation, Friends of the Earth, and the Environmental Defense Fund, also flourished during these years.

There was a strong antibusiness bias to the consumer protection and environmental movements. The consumer advocate-environmentalists often found themselves pitted against oil-drilling companies, the nuclear power and chemical industries, timber and mining firms, drug companies, and steel makers in their battle to limit or regulate extractive or manufacturing processes. In addition some of the newer groups, including Nader and his associates, were products of the insurgent mood of the 1960s. Their survival into the 1970s and 1980s represented a long epilogue for 1960s radicalism and the counterculture. Their critics often accused them of opposing all economic growth through some romantic attachment to an imagined utopian, preindustrial past.

If their ideology had been their sole appeal, the consumer advocate-environmentalists would probably not have made much headway. But they also touched the public's instinct for self-preservation. Many Americans, not just those disposed to dislike business or yearn for the Garden of Eden, were made nervous by the dangerous by-products of modern industrial processes and wished to protect themselves and their piece of America.

It was this mood that led even the probusiness Nixon administration to support environmental legislation. On January 1, 1970 Nixon signed into law the National Environmental Policy Act, requiring federal agencies to issue an "impact statement" for each major project they proposed. In April, following a damaging oil spill in the Santa Barbara Channel off the California coast, Congress passed the Water Quality Improvement Act authorizing the government to clean up oil spills and levy charges on those responsible. In 1970 Nixon also recommended and got an Environmental Protection Agency (EPA) to administer all federal programs to combat pollution. At the same time he proposed a National Atmospheric Administration to deal with the problems of the oceans and the atmosphere. In 1972 Congress passed the Federal Environmental Pesticide Control Act, giving the EPA power to control the manufacture, use, and distribution of pesticides. Soon after, EPA administrator William Ruckelshaus banned DDT from all further use.

Space

One striking triumph of Nixon's first year in office was the moon landing in July 1969. This was the culmination of President Kennedy's 1961 promise to land a man on the moon "before this decade is out" and Lyndon Johnson's continued commitment to that goal. Yet it was in Nixon's administration that, after many billions of dollars and countless man-hours, the manned space program finally achieved Kennedy's end. On July 16 the Apollo 11 mission, with Michael Collins, Edwin Aldrin, Jr., and Neil Armstrong aboard, blasted off from the Kennedy Space Center (Cape Canaveral) in Florida and headed for earth's only natural satellite. Three days later the astronauts placed their command vessel into orbit around the moon, and on Sunday, July 20 Armstrong and Aldrin descended in the *Eagle* landing module to the broken lunar surface. At 10:56 P.M. Eastern Daylight Time, as over half a billion people worldwide watched and listened, Armstrong left *Eagle* and took humankind's first step onto the surface of any celestial body other than earth. Joined by Aldrin, he planted a television camera on a pole, and delighted viewers could see the two men bounding like

July 1969: earthlings walk on the moon for the first time. (UPI/Bettmann Newsphotos)

kangaroos over the stark lunar terrain (the moon's gravitational pull is only one-sixth of the earth's).

Two hours later, after collecting fifty pounds of moon rocks and soil for testing, and planting an American flag and various scientific devices on the surface, the astronauts returned to their mother ship *Columbia* and blasted off for earth. On July 24 the *Columbia* splashed down in the Pacific. President Nixon was on the bridge of the aircraft carrier *Hornet,* waving his binoculars, when the *Columbia* descended on its orange and white parachutes.

Apollo 11 was followed by five other American-sponsored moon landings, each of which gathered additional information about the moon's composition and geology and revealed fascinating data about the nature of the solar system. But then the landings ceased. The Apollo 17 expedition, which returned to earth in December 1972, was the last of the series and, so far, the last time humans touched down on the moon.

By this time the novelty of the moon landings had worn off and enthusiasm had waned. The Apollo series had cost $25 billion, a sum that appalled citizens who worried about the plight of America's needy and underprivileged. Critics claimed, moreover, that the costs had been unnecessary from a strictly scientific point of view: as much or more information could have been garnered by sending unmanned probes at far lower cost. America had been moved more by rivalry with the Soviet Union than by thirst for knowledge, many claimed.

But another explanation of the space program's winding down also fits the facts. Launched in the full enthusiasm of the buoyant early sixties, it expressed the American people's confidence in limitless possibility. By 1970 times had changed. Americans were no longer confident; they also no longer felt flush. Apollo fell victim to the spiritual and material malaise that was creeping across the country by the early 1970s. Its termination, in turn, reinforced the erosion of national morale.

Nixonomics

Declining morale was also linked to economic decline. The decade following 1968 was a period of slowdown, a time when growth rates diminished and America's place in the world economy deteriorated. The effects would reverberate through many areas of national life.

During the twenty year period 1947–1967 the nation had ridden an extraordinary economic wave. Total gross national product (GNP) growth rates had averaged 3.9 percent per year. Productivity per man-hour, an important measure of economic vigor, had grown at a 3.2 percent average annually. Unemployment during this period had run a small 4.7 percent of the labor force. Then about the time Nixon took office, the boom ran out of steam. Between 1967 and 1979 GNP growth slowed to 2.9 annually, productivity increases declined to 1.5 percent each year, and unemployment rose to an average of 5.8 percent. Worst of all, inflation returned with a roar. In the 1947–1967 period consumer price increases had held to about 2 percent yearly; by 1973 they had soared to over 9 percent. In 1979 consumer prices would rise by 13 percent, one of the highest inflation rates in American history. (See Figure 5–1.)

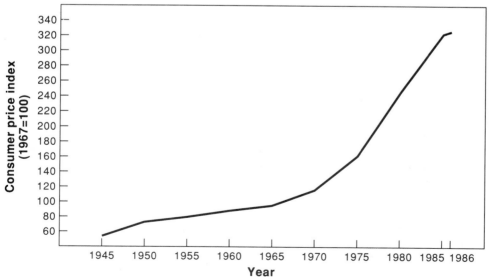

Figure 5–1   The Consumer Price Index, 1945–1986 (1967 = 100)

Sources: *Historical Statistics of the United States* (Washington: U.S. Bureau of the Census, 1975), p. 210, and *Statistical Abstract of the United States, 1988* (Washington: U.S. Bureau of the Census, 1987), p. 450.

The Causes of the Economic Problems

Nixon was not responsible for the national economic slowdown. The start of the inflation surge, for example, was largely the result of Johnson's reluctance to follow pay-as-you-go policies for the Vietnam War and his reliance on federal deficits to pay the nation's bills.

The growth rate decline had even more distant roots. In part America's economic achievements had been due to its easy domination of postwar international markets. This success was as much a product of other nations' limitations following World War II as its own prowess. But by the late sixties the war-torn regions abroad had recovered, and Germany and Japan, especially, had fully modernized their industrial plant. It did not take long before they had become formidable competitors to the United States, not only cutting into America's overseas markets, but winning millions of customers for their products in the United States itself.

This development caught the United States unprepared. As the engine of the free world economy after 1945, America had been a major exporter of capital and under the 1947 General Agreement on Tariffs and Trade had kept its markets open to foreign producers. Along with generous Marshall Plan aid and American willingness to shoulder the immense burden of anti-Communist military defense, this policy had helped revive the free world economy. But as the 1960s drew to a close, American producers found themselves unable to match the costs and the quality of German and Japanese wares, especially in electronics, optical goods, and automobiles. By 1970 German Volkswagens and Mercedes and Japanese Toyotas and Datsuns had begun to flood American streets and highways, cutting deeply into the sales of GM, Ford, and Chrysler. By that time too the thirty-five millimeter camera had become an exclusive Japanese-German preserve and more and more American companies had abandoned television production to Sony, Panasonic, and other Japanese electronics firms. As the new decade began, even the steel industry, the very symbol of America's earlier industrial preeminence, was in serious financial trouble, unable to compete with foreign producers.

The picture was not all dark. American agriculture remained the most advanced and productive in the world, and the United States was able to meet not only its own food needs but the shortfalls of other nations, including the Soviet Union. Furthermore American firms such as Boeing and Douglas supplied the world with most of its civilian airliners. The most advanced sector of American industry was semiconductors and the dazzling computers they made possible. The major breakthroughs in computer science, as in electronics generally, were achieved in American laboratories. In electronics the Japanese had been more skillful in converting basic technology into successful consumer products. Not so with computers, where firms such as IBM, Wang, Cray, and other companies were soon far ahead of everyone else in building large "number crunchers" that enabled industry, financial firms, and government agencies to make their operations more efficient. Still, although there were islands of excellence and competitiveness in the economy, as the sixties gave way to the seventies it was clear that the United States was facing an economic challenge from abroad without precedent since the previous century.

Sagging American exports and soaring American imports in turn created severe financial problems. By 1970 American exports dipped below American imports for the first time in many decades. Americans paid for the excess of imports with dollars and our major trading partners were soon awash with them. By 1971 the West German government alone held more dollars then there was gold in Fort Knox. Because foreigners now had more dollars than they wanted, they sought to exchange them for American gold, a procedure allowed by both American law and the Bretton Woods Agreement negotiated in 1944 as World War II wound down. The drain soon threatened to exhaust the American gold stock.

Nixon's Economic Policies

Nixon dealt with these dangers ineptly. His answer to America's deteriorating trade position was to end the convertibility of American dollars into gold on demand in August 1971. Soon after, in hopes of lowering American prices to foreign customers, the United States devalued the dollar in terms of other national currencies. These moves stopped the gold drain but did little to check the long-term decline of America's productivity and competitiveness relative to other nations.

Nixon's move against inflation was little better. The president, as we saw, inherited the problem from his predecessor. He had long professed to despise tight economic controls by government, but faced with a possible runaway inflation, and fearing its effects on his reelection chances, in 1971 he abruptly changed course. On the same day that he ended the dollar's gold redeemability, Nixon announced that all prices, wages, dividends, and rents would be frozen at existing levels for three months. Compliance by employers, firms, and landlords would be imposed by a Cost of Living Council headed by Treasury Secretary John Connally. Over the next few months the inflation rate slowed, and Nixon announced "Phase Two," which replaced compulsion with voluntary compliance. Phase Two proved largely ineffective; price increases once more accelerated.

Nixon and Foreign Policy

But at best Nixon dealt with domestic problems almost as an afterthought. It was in the shaping of America's relations with other nations that he would, he believed, make his mark in history. Nixon's first secretary of state was William Rogers, a smooth New York lawyer who had served as Eisenhower's attorney general. But Rogers had little to do with the management of foreign policy. Nixon reserved much of the field for himself and in any case preferred to consult his more congenial National Security Adviser Henry Kissinger, a former Harvard professor of government who was a proponent of unsentimental *realpolitik* in the conduct of foreign affairs. Nixon and Kissinger seemed to enjoy intrigue, preferring to deal with foreign leaders by hidden "back channel" routes rather than through the State Department and the usual ambassadorial officials.

Nixon and China

Although progress toward disengagement in Vietnam at first proved slow and discouraging (see Chapter 4), the Nixon-Kissinger team could claim major foreign policy advances on other fronts.

Nixon was no friend of the China Lobby, that group of conservative Americans who abhorred the Chinese Communist regime and had successfully fought every attempt to get the United States to recognize the Beijing (Peking) government and allow admission of the People's Republic to the UN. The president, although a dyed-in-the-wool anti-Communist, understood that Red China would not simply go away if the United States refused to establish diplomatic relations. He also perceived that a major breach was opening between the two largest Communist nations, China and the Soviet Union. Establishing relations with Beijing might enable the United States to use one Communist nation against the other to advance its own interests. In this case Nixon's long-established conservative and anti-Communist reputation stood him in good stead. The political right could not accuse him, as they would a liberal Democrat who sought to deal with China, of betraying his country.

The initial move came from the Americans when in March 1971 the State Department lifted a long-imposed ban on American travel in the People's Republic. By now China had abandoned its bizarre and tumultuous Cultural Revolution and was prepared to deal rationally with its problems. In April the Beijing government responded by inviting the American table tennis team, then playing in Japan, to tour mainland China, all expenses paid. The Soviets recognized the meaning of the event and called the invitation "unprincipled."

The American team was given the red-carpet treatment, and to flatter their guests the Chinese discretely avoided sending their best players to the meets. The positive response of the American people in turn encouraged Kissinger and Nixon to proceed. During the next few months Kissinger made a secret visit to the Chinese capital where he talked at length with foreign minister, Chou En-lai. On July 14, 1971, Nixon informed the American people of Kissinger's visit on national television and declared that he expected to go soon to Beijing himself. Although seeking a new relationship with Beijing, the United States sought to avoid sacrificing its old Kuomintang friends on Taiwan. Nixon tried to pursue a "two Chinas" policy that included keeping Taiwan in the UN. But fired up by the breakthrough, the members of the UN General Assembly voted to exclude Taiwan and admit Red China regardless of the American president's wishes.

In late February 1972 Nixon, his wife, Pat, and an entourage of journalists and advisers flew to Beijing to meet with the Chinese leaders. Relatively little was accomplished in the formal talks beyond an American agreement to withdraw U.S. troops from Taiwan, but the visit prepared the ground psychologically for full diplomatic relations. Americans watched on television in amazement as their president, once the arch anti-Communist, walked along the Great Wall and shook hands with Mao Tse-tung (Mao Ẑedong). After more than twenty years the two great nations, once close friends, had resumed relations.

Improved Soviet Relations

Kissinger and Nixon also succeeded in improving relations with the Soviet Union, a policy labeled *détente*. For months the national security adviser had been holding secret talks with Soviet Ambassador Anatoly Dobrynin without consulting Secretary Rogers. These had led to closer economic ties with the Soviets, including major grain sales to compensate for the Soviet Union's chronic shortfall in wheat production. But the president and his chief adviser were out for bigger game than improved trade relations. They wanted the Soviet Union to pressure the North Vietnamese into a more reasonable negotiating position at the Paris peace talks and hoped to slow the nuclear arms race and reduce Cold War tensions.

For a time in the spring of 1972 improved Soviet-American relations were endangered when the United States resumed bombing attacks on Hanoi and mined Haiphong harbor, the major North Vietnamese entry port for Soviet supplies. The bombers sank a Soviet ship in the harbor, killing several on board. Fortunately the Soviets chose to ignore the attack. On May 22 Nixon visited Moscow and was greeted cordially by Soviet Premier Leonid Brezhnev. Amid the festivities some actual business was concluded. The United States and the Soviet Union agreed to a series of joint research projects in medicine, to cooperation in space and on environmental matters, and to an end to hostile encounters on the high seas. Most important were a series of agreements on nuclear arms limitations that capped years of negotiations. When incorporated into the Strategic Arms Limitation Treaty (SALT I) of August 3, 1972, these agreements limited the defensive antiballistic missiles that both sides could position and froze offensive nuclear weapons to those already in existence or still under construction.

The Middle East

The Middle East had long been a major trouble spot for the United States. There Israel and its Arab neighbors remained implacable enemies, with the Arabs determined to destroy what they perceived as a Western intruder in their region. Israel's stunning victory in the 1967 Six Day War had expanded its boundaries to include all of Jerusalem, part of Syria, Egypt's Sinai Peninsula, the Gaza Strip, and the West Bank of Jordan. (See Figure 5–2.) The victory had created a new sense of security, even complacency, among Israel's beleaguered people, but it had also increased the hostility of its Arab neighbors and added immeasurably to its dilemma over the Palestinians, the predominantly Muslim inhabitants of what had been the British Palestine mandate, who were now, in much larger numbers, under Israeli rule.

On October 6, 1973, during the Jewish holiday of Yom Kippur, Egypt, now led by Anwar Sadat, and Syria attacked Israel. Caught unaware, the Israelis for several critical days retreated, suffering heavy losses in men and equipment, particularly on the Egyptian front. The war soon looked as if it might become a superpower confrontation, for although the Egyptians had recently thrown out their Soviet advisers, the Soviet Union quickly supplied them with new weapons and when it looked as if the Israelis might be defeated, the United States airlifted enormous amounts of replacement supplies to Israel.

In a few days the tide of battle turned. Israel halted the Arab advance and then launched a counterattack that threatened to destroy the entire Egyptian invasion army. At this point the Soviets intervened politically on behalf of Egypt. They warned that if the Israelis did not desist, they would send troops to stop them. The United States

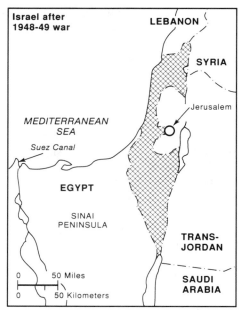

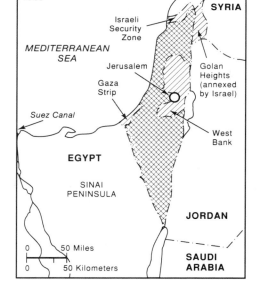

Figure 5–2   Israel and the Middle East

responded by placing its military forces on worldwide alert. Fortunately the Israelis agreed not to proceed any further and to accept a truce with UN forces to supervise the cease-fire.

The Yom Kippur War had repercussions far beyond the eastern Mediterranean. By now many of the industrialized nations, including the United States, had become dependent on middle eastern oil for automobile gasoline, heating fuel, and electric power production. This reliance placed them at the mercy of the Arab oil producers who dominated the Organization of Petroleum Exporting Countries (OPEC). In response to the support of Israel by the United States and several European countries, the Arab producers cut their crude oil production by 5 percent and imposed a complete oil embargo on nations considered friendly to Israel. The embargo itself was soon lifted, but the experience left the Arab nations with a new sense that oil was a powerful international weapon and a new willingness to cooperate for the purpose of raising oil prices. In the next few years, as world petroleum prices quadrupled, Americans and Europeans would hear much of OPEC's economic power, invariably to their dismay.

The Yom Kippur War had another significant and more welcome effect. Although in the end Israel gained the upper hand, the Egyptians' near-victory instilled in them a new confidence. No longer obsessed by a sense of inferiority, they were able to act more generously toward their enemies. When Kissinger, then secretary of state, began a series of whirlwind trips among the various Middle Eastern capitals during the fall and winter of 1973–74 ("shuttle diplomacy"), he managed to negotiate several agreements between Israel and Egypt regarding troop disengagement and other matters. He also won the confidence of Anwar Sadat and was able to draw Egypt into the American orbit.

The 1972 Election and Watergate

Nixon had campaigned hard for Republican candidates during the 1970 congressional elections and sought to use incidents of student heckling and rock-throwing to malign the Democrats. The tactic did not work well. The Democrats gained twelve House seats and eleven governorships.

By the time Nixon returned from his Moscow trip, the country was gearing up for the 1972 presidential campaign. On the Democratic side the obvious front-runner would have been Senator Edward Kennedy of Massachusetts, the only surviving senior Kennedy male and heir to the family mystique. But Kennedy had destroyed his chances in July 1969 when, at Chappaquiddick near Martha's Vineyard, a fatal accident occurred. Leaving a hard-drinking party with a young woman who had been a political worker for his brother Robert, the senator drove his car off a bridge and the young woman drowned. Kennedy himself escaped serious injury. Despite his denials the public believed that he and the girl had left the party for romantic reasons and in his drunken state he had taken a wrong turn. They were also skeptical of his story of how he had tried many times, at risk to himself, to save her. A married man, the senator already had a reputation for infidelity, and the awful incident further damaged his public image.

With Kennedy out, Senator Edmund Muskie of Maine, the Lincolnesque Humphrey running mate of 1968, was the front-runner as the Democratic convention in Miami approached. But Muskie ruined his chances when, viciously attacked by the far-right *Manchester Union Leader* during the New Hampshire primary campaign, he apparently broke down and wept while defending his wife. The public took this as a sign of weakness and Muskie's campaign thereafter collapsed. The backlash-voter hero George Wallace, now back in his home Democratic party, also seemed a serious contender until he was shot and paralyzed while campaigning in Maryland by a publicity-seeking would-be assassin.

Senator George McGovern of South Dakota, a former history professor who belonged to the party's most liberal and dovish wing, soon moved to front place. McGovern benefited from major rule changes adopted at Chicago in 1968 that were designed to open up the party to outsiders. These mandated a better "balance" at national conventions by requiring that in the future there be more African-Americans and other racial minorities, more women, and more young people among convention delegates. No longer would the professionals, the trade union leaders, and the white male politicos determine the results.

At Miami the new groups were present in force; the California delegation even boasted a contingent of people on welfare. The convention seemed a holdover from the sixties with elements of the political left, the counterculture, and various "liberationist" groups highly visible and vocal. These "New Politics" groups controlled the convention, excluding many traditional Democrats from the proceedings and repudiating more conservative views. The convention adopted a left-liberal, strongly antiwar platform and nominated McGovern on the first ballot. It seemed to shrewd observers a pyrrhic victory for the McGovern forces, however. Many conservative and middle-of-the-road Democratic voters watching the proceedings on television felt alienated by the spectacle of the party's conquest by the left. They would not be enthusiastic supporters of the ticket in November.

Nixon and Agnew won renomination without serious opposition at the Republican convention in August on a conservative platform. After the president's opening to China and détente with the Soviet Union, his reputation had soared. Against the unorthodox Democrats his victory seemed a sure thing.

Watergate: Opening Phase

But Nixon and his advisers decided to leave nothing to chance. Running the campaign, under the direction of former Attorney General John Mitchell, was the Committee for the Re-Election of the President (CRP). This committee, soon called "CREEP" by the Democrats, was determined to win and win big in November for the president—and at any cost.

The collection of crimes called *Watergate* grew out of this win-at-all-cost attitude. It also was sustained by Nixon's special failings as a political leader. However skilled in diplomacy, he was politically insecure, suspicious of his opponents, and uncomprehending of the rules of the American political game. His chief advisers—men such as John Mitchell; John D. Ehrlichman, Nixon's domestic affairs adviser; White House Chief of Staff H. R. Haldeman; and John Dean, White House counsel—were even worse. Drawn mostly from the business community where sharp dealing was often the norm, unused to the compromises and restraints of the nation's mainstream political culture, and deeply imbued with the security obsessions that marked the era, they accepted the principle that anything goes in the pursuit of victory. To win in 1972, the public later learned, they were willing to subvert the laws and the spirit of the constitutional processes by which the nation lived.

By the summer of 1972 CRP was rolling in money, much of it extracted from large corporations induced to contribute by promises of favors. After "laundering" in Mexico to disguise their origins, these funds were deposited in secret party accounts or crammed into CRP safes. The flood of green would be used to bury the Democrats in a wave of media ads and massive rallies in the fall.

Another phase of the projected Nixon campaign was "dirty tricks," a "disinformation" and espionage campaign to confuse and obstruct the Democrats. Run by a White House Special Investigations Unit, nicknamed the "plumbers," it had begun as an attempt to plug leaks of confidential administration discussions and activities. The most bothersome of these leaks had been the theft by former Kissinger aide Daniel Ellsberg of the *Pentagon Papers*—hundreds of documents on Vietnam collected as an internal Defense Department report—and their publication in the *New York Times* in June 1971. That September a unit of the plumbers broke into the office of Ellsberg's Los Angeles psychiatrist in search of information that might tarnish Ellsberg's reputation.

CRP borrowed the plumbers' approach and some of their personnel. It funded Republican zealot Donald Segretti's spying and infiltration operations against the Democrats and his scheme to sow dissension in their ranks by mailing letters on bogus Muskie campaign stationary charging other Democratic candidates with sexual indiscretions. Other CRP-financed dirty tricks included an attempt to sabotage Ted Kennedy by concocting phony cables implicating his dead brother John in the assassination of the South Vietnamese leader Ngo Dinh Diem and encouraging Internal Revenue Service audits of prominent Democrats' tax returns to distract them from political activities.

The dirty trick that would backfire and eventually destroy Nixon was the June 1972 break-in at Democratic National Committee headquarters in the Watergate Hotel and office complex in downtown Washington to steal confidential Democratic documents. The operation was conceived by G. Gordon Liddy, counsel to CRP, a man with a James Bond imagination. At one point CRP had considered a million-dollar sequence of kidnappings, phone-tappings, and sexual blackmail operations against Democrats that made even Mitchell blanch. In the end Liddy settled for a much cheaper break-in at the Watergate to rifle the Democrats' files and bug their telephones for useful or incriminating information.

On the evening of June 17, after the failure of an earlier attempt, James W. McCord, Jr., security coordinator of CRP, and four anti-Castro Cuban accomplices succeeded in entering the empty Democratic offices. But the break-in was detected by a security guard and McCord and his four colleagues were caught. When booked at the police station, they all gave aliases and refused to say what they had been doing. Observing the arrest from the balcony of a nearby motel were several other members of CRP, including E. Howard Hunt, a White House consultant.

News of the arrests reached CRP leaders in Los Angeles the next morning when Liddy called long distance. Their immediate reaction was to try to conceal the connection between the break-in and the president's reelection campaign. Unfortunately for CRP it did not take long before the link between the burglars and the Republicans leaked out. On June 19 the police discovered Hunt's name in an address book in possession of one of the arrested Cubans.

At this point, hindsight shows, it would have been politically smart for the president to have admitted that Republican zealots had violated the law and then condemned their acts. Instead Nixon and his staff, under pressure from the indicted men to supply money for legal defense and for their families, agreed to protect the burglars by making the break-in appear to be an anti-Castro Cuban caper. On June 20 the president told White House aide Charles Colson, "We are just going to leave this where it is, with the Cubans." In short order documentary evidence of the operation went into the paper shredders. Other incriminating documents were sent to FBI Director L. Patrick Gray, who, on instructions, burned them. At the same time CRP drew on its vast pool of funds and sent $500,000 in hush money to the indicted men.

The *Washington Post* carried news of the break-in the day after it happened. But at first almost no one paid much attention. At a briefing for reporters on June 19 Press Secretary Ronald Ziegler dismissed the break-in as "a third-rate burglary attempt" too insignificant to comment on. As pressure grew, however, Nixon could not ignore the issue. Finally on August 29 he told reporters that he had already ordered an investigation of the affair by Chief White House Counsel John Dean, and the results had shown that "no one in the White House Staff, no one in this Administration presently employed, was involved in this very bizarre incident" Dean later said this was the first he had ever heard of this "investigation."

Nixon Reelected

By now the presidential election was entering the home stretch. McGovern proved to be an inept campaigner. He had chosen as his running mate the young senator from Missouri, Thomas Eagleton. When shortly after the convention Eagleton confessed that he had twice been hospitalized for emotional problems, McGovern at first defended him and then forced him off the ticket, choosing in his place Sargent Shriver, the former Office of Economic Opportunity head. The incident made McGovern seem both indecisive and self-righteous.

The Democratic candidate tried to recoup by attacking the administration for being too close to business, for its opportunistic economic controls policy, for favoring the rich over the poor, and for spending too much on defense and not enough on domestic welfare programs. He mentioned the Watergate break-in as an example of the administration's disregard of law, but in the absence of any hard evidence of White House involvement, the charge did not stick. McGovern took particular aim at the administration's continued involvement in Vietnam. This too missed its mark. By now Vietnamization had reduced American casualties to the vanishing point.

The election results were not surprising. In the end McGovern got only 37.5 percent of the popular vote to Nixon's 60.7 and won only the liberal state of Massachusetts and the District of Columbia, a predominantly African-American community. There was a massive defection of traditional white Democratic voters. McGovern had not succeeded in surmounting the perception that the party had fallen into the hands of minorities, radicals, and eccentrics, and many Democrats—ethnics, the white South, trade union families—deserted their party. Some obviously voted Republican, yet many Americans still did not like the man in the White House and refused to vote at all. The voter turnout was the smallest in twenty-four years.

Watergate Unravels

By the time of Nixon's second inauguration in January 1973 the Watergate burglars along with Hunt and Liddy were under indictment. As yet no one could pin anything on the president's staff, certainly not on the president himself, although two *Washington Post* reporters, Carl Bernstein and Robert Woodward, had begun to dig deeply into the scandal.

But then, soon after the beginning of Nixon's second term, the White House cover-up plan began to fall apart. The trial in Washington of the Watergate burglars, presided over by "Maximum John" Sirica, a tough federal judge, concluded on January 30, 1973, with their conviction on a variety of charges. At the sentencing in March Sirica read aloud a letter from McCord declaring that "perjury had occurred during the trial" and that "there was political pressure applied to the defendants to plead guilty and remain silent." Clearly, the judge stated, the full Watergate story had not been told.

The McCord statement blew the Watergate affair wide open. In early February the Senate appointed a Select Committee on Presidential Campaign Activities to investigate. The committee was headed by the white-haired, folksy, but Harvard-educated Democrat, Sam Ervin of North Carolina. Over the next few months a parade of witnesses came before the Ervin Committee to testify under oath about their knowledge of the break-in. Meanwhile the Watergate defendants, as yet unsentenced and worried about their futures, remained a serious danger to the administration. On March 22 John Dean told Nixon that Watergate was "a cancer growing on the presidency" and that something must be done to stop its growth. Soon after, he, Haldeman, and the president considered further demands by the Watergate burglars for money and for possible clemency. Nixon told the others that money would be no problem: "You've got to keep the cap on the bottle . . . in order to have any options." He advised that all those who were forced to testify should avoid the risk of perjury charges by claiming faulty memories. Their defense should be that the break-in was connected to national security. The following day in a private discussion with John Mitchell he further declared: "I don't give a shit what happens. I want you all to stonewall it, let them plead the Fifth Amendment, coverup or anything else, if it'll save it—save the plan . . . . Up to this point, the whole theory has been containment, as you know John."

For the next year the intertwined set of scandals called Watergate was never far from headline news. The public absorbed the revelations of reckless disregard for truth, contempt for constitutional processes, and the plain violations of criminal law with fascinated horror as they poured from the televised Ervin Committee hearings, continued grand jury investigations, and the reports of Woodward and Bernstein in the *Washington Post*. Each day, it seemed, brought its appalling disclosures of gross breaches of trust by the administration. Americans learned about the break-in at Elleberg's psychiatrist's office and then the attempt by Ehrlichman at Ellsberg's trial for espionage and theft of the Pentagon documents to suborn the judge by offering him the vacant FBI directorship. They heard about a White House "Enemies List" of antiadministration politicians, professors, and journalists who were tagged for harassment by the Internal Revenue Service and other federal agencies. Ultimately a raft of secondary scandals also came to light: how the administration had settled an antitrust suit in favor of the International Telephone and Telegraph Company in exchange for political contributions, how Nixon had been allowed improper tax deductions for donating his vice presidential papers to the National Archives, how he had used federal funds to improve the grounds of his personal homes at Key Biscayne, Florida, and San Clemente, California.

As the investigators closed in, Nixon was forced to throw some of his staff to the wolves. On April 30, 1973, two weeks after declaring that he was launching searching new inquiries, he announced the resignations of Haldeman, Ehrlichman, and of Attorney General Richard Kleindienst, Mitchell's successor, and the firing of John Dean.

In early May the new attorney general, Elliot Richardson, agreed to appoint a special prosecutor to investigate all aspects of the Watergate affair. On Richardson's advice Nixon chose Harvard Law Professor Archibald Cox for the post on May 18.

The Watergate hearings proved to be as riveting as the Army-McCarthy hearings twenty years earlier. Despite the administration's attempt to prevent the testimony of high officials by invoking the doctrine of executive privilege, Mitchell, Haldeman, Ehrlichman, Dean, and others appeared before the Ervin Committee and revealed much of what had taken place in secret conclaves in the White House and elsewhere. But no one except Dean was willing to accuse the president himself of guilty knowledge or of trying to prevent disclosure of the full facts.

Then on July 16 former White House aide Alexander Butterfield remarked almost casually that for the previous two years all White House conversations had been taped. If the tapes could be procured, it would become possible to know without fail—in the words of Senator Howard Baker of Tennessee—"what the president knew and when he knew it."

Both Cox and the Ervin Committee subpoenaed tapes for key periods. Nixon, claiming executive privilege once more, refused to release them. Cox asked the courts to compel the president's compliance, and Nixon, fearing the prosecutor's zeal and independence, asked Richardson to fire him. When the attorney general refused, the president dismissed him. Nixon then asked the deputy attorney general to do the deed. He too refused and was fired. Finally, concluding this "Saturday night massacre," Solicitor General Robert Bork became acting attorney general and dismissed Cox.

Impeachment and Resignation

Cox's departure did little to help Nixon. Public outrage compelled the president to appoint another special prosecutor. His choice fell on Leon Jaworski, a conservative Houston lawyer who could be expected to be more favorable to the Republican administraton than his predecessor. Meanwhile in October the House Judiciary Committee, under Peter Rodino of New Jersey, began to hold preliminary hearings on the possible impeachment of the president.

While these events were unfolding a scandal erupted around Vice President Spiro Agnew, a man who had become the administration's hard-line voice against the militant students, the peace activists, and the "eastern liberal establishment." Accused of taking kickbacks from contractors while governor of Maryland and of evading income taxes, Agnew resigned on October 10. Following the terms of the twenty-fifth Amendment, Nixon nominated Gerald Ford of Michigan, the House minority leader, to succeed Agnew.

In April 1974 the White House's last-ditch effort to conceal the cover-up began to come apart. On April 11 the Rodino Judiciary Committee subpoenaed forty-two White House tapes; soon after this Special Prosecutor Jaworski, less compliant than had been expected, also demanded to see White House tapes. Nixon resisted bitterly, but on April 30 he released over a thousand pages of edited transcripts, although not the tapes themselves or even transcripts of all the tapes requested. Yet even these revealed the president and his colleagues as unfocused, inarticulate, often truculent, and bigoted men. They also pointed at efforts to prevent the full revelation of Watergate misdeeds. But they failed to reveal any "smoking gun."

In July the House Judiciary Committee began televised discussions of impeachment and at the end of the month voted three articles of impeachment against Nixon: for engaging "personally and through his subordinates and agents in a course of action designed to delay, impede, and obstruct the investigation" of the Watergate break-in and to "cover up, conceal, and protect those responsible" for the break-in; for "violating the constitutional rights of citizens [and] impairing the due and proper administration of justice"; and for defying committee subpoenas, thereby hobbling the impeachment process. But it turned out that the articles, the first voted against a president since 1868, never had to be weighed by the Senate in an impeachment trial.

On August 5 after the Supreme Court had denied Nixon the right to withhold any of the tapes, he surrendered the tapes to Jaworski. One of these, for June 23, 1972, contained the smoking gun. On that day, less than a week after the burglary, the President had discussed the break-in with Haldeman and had told his assistant to stop the CIA and the FBI from proceeding any further on the case. They should be told, he said, that if the purposes of the break-in were revealed it would jeopardize national security. (See Reading 5.)

The publication of the June 23 conversation made it certain that the president would have to leave office. On August 7 senators Barry Goldwater and Hugh Scott, representing respectively the conservative and liberal wings of the Republican party, visited the White House to tell Nixon he must resign to spare the country the long agony of an impeachment trial. That evening Goldwater told reporters he could not count more than fifteen senators who would vote against conviction.

At 9 P.M. Eastern time on August 8, Nixon spoke to the nation on television. He would resign the presidency at noon the next day, he said. The next morning, after a brief farewell to his staff in the East Room of the White House, he and his family flew off for California and retirement from public life. At a little after noon that day Gerald Ford took the oath of office as president of the United States.

READING 5

The Watergate Cover-up

Nixon was by no means the most incompetent man who sat in the White House, but he may have been the most devious. Insecure, suspicious, often mean-spirited, he encouraged the deceit and chicanery that led to the Watergate break-in and then fostered the cover-up that turned it into a constitutional crisis. This reading comes from the famous taped private conversations between the president and key White House aides in the weeks after the Watergate burglars were caught. H. R. Haldeman was Nixon's chief of staff; John Dean a White House counsel. These conversations and others like them constituted the smoking gun of presidential complicity in the cover-up attempt that ultimately forced Nixon out of office.

June 23, 1972

Haldeman: Now, on the investigation, you know the Democratic break-in thing, we're back in the problem area because the FBI is not under control, because [Director Patrick] Gray doesn't exactly know how to control it and they have—their investigation is now leading into some productive area. . . . They've been able to trace the money—not through the money itself—but through the bank sources—the banker. And it goes in some directions we don't want it to go. Ah, also there have been some [other] things—like an informant came in off the street to the FBI in Miami who was a photographer or has a friend who is a photographer who developed some films through this guy [Bernard] Barker and the films had pictures of Democratic National Committee letterhead documents and things. So it's things like that that are filtering in. . . . [John] Mitchell came up with yesterday, and John Dean analyzed very carefully last night and concludes, concurs now with Mitchell's recommendation that the only way to solve this . . . is for us to have [CIA Assistant Director Vernon] Walters call Pat Gray and just say, "Stay to hell out of this—this is ah, [our] business here. We don't want you to go any further on it." That's not an unusual development, and ah, that would take care of it.

President: What about Pat Gray—you mean Pat Gray doesn't want to?

Haldeman: Pat does want to. He doesn't know how to, and he doesn't have any basis for doing it. Given this, he will then have the basis. He'll call [FBI Assistant Director] Mark Felt in, and the two of them—and Mark Felt wants to cooperate because he's ambitious—

President: Yeah.

Haldeman: He'll call him in and say, "We've got the signal from across the river to put the hold on this." And that will fit rather well because the FBI agents who are working the case, at this point, feel that's what it is.

President: This is CIA? They've traced the money? Who'd they trace it to?

Haldeman: Well, they've traced it to a name, but they haven't gotten to the guy yet.

President: Would it be somebody here?

Haldeman: Ken Dahlberg.

President: Who the hell is Ken Dahlberg?

Haldeman: He gave $25,000 in Minnesota and, ah, the check went directly to this guy Barker.

President: It isn't from the Committee though, from [Maurice] Stans?

Haldeman: Yeah. It is. It's directly traceable and there's some more through some Texas people that went to the Mexican bank which can also be traced to the Mexican bank—they'll get their names today.

President: Well, I mean, there's no way—I'm just thinking if they don't cooperate, what do they say? That they were approached by the Cubans? That's what Dahlberg has to say, the Texans too.

Haldeman: Well, if they will. But then we're relying on more and more people all the time. That's the problem and they'll [the FBI] . . . stop if we could take this other route.

President: All right.

Haldeman: [Mitchell and Dean] say the only way to do that is from White House instructions. And it's got to be to [CIA Director Richard] Helms and to—ah, what's his name? . . . Walters.

President: Walters.

Haldeman: And the proposal would be that . . . [John] Ehrlichman and I call them in, and say, ah—

President: All right, fine. How do you call him in—I mean you just—well, we protected Helms from one hell of a lot of things.

Haldeman: That's what Ehrlichman says.

President: Of course; this [Howard] Hunt [business.] That will uncover a lot of things. You open that scab there's a hell of a lot of things and we just feel that it would be very detrimental to have this thing go any further. This involves these Cubans, Hunt, and a lot of hanky-panky that we have nothing to do with ourselves. Well, what the hell, did Mitchell know about this?

Haldeman: I think so. I don't think he knew the details, but I think he knew.

President: He didn't know how it was going to be handled though—with Dahlberg and the Texans and so forth? Well who was the asshole that did? Is it [G. Gordon] Liddy? Is that the fellow? He must be a little nuts!

Haldeman: He is.

President: I mean he just isn't well screwed on, is he? Is that the problem?

Haldeman: No, but he was under pressure, apparently, to get more information, and as he got more pressure, he pushed the people harder.

President: Pressure from Mitchell?

Haldeman: Apparently. . . .

President: All right, fine, I understand it all. We won't second-guess

Mitchell and the rest. Thank God it wasn't [special White House counsel Charles] Colson.

Haldeman: The FBI interviewed Colson yesterday. They determined that would be a good thing to do. To have him take an interrogation, which he did, and the FBI guys working the case concluded that there were one or two possibilities—one, that this was a White House (they don't think that there is anything at the Election Committee) they think it was either a White House operation and they have some obscure reasons for it—non-political, or it was a—Cuban [operation] and [involved] the CIA. And after their interrogation of Colson yesterday, they concluded it was not the White House, but are now convinced it is a CIA thing, so the CIA turnoff would—

President: Well, not sure of their analysis, I'm not going to get that involved. I'm (unintelligible).

Haldeman: No, sir, we don't want you to.

President: You call them in.

Haldeman: Good deal.

President: Play it tough. That's the way they play it and that's the way we are going to play it. . . .

* * *

President: O.K. . . . Just say (unintelligible) very bad to have this fellow Hunt, ah, he knows too damned much. . . . If it gets out that this is all involved, the Cuba thing, it would be a fiasco. It would make the CIA look bad, it's going to make Hunt look bad, and it is likely to blow the whole Bay of Pigs thing which we think would be very unfortunate—both for CIA, and for the country, at this time, and for American foreign policy. Just tell him to lay off. Don't you [think] so?

Haldeman: Yep. That's the basis to do it on. Just leave it at that. . . .

September 15, 1972

President: We are all in it together. This is a war. We take a few shots and it will be over. We will give them a few shots and it will be over. Don't worry. I wouldn't want to be on the other side right now. Would you?

Dean: Along that line, one of the things I've tried to do, I have begun to keep notes on a lot of people who are emerging as less than our friends because this will be over some day and we shouldn't forget the way some of them have treated us.

President: I want the most comprehensive notes on all those who tried to do us in. They didn't have to do it. If we had had a very close election and they were playing the other side I would understand this. No—they were doing this quite deliberately and they are asking for it and they are going to get it. We have not used the power in this first four years, as you know. We have never used it. We have never used it. We have not used the Bureau, and we have not used the Justice Department, but things are going to change now. And they are either going to do it right or go.

Dean: What an exciting prospect.

President: Thanks. It has to be done. We have been (adjective deleted) fools for us to come into this election campaign and not do anything with regard to the Democratic Senators who are running, et cetera. And who the hell are they after? They are after us. It is absolutely ridiculous. It is not going to be that way any more.

March 13, 1973

President: How much of a crisis? It will be—I am thinking in terms of—the point is, everything is a crisis. (expletive deleted) it is a terrible lousy thing—it will remain a crisis among the upper intellectual types, the soft heads, our own, too—Republicans—and the Democrats and the rest. Average people won't think it is much of a crisis unless it affects them. (unintelligible)

Dean: I think it will pass. I think after the [Senator Sam] Ervin hearings, they are going to find so much—there will be some new revelations. I don't think that the thing will get out of hand. I have no reason to believe it will.

President: As a matter of fact, it is just a bunch of (characterization deleted). We don't object to such damn things anyway. On, and on and on. No, I tell you this it is the last gasp of our hardest opponents. They've just got to have something to squeal about it.

Dean: It is the only thing they have to squeal—

President: (Unintelligible) They are going to lie around and squeal. They are having a hard time now. They got the hell kicked out of them in the election. There is not a Watergate around in this town, not so much our opponents, even the media, but the basic thing is the establishment. The establishment is dying, and so they've got to show that despite the successes we have had in foreign policy and in the election, they've got to show that it is just wrong, just because of this. They are trying to use this as the whole thing.

March 21, 1973

Dean: So that is it. That is the extent of the knowledge. So where are the soft spots on this? Well, first of all, there is the problem of the continued blackmail which will not only go on now, but it will go on while these people are in prison, and it will compound the obstruction of justice situation. It will cost money. It is dangerous. People around here are not pros at this sort of thing. This is the sort of thing Mafia people can do: washing money, getting clean money, and things like that. We just don't know about those things, because we are not criminals and not used to dealing in that business.

President: That's right.

Dean: It is a tough thing to know how to do.

President: Maybe it takes a gang to do that.

Dean: That's right. There is a real problem as to whether we could even do it. Plus there is a real problem in raising money. Mitchell has been working on raising some money. He is one of the ones with the most to lose. But there is no denying the fact that the White House, in Ehrlichman, Haldeman and Dean, are involved in some of the early money decisions.

> ***President:*** How much money do you need?
>
> ***Dean:*** I would say these people are going to cost over a million dollars over the next two years.
>
> ***President:*** We could get that. On the money, if you need the money. you could get that. You could get a million dollars. You could get it in cash. I know where it could be gotten. It is not easy, but it could be done. But the question is who the hell would handle it? Any ideas on that?
>
> ***Dean:*** That's right. Well, I think that is something that Mitchell ought to be charged with.
>
> ***President:*** I would think so too.
>
> *Source:* From *Hearings Before the Committee on the Judiciary, House of Representatives, 93rd Congress, 2nd Session* (Washington: Government Printing Office, 1974).

The Ford Presidency

Ford's first words to the American people, uttered moments after the swearing-in ceremony, were reassuring. The country's "long national nightmare" was over, he declared. "Our Constitution works. Our great republic is a government of laws and not of men." But many people were not certain that "the system" had "worked" all that well. Without the lucky break of the tapes, after all, Nixon and company might well have succeeded in concealing their illegal cover-up. Doubts were reinforced when the new president pardoned the ex-president, thereby preventing his prosecution for criminal activity. The act seemed all the more misguided in light of the ultimate trial and conviction of most of Nixon's close advisers.

Yet the public wanted very much to like this first unelected president. Ford seemed a solid and personally agreeable, if dull and unimaginative, man. To make up for his lack of foreign policy experience, he retained Henry Kissinger as secretary of state. Since Ford's elevation to the presidency had vacated the vice presidential office, he was charged with selecting his successor. For this post he chose the Republican party's liberal gadfly, Nelson Rockefeller of New York. Both appointments seemed wise choices for a man without a popular mandate.

Economic Policy under Ford

Ford's chief domestic problem was the accelerating inflation. By 1974 prices were rising at the double-digit rate of 11 percent. The next year they slowed somewhat but then in 1979 and 1980 they soared to 12 and then to 13 percent. Inflation would be the most severe economic problem of the late seventies.

Some of this surge could be traced to petroleum price rises by the OPEC oil cartel, newly confident of its strength following the Yom Kippur War. For decades the United States had been a major oil producer and exporter. Gasoline and other petroleum derivatives had been cheap, and Americans had been extravagant in their use of energy. American automobiles, for example, had been notorious gas-guzzlers, getting often no more than 8 or 10 miles per gallon. By the mid-seventies, however, the United States no longer produced enough oil for its needs and was importing millions of barrels annually.

Dependence on imported oil made the OPEC price rises reverberate through the economy. Every item that used large amounts of energy to manufacture immediately leaped in cost. In addition, the soaring price of energy required major redesign of automobile engines, electric generator stations, and housing insulation systems to increase energy efficiency. All of these efforts were expensive and all added further impetus to inflation.

But soaring oil prices were not the only economic problem. By the mid-seventies the United States was suffering from a condition that the wordsmiths called "stagflation." This was the worst of two worlds: stagnation and inflation simultaneously. Not only were prices rising, economic growth was slowing. Annual increases in GNP, which had averaged almost 4 percent a year the previous decade, slowed to about 3 percent during the 1970s. This leveling off was felt in the paycheck of American working people. From 1948 to 1966 average yearly growth in real spendable earnings had run 2.1 percent. Between 1966 and 1973 it dropped to half that rate. During the last two or three years of the 1970s real spendable income actually declined, on average, for American wage and salary earners. Family incomes would continue to rise slowly, but only because more family members, especially wives and mothers, joined the work force.

Accompanying the slower growth was rising unemployment. In the late sixties the jobless rate had averaged under 4 percent; in 1975 it reached 8.5 percent. (See Figure 5–3.) In the past inflation and unemployment had been trade-offs; now the country was afflicted with both of them at the same time.

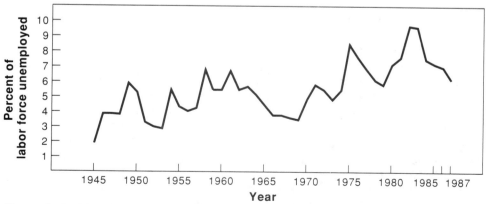

Figure 5–3   Unemployment, 1945–1987

Sources: *Historical Statistics of the United States* (Washington: U.S. Bureau of the Census, 1975), p. 135; *Statistical Abstract of the United States, 1985* (Washington: U.S. Bureau of the Census, 1984), p. 390; *Statistical Abstract of the United States, 1988* (Washington: U.S. Bureau of the Census, 1987), p. 365; and *Monthly Labor Review* (September 1988), p. 65.

The reasons for the stagflation were not clear. Conservative economists blamed government policies. High social security and personal income taxes, overgenerous unemployment insurance benefits, excessive regulation, and heavy taxation of capital gains had either discouraged investment or drained the economy of needed capital funds, they said. Yet at the same time an exaggerated concern with social misfortune and the desire to maintain full employment impelled the government to spend more than it took in, thus pumping up consumer demand and fueling inflation. The conservative experts also tended to believe that American workers were overpaid. Powerful unions, especially in steel, mining, and automobiles, had worked out deals with management that provided ever larger wage hikes without corresponding increases in worker output. The net effect of all of this was inflationary price rises.

Liberal economists tended to blame stagflation on distorting "structural" factors. Inflation, of course, owed much to OPEC's price rigging. But in addition American businessses and industries were themselves responsible for artificially high prices, a result achieved by price collusion and inefficient forms of production, such as annual automobile model changes, that added nothing but costs to the price of a car. Furthermore the vast government outlays on defense were wasteful; not only did they pump money into the economy, they starved it of needed skills and resources. Racism and sexism also exacted high economic costs by wasting the skills of major segments of the American population. Finally there were the shifts from blue-collar heavy industry jobs to white-collar knowledge industry jobs that marked the maturing of the economy. This process had left millions without the skills needed for the job market. No matter how much purchasing power the government created by deficits, these workers would remain unemployed unless and until they were retrained.

Different views led to different prescriptions. Conservatives wanted to lower taxes, especially on capital gains and on people with higher incomes, to encourage investment and creative enterprise. They wanted to offset the government's smaller revenues by cuts in government spending, especially on welfare programs. They also wanted to encourage stiffer domestic competition by ending government regulation, even if this entailed some risk to the environment or to the survival of weaker firms. By the end of the decade conservative economists with views such as these would be called *supply-siders*.

Liberals instead favored sharp cuts in defense spending; a marked increase in government outlays for retraining programs, education, and research and development; and various federal incentive policies focused on specific industries. One unusual development among liberal thinkers was the appearance of high tariff, protectionist views. These were not based on theory, but were a response to foreign competition that threatened the jobs of American industrial workers.

President Ford dealt ineffectively with the economy's problems. A conservative Republican, he was far more concerned with rising prices than with rising unemployment. The president sought to slash government spending for housing, education, and public works and at the same time urged a tax increase to cut down on consumer purchasing power. He also launched a psychological attack on inflation expectations that featured buttons inscribed with the motto WIN (Whip Inflation Now). The campaign accomplished little and critics laughed at its triviality. In truth there were no easy solutions to the stagflation problem, and the president was not wrong in believing that persistent federal deficits were an important part of the problem. The public wanted expensive programs—aid to education, better roads, superior health care, and national security—but preferred borrowing to pay for them rather than taxing themselves.

Legislation and Foreign Policy

Several pieces of legislation during the Ford years reflected the lessons learned during Watergate. In October 1974 Congress strengthened an earlier Freedom of Information Act to allow the public access to data accumulated by the federal government concerning individuals. Ford vetoed the measure on the grounds that it might jeopardize national security. Congress passed it over his veto.

The president approved, however, a new law to reduce the influence of money in politics. The Campaign Finance Law of 1974 established spending limits for primary campaigns, required disclosure of sources and uses of campaign money, and allowed taxpayers to contribute money to presidential campaigns through a tax deduction from their income tax returns. The new law was intended to help make candidates less dependent on fat-cat campaign contributors and lobbyists, but it did not. With each campaign the costs of embarking on the long ordeal of caucuses, primaries, and conventions that preceded nomination continued to grow. Despite the law's intent, money continued to count. In fact with each successive national election there were more numerous and more powerful political action committees (PACs) representing special ideologies or special social and economic interests. Critics claimed that if existing trends persisted the United States would become a plutocracy, a nation ruled by the wealthy.

Ford's foreign policy was an extension of Nixon's. Since most Americans considered the disgraced president more successful at foreign than domestic affairs, this was not surprising. Ford and Kissinger continued to seek some sort of peace between Israel and its Arab neighbors. Like his predecessor the new president visited China and reaffirmed Sino-American friendship. In November 1974 Ford met with Soviet Premier Leonid Brezhnev in Vladivostok and the two continued the nuclear arms limitation process launched with the SALT I agreements by signing a document limiting the number of each country's missile launchers, warheads, and other strategic weapons. Proponents of nuclear disarmament hoped that the agreement would soon be incorporated into formal treaties as SALT II.

The Bicentennial

The highpoint of the Ford years was the 1976 bicentennial celebration of American independence. One hundred years earlier, the country had mounted an international exposition in Philadelphia to commemorate the centennial of American independence. The great 1876 Philadelphia World's Fair had displayed the confident nation's new industrial might and technological prowess. It was here that Alexander Bell's great invention, the telephone, was unveiled.

But in 1976 a vastly richer nation could not find an equivalent focus for the celebration. World's fairs were now enormously expensive events that often produced

The "tall ships" sail through New York Harbor on July 4, 1976. (Black Star/Ted Hardin)

large deficits. The nation was also too divided. Attempts by Philadelphia promoters to organize an international exposition fell afoul of racial squabbling over employment, land use, and other matters. Moreover newer parts of the country wanted their own local celebrations.

In the end, the bicentennial became a decentralized, scattershot affair. Washington, D.C., held a major parade down Pennsylvania Avenue with 500,000 spectators, 60 floats, and 90 marching bands. In San Francisco 6000 people gathered at Golden Gate Park to celebrate both the U.S. bicentennial and the two hundredth anniversary of the arrival of the first Spanish settlers at the site of the future city. The closest thing to a national event took place in New York harbor as sailing ships from many lands cruised through the harbor while millions of spectators watched the tall ships' stately procession. Most Americans did feel a surge of pride on the nation's two hundredth birthday; yet those with a sense of history felt the occasion also reflected a nation afflicted with a new sense of limits.

The 1976 Election

In 1974 the voters expressed their dismay over Watergate by giving the Democrats a smashing victory in the midterm congressional elections. Even Ford's own congressional district, which had been safely Republican since 1912, went Democratic. As the 1976 presidential election approached, it looked as if the national mood had made nonsense of Kevin Phillips' predictions that the Republicans were becoming the normal majority party.

The chief beneficiary of the Democratic surge was the one-term governor of Georgia Jimmy Carter, a Naval Academy graduate, a southerner, and a born-again Christian. Carter's chances for the Democratic presidential nomination would have been virtually nil if not for Watergate. That chamber of political horrors had made millions of voters skeptical of old politicos like Nixon and anxious for a fresh face. The former governor, who prayed daily, also seemed a deeply moral man who would never permit the sort of shabby behavior that had pervaded the White House during the Nixon years. True, Gerald Ford was an honest man, but he was closely identified with the Washington establishment and he had squandered much of his moral capital by pardoning Nixon.

Starting with a name-recognition factor of only 2 percent, Carter campaigned ceaselessly for delegates during the primary period. By the time of the 1976 Democratic convention in New York he had the nomination sewed up and won on the first ballot. He chose for his running mate Senator Walter Mondale of Minnesota.

An incumbent president seldom encounters serious competition for his party's renomination, but Ford, who had not been elected to the office and was a man without much personal magnetism, had to beat off the serious challenge of Ronald Reagan, the conservative former governor of California. Ford narrowly won on the first ballot. He chose Senator Robert Dole of Kansas as his vice presidential running mate.

The Democrats campaigned as friends of the "little man" and enemies of the big corporations. They appealed to African-American voters and women but avoided too close an identification with the "outsiders" who had been such a prominent part of McGovern's campaign four years earlier. Ford campaigned as the more experienced leader and attacked Carter as a man with only the vaguest idea of what he would do as president. As the weeks passed the voters, initially enthusiastic about Carter, began to waver and on election day gave the Democratic candidates a shaky victory of 40.2 million popular votes to their opponents' 38.6 million, and 297 electoral votes to the Republicans' 241. When the analysts examined the returns they concluded that Carter had fashioned his victory from a combination of the South, including states that had been recently drifting into the Republican column, and the traditional Democratic constituency of northern African-American, ethnics, Catholics, Jews, and trade unionists. It seemed doubtful, however, that anyone but a southerner could have carried it off. (See Figure 5–4.)

Jimmy Carter: The Early Months

Despite the narrow victory Carter began his administration on a wave of hope and popular approval. The public liked his common touch. For the swearing-in ceremony he wore a $175 dollar three-piece business suit and took his oath of office with his hand on an old family Bible. After the ceremony he and his wife, Rosalynn, and their daughter Amy walked, rather than rode, at the head of the procession to the White

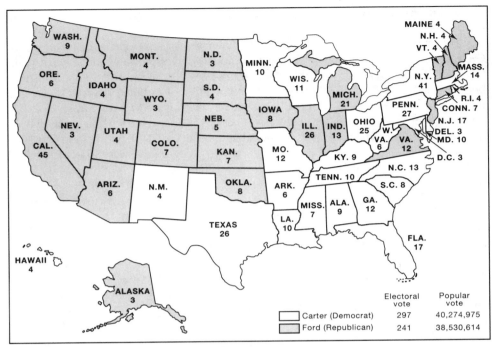

Figure 5–4   The 1976 Presidential Election

President and Mrs. Carter walking up Pennsylvania Avenue after the president's inauguration, January 20, 1977.

House. To further demonstrate their democratic values the Carters enrolled Amy at the local, predominantly African-American, Washington public school.

Energy

The new administration's domestic policies were dominated by the energy crisis. After the OPEC nations lifted the oil embargo in March 1974, petroleum and gasoline once more became abundant, although at much higher prices than ever before. Meanwhile Americans continued to consume energy supplies wastefully, daily increasing American dependence on the Middle East and other foreign regions for their oil supply.

Carter, a former nuclear submarine officer, understood the dangers of American oil dependence. The world's most powerful nation could not permit itself to become hostage to the goodwill of Middle East oil sheiks; Saudi Arabia could not be allowed to make American foreign policy. There was also the matter of international economic relations. If America continued to be dependent on foreign oil, it would have to pay out billions of dollars to the Middle East. This would worsen an already large balance of payments deficit.

The energy dearth also created problems by shifting the nation's regional power balance. The South and West, with their lower cost of living and their warm climate, had long attracted retirees from the North. By midcentury, with so many Americans living into their seventies and even eighties and with federal and private pension plans giving people the freedom to live anywhere in the country, the populations of Florida, Arizona, California, Texas, and other Sunbelt states soared.

Now rising oil prices engineered by OPEC brought further prosperity to Texas, Oklahoma, Louisiana, and other states in the southwestern "oil patch" while simultaneously hurting the northern industrial and farm regions that consumed energy but produced relatively little of their own. Oil patch residents were not always generous in their response to the plight of other Americans. Observers during these years reported bumper stickers on cars in Texas and other oil-producing states saying "Freeze a Yankee" and "Let the SOB's Freeze in the Dark."

Carter first addressed the energy crisis soon after the inauguration in the midst of one of the most severe eastern cold snaps in years. Before the cameras the president wore a heavy wool sweater to show the need to keep home thermostats low. On this occasion he said that his program would "emphasize conservation" and he asked the public to lower its thermostats to 65 degrees during the day and 55 at night. In late April he appeared before Congress and outlined a major energy program. The prices of petroleum, natural gas, and other fuel sources, until now held down artificially by government regulation, should be deregulated to find their own level. This would stimulate exploration for oil and natural gas and help increase domestic sources of supply. At the same time the government should encourage conservation by placing a high tax on imported oil and providing tax credits for people who insulated their houses. But the president's energy program, incorporated into over a hundred separate measures, quickly stalled in Congress.

Part of the problem was regional rivalries. The program promised to shift wealth still further from the North and East to the Sunbelt, where most of the nation's energy derived. There were also ideological difficulties. Liberal critics claimed that making higher prices the chief incentive to conservation hurt the poor far more than the rich. Conservatives responded that the only alternative was some unacceptable bureaucratic system of rationing.

Nuclear Energy and the Environment

The public was also divided over the role of atomic power in any scheme to ease the energy shortage. Since the 1950s the number of power-generating stations based on radioactive fuel had been increasing across the nation. It soon became clear that atomic energy was not the revolutionary breakthrough to cost-free energy that had been predicted just after World War II, but by the late 1970s about 3.5 percent of all U.S. electricity was generated by nuclear power plants.

This was a smaller proportion than in many major industrial nations, yet it raised a storm of controversy. As we have seen, ever since Rachel Carson's *Silent Spring* (1962) the public had worried about human-made environmental disaster and Congress had acted to limit sources of air and water pollution. The passionate environmentalists felt that these controls were too feeble and pointed to recent disasters as warnings: major oil spills along the California coast that threatened to damage Pacific coast ecology; forest damage inflicted by acid rain, the by-product of northeastern and midwestern fossil-fuel consumption; the disastrous erosion of the quality of life by unrestricted suburban growth. The country, they said, must clamp down hard on dangerous environmental practices, even if this meant limits on economic growth.

The proper response to the energy shortage, they insisted, was conservation —lowering energy use. Cars must be made smaller and more fuel efficient; houses must be better insulated; people must lower their thermostats, walk more, and turn off their lights. If energy output had to be increased it should be done by harnessing wind power and natural thermal power. For a time solar panels that could convert the sun's rays into hot water became the rage in some parts of the country. Often connected with such views was a concern for population limitation. People polluted the environment and used up scarce resources, and the sooner the country brought its rate of natural increase down to bare "replacement level," the better.

The environmentalists particularly deplored nuclear energy. Atomic energy plants produced thermal pollution of the water used to cool them, thereby endangering fish and local flora. Their spent nuclear fuel created severe problems of radioactive waste disposal. Most serious of all was the possibility of nuclear accident where failure of equiment or human error might cause a radioactive leak, or worse, a meltdown that would release vast quantities of radioactive gas and soot into the atmosphere. If such an accident occurred thousands might die or contract cancer.

In the last half of the seventies environmental groups used the protest tactics of the sixties to block construction or completion of nuclear power plants. In April 1977 for example, 2000 Clamshell Alliance demonstrators occupied the construction site of a new atomic energy plant going up at Seabrook, New Hampshire. The police arrested 1400 demonstrators. The antiatomic energy groups also pressed legal challenges to nuclear power plant construction. The antinuclear cause received a big lift when a leak developed at the nuclear power plant at Three Mile Island, near Harrisburg, Pennsylvania, in March 1979. Although the leak was contained and no one died, the American public quaked at the apparent narrow escape from a meltdown. Conservatives and power industry spokespeople continued to insist that atomic energy was safe and potentially cheap, but by the early 1980s it had become too difficult and expensive to overcome the public's fears and the environmentalists' challenges. The atomic energy industry soon stopped dead in its tracks. Half-completed plants were abandoned; planning for new ones ceased.

Carter's Political Failings

But the slow progress of Carter's energy program was not just a product of ideological and regional differences. There were serious flaws in the president's way of presenting the energy problem to the American people. Carter often sounded like a preacher calling his flock to repentance. He scolded the public for its energy extravagance. It was their disregard of the future, he said, that had gotten the United States into its current energy bind in the first place. He referred to "limits" and the need to accept a future less prosperous than the past. In July 1979, in a talk from his Camp David retreat often referred to as the "malaise" address, he described the country's "crisis of confidence" brought on by the energy crisis. Soon after, to signal a new beginning for his administration, he fired three of his cabinet members.

Much of what the president said was valid, but the American public did not enjoy being told that it could not have its cake and eat it too. Carter's political sermonizing, moreover, seemed self-righteous and depressing.

The president and his staff also proved inept in the infighting and horse-trading that marks legislative success in Washington. Carter had no experience of the federal government. Indeed that had been one of his political assets in the eyes of the post-Watergate public. But his ignorance and the arrogance of his young staff hurt him seriously in his relations with Congress. The administration offended Democratic leaders by not informing them of impending nominations for major executive positions or by failing to consult powerful members of Congress on matters that came under their legislative purview. Early in his administration Carter vetoed nineteen pet water projects for the West without telling their congressional sponsors in advance; many learned about the action only from their local newspapers. Even in small things the Carter staff lacked tact and courtesy. Hamilton Jordan, a close Carter aide, refused to grant House Speaker Thomas ("Tip") O'Neill's request for extra seats to the inaugural festivities. Thereafter O'Neill always referred to Jordan as "Hannibal Jerkin."

Some of the administration's severest setbacks came on the economic front. As we have seen, ever since the lifting of the Nixon price ceilings, inflation had soared out of control. As prices rose, so did interest rates, in part to discount higher prices and ensure lenders a reasonable return on their money in the future. High interest rates in turn depressed the housing industry because home buying depended on borrowed mortgage money. After 1979 the new head of the Federal Reserve Board, Paul Volcker, deliberately raised the Fed's rediscount rate, its interest charge to private banks, to reduce consumption and hold down prices. The move was unavoidable, but positive results were slow in coming.

For a time in the late 1970s it looked as if inflation had become a way of life and people sought to accommodate to its effects. The results were deplorable. Investors shifted their money from income-generating factories and enterprise into real estate and "collectibles," anything that promised to appreciate in price. The inflation surge also discouraged efficiency. If each month prices were higher, businesspeople, no matter how wasteful their practices, could count on profits. The incentive to increase productivity fell sharply. The inflation also shifted income from some groups to others. People who could pass along their costs to others gained; those on fixed incomes lost.

Carter seemed to have no answers. He favored reduced federal spending and continued high taxes to cool the economy but was unable to inspire the public or Congress with any clear policy. During much of his administration the economy just drifted with inflation seemingly built into the system.

Carter's Foreign Policy

The president's foreign policy balance sheet showed both debits and credits. Carter was determined to put the Vietnam era behind him and to ease Cold War tensions further. In his view this meant avoiding the hard-nosed Kissinger era response of putting America's short-term advantage first. The United States would no longer support authoritarian regimes abroad but use its good offices to induce undemocratic foreign governments to respect human rights. Washington would criticize harsh Soviet policy toward its dissidents who opposed Moscow's repressive domestic policies or who, as Jews, suffered religious persecution. Few Americans quarreled with this response. But the human rights principle was applied inconsistently. At times Washington attacked anti-Communist, pro-American authoritarian governments in the Americas and elsewhere. Conservatives, placing success in the Cold War first, deplored such attacks. At other times the administration overlooked the human rights violations of the United States' authoritarian friends. On these occasions liberals, less concerned with gaining Cold War advantages than with perceived international injustice, complained.

The president offended anti-Communist hard-liners by going beyond Nixon and opening formal diplomatic relations with the People's Republic of China in January 1979. The previous year he had succeeded in inducing the Senate to approve a new treaty with Panama that provided for the eventual transfer of control over the Panama Canal and the Canal Zone from the United States to Panama. Various superpatriot groups considered the treaty a shameful surrender of American rights.

Carter and the Soviet Union

Carter's policy toward the Soviet Union seemed naive to conservatives. Although he condemned Soviet human rights violations, he acted as if the Soviet Union were otherwise trustworthy. In June 1979 he completed negotiations for another Strategic Arms Limitation Agreement (SALT II). This treaty was pending in the Senate when, abruptly in late 1979, the Soviets sent troops into Afghanistan to support a puppet government threatened with overthrow by its domestic opponents.

Afghanistan was close to the Persian Gulf, the vital sea outlet for much of the Middle East's oil supply, and the move shocked the president and the American public. In response Carter withdrew the SALT II treaty from the Senate, canceled large Soviet grain purchase contracts with the United States, embargoed shipments of high technology wares to the Soviet Union, forbade Americans to particpate in the 1980 summer Olympic games in Moscow, and asked Congress for legislation to require draft registration of all nineteen- and twenty-year olds. In his January 1980 State of the Union Address he warned the Soviet Union that the United States considered the Persian Gulf region essential to U.S. national security.

Carter and the Middle East

More than even his predecessors Carter found his administration caught up in the intricacies of Middle Eastern affairs. The president won applause at home for his success in getting long-time enemies Israel and Egypt to agree to a peace treaty.

The possibility of such a pact had appeared unexpectedly in November 1977, when Egyptian leader Sadat visited Israel to discuss differences between the two countries. This was the first break in the Arab line against recognition of Israel, and it made Sadat a marked man to the anti-Israeli Palestine Liberation Organization (PLO) and its supporters in the Arab world. In August 1978 after it appeared that the peace process between Egypt and Israel had stalled, Carter invited Sadat and Israel's Prime Minister Menachem Begin to the presidential retreat at Camp David in Maryland to resume negotiations.

After weeks of hard bargaining that tested Carter's powers of persuasion severely, the two sides reached an agreement. Israel would evacuate the oil-rich Sinai region, occupied after the 1967 war, and return it to Egypt. In return Egypt would recognize Israeli independence and exchange diplomatic representatives with its former enemy. Unfortunately, on the all-important issue of the displaced Palestinians, the agreement settled for vague promises of a future accommodation, terms that the PLO and its Arab supporters rejected. During the next few years Arab resentment of Israel continued and new hatred was spawned against Egypt and the United States. At times it would take the form of terroristic hijacking of American airplanes, kidnappings, and bombings at airports abroad used by American tourists. Yet despite these responses the American public and much of the free world hailed the Camp David results as a major Carter success.

The Iran Hostage Crisis

Almost wholly negative in its consequences and ultimately disastrous for the Carter administration was the triumph of Islamic fundamentalism in Iran. Early in 1979 Shah Mohammad Reza Pahlevi of Iran, the authoritarian ruler who America had helped regain his throne in 1953 (see Chapter 2), was overthrown by a coalition of opponents from his left and right. The shah eventually came to the United States, where he entered a hospital for treatment of cancer. Soon after, Shiite Muslim fundamentalists led by the Ayatollah Ruholla Khomeini gained the upper hand in Iran and brutally suppressed their enemies—both the shah's supporters and the leftists—and imposed a strict religious regime on the Iranian people.

The ayatollah and his followers represented a powerful new force in the Middle East. Violently anti-Western, a throwback to the days of Islamic ultraorthodoxy and religious rule, they appealed to a strong Shiite minority in the Muslim world that resented both the Sunni majority and the modernizing tendencies represented by the West. Their sworn enemies were Israel and the United States, the latter seen as a "great Satan."

In November 1979 a group of fanatical young militants, probably with the approval of the ayatollah, seized the U.S. Embassy in Tehran and refused to release seventy American employees and diplomats. They would hold the hostages, they said, until the United States agreed to surrender the shah and his ill-gotten wealth to the Iranian authorities and apologized for America's past actions toward Iran.

This violation of diplomatic protocol and the law of nations shocked the American people and riveted their attention on events in Tehran for over a year. In retrospect it is clear that Americans allowed their concern for the hostages to eclipse too many other interests and absorb too many energies. The seizure was outrageous, but extricating the hostages and punishing the culprits should not have become an obsession.

Yet it did. Month after month while the United States maneuvered and argued—in the World Court, at the UN, among the other Muslim states—the hostage

American hostages being paraded in Tehran, Iran, in November 1979. (UPI/Bettmann Newsphotos)

crisis smothered all other news. The American government froze several billion dollars of Iranian funds in the United States and cut off all trade in weapons and other goods to Iran. Individual Americans sometimes vented their frustration by acts of revenge against innocent Iranian students in the United States. On November 17 the Iranians, courting world opinion, released thirteen women and African-American hostages not suspected of espionage but refused to free the remaining fifty-three.

By early 1980 with the presidential election approaching, Carter became desperate. The American hostages were certain to become an important issue in the campaign. In late April, over the opposition of Secretary of State Cyrus Vance, the administration launched a rescue operation by heavily armed helicopters from American naval vessels in the Persian Gulf. This failed dismally. Eight men died in the attempt and the operation had to be aborted. Millions of citizens now felt even more impotent and angry and much of their rage was directed at their own president.

The 1980 Election

Despite the increasing public disenchantment with Carter and a serious challenge from Senator Edward Kennedy, the president could not be denied renomination by the Democrats in 1980. The Republicans turned to Ronald Reagan, the former two-term governor of California and heir of the Goldwater right within the party. They gave the vice presidential nomination to George Bush, a man closer to the Republican center. Some voters who did not like either Carter or Reagan supported Congressman John B. Anderson, a liberal Republican from Illinois, who ran on the Independent ticket.

A former movie actor and erstwhile New Deal liberal, Reagan had drifted to the political right in the 1950s and for a time, after his movie career declined, become a paid spokesman for General Electric. He had been carried into the California governor's mansion in 1966 on a wave of resentment against high taxes and student militancy. In Sacramento Reagan painfully learned the art of compromise and, despite predictions, had moved to the political center.

Yet in 1980 liberals saw his nomination for the presidency as a dangerous challenge to the entire post-twenties political era, and some indulged in loose talk of the coming "fascism" if he won.

In fact, like George Wallace and Richard Nixon before him, Reagan *did* appeal to the backlash against the perceived excesses of the sixties and early seventies. By 1980 African-American militancy, student unrest, and peace marches were things of the past, yet the old resentments—on both sides—lingered.

Reagan profited especially from the seventies' surge of Protestant fundamentalism. He was a product of fundamentalist education—although a divorced man and a lax churchgoer—and he appealed to the fundamentalists' ardent anticommunism, their concern for traditional "family values," their opposition to abortion (which had been legalized by the Supreme Court in 1973) and militant feminism, and their desire to encourage traditional Christianity over a "secular humanism" they claimed had become the nation's predominant faith.

The struggle between fundamentalism and religious liberalism had been part of American cultural life since early in the century. But never before had the fundamentalists been so militant and so well organized politically. During the campaign fundamentalist leaders such as the Reverend Jerry Falwell and Pat Robertson, mobilized as the "Moral Majority," helped rally the devout and raise funds for Reagan. They had the support of Richard Viguerie, a right-wing former Texas lawyer, who organized effective direct-mail fund-raising campaigns for right-wing causes.

Reagan also appealed to voters who felt the Carter administration had ignored growing Soviet strength and had let the United States be pushed around by Iran and other minor powers who no longer feared American might. "Is America as respected throughout the world as it was?" he asked. "Do you feel our security is safe?" Under his administration the country would once more "stand tall."

The highpoint of the campaign was the Carter-Reagan debate on national television. The president proved himself the better informed man, yet Reagan probably "won." The challenger was relaxed and charming, obviously no fascist threat to anyone. How could a man so pleasant, so full of apparent goodwill, harm anyone? The debates helped calm voter fears about a man who had seemed to many at the far-right fringe of American politics.

Yet for a time it seemed that Carter, by getting the embassy hostages released before election day, might pull off a victory. But the Iranians toyed with the United States, and on November 4 they were still captives. Not until January 20, Inauguration Day, did they leave Iran for home. The voting result was a near-Reagan landslide, with the Republican candidate nearly 44 million votes to Carter's 34.7 million. Reagan carried all but four states, winning 489 electoral votes to Carter's 49. (See Figure 5–5.) He would also have a Republican Senate to work with and an ideological, although not a party, majority in the House.

From Nixon to Reagan

The decade that followed the 1960s were depressing years for most Americans. Although Richard Nixon had ended the Vietnam War and lowered tensions between America and the People's Republic of China and the Soviet Union, by the last year of Jimmy Carter's administration Soviet-American relations were worse than during the 1960s. Still more disturbing was the 1980 taking of American hostages by revolutionary Iran Revolution. The hostage crisis tremendously frustrated Americans and reinforced their sense that their country had lost standing in the world.

Conditions at home also gave Americans reasons for gloom. The giant leap of energy prices that followed the OPEC oil embargo of 1973, precipitated a burst of runaway inflation unequalled since the mid 1940s. Many citizens were convinced that the good years of buoyant growth were gone forever.

And political events reinforced the crisis of confidence. Nixon confirmed his enemies' suspicions by plunging the nation into the worst political scandal in its history. Although the country survived Watergate, it emerged with its morale damaged. Carter, the man who might have repaired the nation's collective self-

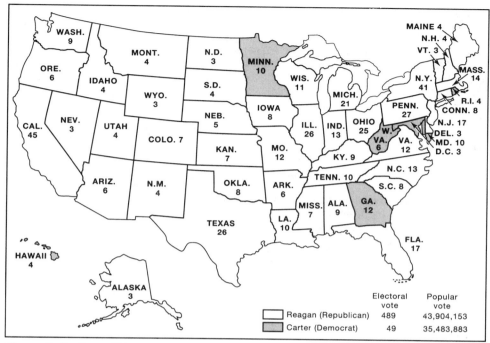

Figure 5–5 The 1980 Presidential Election

esteem, proved ineffectual. He only succeeded in making Americans feel peevish and ill-tempered.

Ronald Reagan was the beneficiary of the public's testy mood as the 1970s ended. The next few years would tell whether he could restore public confidence, revive a faltering economy, and reestablish America's international preeminence.

FOR FURTHER READING

On the Nixon personality see Garry Wills, *Nixon Agonistes: The Crisis of the Self-Made Man* (1971); also Bruce Mazlich, *In Search of Nixon* (1972), a psychoanalytical study.

On the rise of the South to political power see Kirkpatrick Sale, *Power Shift: The Rise of the Southern Rim and its Challenge to the Eastern Establishment* (1975). Peter Carroll, *It Seemed Like Nothing Happened: The Tragedy and Promise of America in the 1970s* (1982) deals with that apparently culturally uninteresting decade in an interesting way.

The beginnings of the post–World War II environment issue is dated from Rachel Carson's *Silent Spring* (1962). For environmentalism thereafter see Frank Graham, Jr., *Since Silent Spring* (1970) and Emma Rothschild, *Paradise Lost* (1973).

Nixon and the Arab-Israeli conflict is described in William Quandt, *Decade of Decision: American Policy toward the Arab-Israeli Conflict* (1977). On the energy crisis the reader should consult Daniel Yergin and Robert Stobaugh, *Energy Future: Report of the Energy Project at the Harvard Business School* (1979). Nixon's economic policies are skewered in Leonard Silk, *Nixonomics* (1972). The welfare reform proposals of the Nixon administration are described in Daniel Moynihan, *The Politics of a Guaranteed Income* (1973).

Nixon and China are covered in Lloyd Gardner, *The Great Nixon Turn-Around: America's New Foreign Policy in the Post-Liberal Era* (1973). On the election of 1972 see Robert Sam Anson, *McGovern* (1972). The most recent installment of America's immigration history is described in David Reimers, *Still the Golden Door: The Third World Comes to America* (1985).

The Watergate literature is more than abundant. Some of the best works are Carl Bernstein and Robert Woodward, *All the President's Men* (1974); Theodore White, *Breach of Faith: The Fall of Richard Nixon* (1975); Jonathan Schell, *The Time of Illusion* (1975); John Dean, *Blind Ambition: The White House Years* (1976): and Leon Jaworski, *The Right and the Power: The Prosecution of Watergate* (1976).

Two works on the Ford presidency are Richard Reeves, *A Ford, Not a Lincoln* (1975) and J. F. ter Horst, *Gerald Ford and the Future of the Presidency* (1974). For the 1976 election see Jules Witcover, *Marathon* (1977).

On Carter, the man and his administration, see James Wooten, *Dasher: The Roots and the Rising of Jimmy Carter* (1978); Haynes Johnson, *In the Absence of Power: Governing America* (1980); and Clark Mollenoff, *The President Who Failed: Carter Out of Control* (1980).

Carter's most conspicuous foreign policy failure was the hostage crisis in Iran. See Barry Rubin, *Paved with Good Intentions* (1980) and Hamilton Jordan, *Crisis: The Last Year of the Carter Presidency* (1982).

6
The Reagan Revolution

Ronald Reagan (left) and George Bush at the 1980 Republican National Convention. (UPI/Bettmann)

The "New Right"

Ronald Reagan's victory was hailed by conservatives as a mandate for a rightward political shift. And they were correct. For years Americans who deplored the social "excesses" of the permissive sixties and the political and economic excesses of liberal government had been preparing for the day. These members of the *New Right* were the spiritual descendants of the traditional Americans who had resisted the new social and intellectual forces of the 1920s and of the Harding and Coolidge Republicans who had turned the nation away from the progressive movement's concern over concentrated private economic power. Like their twenties forebears, they came disproportionately from the country's heartland, now located in the Sunbelt rather than the upper Midwest.

The agenda of these eighties conservatives was, in part, an update of their predecessors'. A lot of it dealt with social issues. Much of the New Right was fundamentalist Protestant in its religious affiliations, although it also included, among others, orthodox Jews who deplored irreligious secular trends, and traditional Catholics who rejected Marxist-influenced *liberation theology* and the liberal theological trends since Pope John XXIII. Many of its supporters, especially fundamentalists, deplored the sway of evolutionary teachings in the schools and demanded equal time for *creationist science,* a doctrine based on the biblical version of life's origins. They lamented the growing secularization of American education. The schools should find time for children's prayers; textbooks should not preach godless *secular humanism;* schools should not be allowed to teach immorality under the guise of sex education.

But to the New Right the imperfections of the schools merely reflected the general deterioration of public morality. Since the sixties, civil libertarians and liberal federal courts had made pornography—in books, magazines, film, and recordings—a pervasive influence in American life, corrupting the nation's youth and undermining the moral code.

Feminism too, the New Right said, was corroding conventional moral values as well as the family. In 1973 the Supreme Court in *Roe* v. *Wade,* responding to the new feminist sensibility, had struck down a Texas law forbidding abortion and opened the door to "abortion on demand" during the first three months of pregnancy. The polls showed that a majority of Americans endorsed freer access to abortion, but to many people of traditional religious background abortion seemed indistinguishable from murder. The social conservatives fought for an anti-abortion constitutional amendment and demanded that the federal government limit abortions at veterans' hospitals. A few extremist "pro-life" groups even resorted to bombing abortion clinics to stop the "murder of the innocents."

Still another feminist issue angered the New Right. Disturbed by the slow penetration of African-Americans and women into the professions, government service, and high-paid blue-collar trades, Congress and the courts had pushed the concept of "affirmative action"—preferential, not merely equal, treatment for minorities and women. This policy, said opponents, penalized white males and violated the principle of merit as a measure of preference. Still worse, they insisted,

Anti-abortion protesters in front of the White House, 1986. (UPI/Tim Clary)

was the newer principle of "comparable worth" that sought to equate the salaries of predominantly female occupations with supposedly similar, but higher paying, male job categories. Feminists and minority-group leaders responded that affirmative action was justified compensation for past race and sex discrimination; comparable worth merely eliminated gender-based job bias. Yet the two demands remained a source of irritation to conservative Americans.

The new assertiveness of homosexuals also vexed the New Right. During the late sixties homosexuals, responding to the decade's "liberationist" impulse, had begun to "come out of the closet" and demand changes to end what they perceived as legal, economic, and social discrimination. Social conservatives considered many of these demands—including the right of homosexual couples to adopt children, the legalizing of homosexual "marriages," and the end of discrimination against homosexual schoolteachers—threats to heterosexual mores and dangers to the traditional family. Conservatives fought back. In 1973 Phyllis Schlafly, a lawyer and mother of six, organized the Eagle Forum to oppose homosexual rights activism and free abortion. When in the early 1980s the horrible scourge of acquired immune deficiency syndrome (AIDS) burst on the scene, some of the more militant social conservatives declared that the disease was God's judgment on homosexuals for their wicked sexual practices.

By the end of the seventies the social and religious right had become a formidable organized force. More than 50 million Americans identified themselves as "evangelical" Christians. Not all were militant; not all were political. But many who watched the Reverend Jerry Falwell's "Old Time Gospel Hour" or Jim Bakker's PTL (Praise the Lord) TV ministry also sent money to Falwell's Moral Majority or responded to Richard Viguerie's massive fund-raising letter campaigns for conservative causes and politicians. The support of the religious and social right had been an important component of the Reagan victory in 1980.

The Neoconservative Intellectuals

Many New Right attitudes were visceral responses of people who felt bypassed in American life. They were reacting to the policy of inclusion that had marked the years since the 1960s and that seemed to submerge their values, interests, and visions in favor of those groups who at one time were at the periphery of American society. They were generally ordinary people who came to their views through their churches, the popular magazines and newspapers, and word of mouth.

But the New Right was also informed by a growing conservative intelligentsia. The nation had never lacked an intellectual right, but by the late 1970s it was both larger and more confident than ever before. Some of the conservative thinkers, the so-called *neoconservatives,* were associated with the journals *Commentary* and *The Public Interest.* Some were older men and women, many refugees from the left, driven away, they said, by the radical excesses of the tumultuous sixties. Although they had moved right, they usually retained a strong residual attachment to civil rights and civil liberties.

There were, however, several other clusters of conservative thinkers. There was the group of younger intellectuals attached to new conservative "think tanks" such as the American Enterprise Institute and the Heritage Foundation, organizations funded by conservative businesspeople. The magazine *National Review,* founded by William Buckley in 1955, provided a forum for conservative Catholic activists. Among university economists there were disciples of the free-market thinker Milton Friedman and the supply-siders led by Arthur Laffer. A number of conservative academic political scientists were followers of Leo Strauss, a German-born political philosopher. There was also the curious following of Ayn Rand, a Russian-born novelist and philosophical materialist, who despised democracy and touted an exaggerated elitism. The hero of one of her novels, *The Fountainhead,* was a Frank Lloyd Wright–type genius architect whose housing development design is cheapened by the project's financial backers intent on profit. Rather than accept this compromise with standards, he dynamites the whole thing.

Political Positions of the New Right

The New Right intellectuals, by and large, were more concerned with political and foreign policy issues than the social agenda that attracted the religious right. They deplored "big government" as oppressive. It had taken on too much that should be left to the individual. Government could not make up for the deficiencies in private

READING 6

Ronald Reagan
Lays Out His Agenda

*No one can say that Ronald Reagan did not give fair warning of his in-
tentions both during the presidential campaign of 1980 and in his 1981
inaugural address. Excerpts from that address follow. Reagan said many
times before he actually commenced his duties as president that he would
cut taxes, cut government programs, and make the United States more
powerful militarily. He did indeed accomplish each of these goals but the
process would cost the nation dearly. It would be hard to find a better description of this cost than his own inaugural words for his spendthrift predecessors: they had "piled deficit upon deficit, mortgaging our future and
our children's future for the temporary convenience of the present." By the
time George Bush succeeded Reagan in 1989, the national debt had
climbed to well over $2 trillion, almost three times the figure of eight years
earlier.*

. . . The business of our nation goes forward.

These United States are confronted with an economic affliction of great
proportions.

We suffer from the longest and one of the worst sustained inflations in
our national history. It distorts our economic decisions, penalizes thrift and
crushes the struggling young and the fixed-income elderly alike. It threatens
to shatter the lives of millions of our people.

Idle industries have cast workers into unemployment, human misery and
personal indignity.

Those who do work are denied a fair return for their labor by a tax
system which penalizes successful achievement and keeps us from maintain-
ing full productivity.

But great as our tax burden is, it has not kept pace with public spending.
For decades we have piled deficit upon deficit, mortgaging our future and
our children's future for the temporary convenience of the present.

To continue this long trend is to guarantee tremendous social, cultural,
political and economic upheavals.

You and I, as individuals, can, by borrowing, live beyond our means, but
for only a limited period of time. Why then should we think that collectively,
as a nation, we are not bound by that same limitation?

We must act today in order to preserve tomorrow. And let there be no
misunderstanding—we're going to begin to act beginning today.

The economic ills we suffer have come upon us over several decades.
They will not go away in days, weeks or months, but they will go away.

They will go away because we as Americans have the capacity now, as we have had in the past, to do whatever needs to be done to preserve this last and greatest bastion of freedom.

In this present crisis, government is not the solution to our problem; government is the problem.

From time to time we've been tempted to believe that society has become too complex to be managed by self-rule, that government by an elite group is superior to government for, by and of the people.

But if no one among us is capable of governing himself, then who among us has the capacity to govern someone else? . . .

Well, this administration's objective will be a healthy, vigorous, growing economy that provides equal opportunities for all Americans with no barriers born of bigotry or discrimination.

Putting America back to work means putting all Americans back to work. Ending inflation means freeing all Americans from the terror of runaway living costs.

All must share in the productive work of this "new beginning," and all must share in the bounty of a revived economy. . . .

Our government has no power except that granted it by the people. It is time to check and reverse the growth of government which shows signs of having grown beyond the consent of the governed.

It is my intention to curb the size and influence of the federal establishment and to demand recognition of the distinction between the powers granted to the federal government and those reserved to the states or to the people.

All of us—all of us need to be reminded that the federal government did not create the states; the states created the federal government.

Now, so there will be no misunderstanding, it's not my intention to do away with government.

It is rather to make it work—work with us, not over us; to stand by our side, not ride on our back. Government can and must provide opportunity, not smother it; foster productivity, not stifle it.

If we look to the answer as to why for so many years we achieved so much, prospered as no other people on earth, it was because here in this land we unleashed the energy and individual genius of man to a greater extent than has ever been done before.

Freedom and the dignity of the individual have been more available and assured here than in any other place on earth. The price for this freedom at times has been high, but we have never been unwilling to pay that price.

It is no coincidence that our present troubles parallel and are proportionate to the intervention and intrusion in our lives that result from unnecessary and excessive growth of government.

It is time for us to realize that we are too great a nation to limit ourselves to small dreams. We're not, as some would have us believe, doomed to an inevitable decline. I do not believe in a fate that will fall on us no matter what we do. I do believe in a fate that will fall on us if we do nothing.

So, with all the creative energy at our command let us begin an era of national renewal. Let us renew our determination, our courage and our strength. And let us renew our faith and our hope. We have every right to dream heroic dreams. . . .

In the days ahead I will propose removing the roadblocks that have slowed our economy and reduced productivity.

Steps will be taken aimed at restoring the balance between the various levels of government. Progress may be slow—measured in inches and feet, not miles—but we will progress.

It is time to reawaken this industrial giant, to get government back within its means and to lighten our punitive tax burden. . . .

And as we renew ourselves here in our own land we will be seen as having greater strength throughout the world. We will again be the exemplar of freedom and a beacon of hope for those who do not now have freedom.

To those neighbors and allies who share our freedom, we will strengthen our historic ties and assure them of our support and firm commitment.

We will match loyalty with loyalty. We will strive for mutually beneficial relations. We will not use our friendship to impose on their sovereignty, for our own sovereignty is not for sale.

As for the enemies of freedom, those who are potential adversaries, they will be reminded that peace is the highest aspiration of the American people. We will negotiate for it, sacrifice for it; we will not surrender for it—now or ever.

Our forbearance should never be misunderstood. Our reluctance for conflict should not be misjudged as a failure of will.

When action is required to preserve our national security, we will act. We will maintain sufficient strength to prevail if need be, knowing that if we do so we have the best chance of never having to use that strength.

Above all we must realize that no arsenal or no weapon in the arsenals of the world is so formidable as the will and moral courage of free men and women.

It is a weapon our adversaries in today's world do not have.

It is a weapon that we as Americans do have.

Let that be understood by those who practice terrorism and prey upon their neighbors.

I am told that tens of thousands of prayer meetings are being held on this day, for that I am deeply grateful. We are a nation under God, and I believe God intended for us to be free. It would be fitting and good, I think, if on each inaugural day in future years it should be declared a day of prayer.

Source: Facts on File, January 23, 1981.

character and its attempts to do so only led to permanent dependency. As Reagan, their most effective spokesman, would say, "government is not the solution; government is the problem."

Among government's most troublesome exactions, said the New Right, were the taxes it imposed. These were a brake on enterprise. Creative people were discouraged from innovation when they knew that profits would be taxed away by the government. The existing tax system was especially onerous because of "bracket-creep," the automatic increase in tax rates imposed by inflation-fueled wage and salary increases. Cut taxes drastically, especially in the upper-income brackets, and you would stimulate economic growth by offering new incentives to enterprising people. According to the supply-side economists Arthur Laffer, Jude Wanniski, and Martin Anderson, such an approach need not cause serious budget deficits: the surge in economic output would raise the government's overall tax take, largely offsetting the lower tax rates.

Neoconservatives also found taxes deplorable for the uses to which they were put. The 1960s Great Society antipoverty programs had been a disaster, they said. Rather than enabling the poor to lift themselves out of poverty, they had encouraged more and more able-bodied people to accept handouts permanently and had reduced their incentives to become self-supporting. The result was a permanent underclass of single or abandoned mothers and children living on welfare at the edge of, rather than as part of, society. According to Charles Murray, a conservative social scientist, "we tried to provide more for the poor and produced more poor instead."

Another New Right concern was the apparent decline of America's strength relative to the Soviet Union. Détente had served to mask the Soviet's giant, destabilizing arms buildup, they said. While Americans were lulled by cultural exchanges, Soviet concessions on Jewish emigration, and the like, the Soviet Union had thrown enormous resources into building an all-ocean navy, expanding its nuclear missile arsenal, and pumping up its already vast army. By 1980, many conservatives claimed, the Soviet Union had come even with, or surpassed, the United States in its military might and its ability to win a war of its choosing. This new strength explained the recent Soviet adventurism in Afghanistan and in parts of Africa.

Reaganomics

Thus Reagan came to office in January 1981 backed by a determined army of activists with a bold conservative program. Even millions of Americans who were not New Right ideologues anticipated significant course corrections for the ship of state in economics, social policy, and foreign relations.

Tax Cuts

The first important item on the Reagan agenda was a major tax cut. First suggested in the mid 1970s by Representative Jack Kemp of New York and Senator William V. Roth, Jr., of Delaware (both Republicans), the deep slash was designed to remove the shackles on enterprise and stimulate the economy. Appealing not only to supply-siders, it also won support from the followers of Howard Jarvis, leader of the Proposition 13 tax revolt that had succeeded in trimming California property taxes drastically after 1978. Taking advantage of his election momentum and employing his legendary persuasive powers to good effect, the president induced Congress to pass the biggest federal tax cut in history.

The Economic Recovery Tax Act of 1981 promised to lop $750 billion off the country's tax bill over the succeeding five years, primarily by cutting individual income taxes by 25 percent in three yearly installments. Although these cuts were to be across-the-board, people in the higher income tax brackets would be the largest gainers in total taxes saved. In addition, the law chopped billions off corporation taxes for the purpose of stimulating business.

Critics attacked the cuts as likely to produce giant federal budget deficits. Since deficits had long been among the most heinous crimes in the conservative indictment of liberal Democrats, the matter required explanation. The administration had a number of ready answers. Quoting the supply-siders, it declared that the economy, once freed from the constraining effects of exorbitant taxes, would surge to new levels and increase the Treasury's revenues. The budget would be balanced without pain to anyone. When first expounded by Reagan during the Republican presidential primaries in 1980, George Bush, his chief rival, called this formula "voodoo economics," but in 1981 the public was willing to give it a chance.

The other response—and, some critics said, really the heart of the Reagan tax policy—was that deficits would be avoided by drastically cutting domestic spending programs. Some months later David Stockman, the youthful director of the budget, admitted that "the plan was to have a strategic deficit that would give you an argument for cutting back the programs that weren't desired." In effect the inevitable deficits would force the liberals to accept cuts in social spending whether they liked it or not.

Cutbacks

In fact Stockman wanted to cut more than the benefits to the poor. His goal, he later wrote, was to attack "weak claims," not "weak clients." The boondoggles for the powerful, that is, should be no more exempt from review and cutback than those for the disadvantaged. Thus subsidies for truckers, middle-class college students, and for the nuclear power industry must go; they were special privileges for a few at the expense of the many and the efficiency of the economy as a whole.

It proved harder to reduce domestic programs than the administration thought, however. The president announced that he would retain a "safety net" of welfare programs under the truly indigent, but he and his colleagues took aim at many antipoverty and other entitlement programs that dated back to the Lyndon Johnson Great Society era. In 1981, during the first flush of enthusiasm for the Reagan policies, Congress agreed to sharp cuts in such programs as food stamps, Aid to Families with Dependent Children, child nutrition, Supplemental Security Income, health block grants, and Low Income Energy Assistance. It voted to trim job-training programs, aid for college students, and public-service employment. The administration also imposed limits on unemployment insurance programs and the cost of Medicare and Medicaid health insurance. It also sought to remove benefits from farmers, cities, and favored businesses. All told, during 1982–85 the Reagan forces managed to secure cuts of approximately $175 billion in nonmilitary spending.

But this was only about half of what the president needed to avoid large deficits. In truth many of the social programs were vulnerable. Not all were effective; many were bandages on deep social wounds that really required more drastic treatment. Others were wasteful, payoffs to one group or another without any serious rationale. Yet many had powerful constituencies—their direct beneficiaries and liberal politicians—and the resistance to deep cuts proved formidable and effective. The business and farm groups were even better defended. Lobbyists, local officials, and members of Congress besieged Stockman demanding that their favorite enterprise be exempt from the tax axe. Nor were his opponents only liberal Democrats. Republican Senator Howard Baker of Tennessee defended his pet Clinch River nuclear reactor project against projected cuts. Senator Jesse Helms of North Carolina, one of the most conservative people in Congress, insisted that subsidies to tobacco farmers be retained. Another conservative Republican senator, Orrin Hatch of Utah, defended the Job Corps because, Stockman wrote, the corps had a large office in Utah. Even fellow administration officials refused to cooperate with spending cuts. Secretary of State Alexander Haig, the budget director reported, refused to consider any cuts in the State Department budget on the grounds that foreign policy should be exempt from the economy drive.

Social Security

No program was as tough to take on as social security. By the early 1980s the nation's retirees represented an awesome bloc of alert and militant voters. Over the years they had succeeded in beefing up social security retirement benefits so that by the Reagan era the elderly were no longer, as a group, among the country's most seriously disadvantaged. That distinction had passed to the young. Owing to family breakup, teenage parenting, actual cuts in social programs, and the erosion of welfare benefits by inflation, more and more young children belonged to low-income families. Yet the elderly "gray panthers" refused to see themselves as a privileged group and fought back effectively.

In 1981, in the first flush of pro-Reagan enthusiasm, Congress allowed small cuts in projected social security increases. In May 1981, pleading the need to keep the system from going bankrupt, the administration asked for deeper cuts in social security programs. Its requests fell on deaf ears. By now social security had become a sacred cow and the Senate voted 96 to 0 to reject the proposals.

The problem did not go away. The United States had an aging population, and the millions of retired people in their seventies and eighties promised to be an enormous future economic burden on a proportionately ever smaller group of working people. There were powerful actuarial reasons for either limiting retirement and medicare benefits or hiking social security taxes. But the issue proved to be such a hot political potato that neither party wanted to tackle it, and it required bipartisan action through a national commission to push through modestly scaled-down benefits and higher social security taxes.

At the end of the process the nation's seniors emerged as the most effective pressure group in sight, one that no politician with a normal sense of self-preservation cared to challenge. Some social pundits worried that the 1980s struggle over social security foreshadowed a future confrontation of the generations over how to divide up the social pie.

Reagan and Poverty

All told, if the Reagan administration intended to eliminate the welfare state as constructed by the Democrats since the 1930s, it was unsuccessful. Although many saw flaws in the other person's program, they seldom perceived any in those that benefited themselves. Too many Americans had a stake in the system, and the beneficiaries were not just the nation's outsiders.

But liberals inevitably emphasized the impact on the poor. Notwithstanding the Stockman claim, the Reagan attack, they insisted, penalized those least able to defend themselves and spared the rich and powerful. The administration's policies were helping to swell the number of Americans below the poverty line.

They were right about the number of the poor; they increased. And the poor were more visible than ever before. In the big cities, particularly, homelessness became a major problem. Americans winced when Soviet television in 1986 carried a propaganda program showing people sleeping on the streets of New York and other American cities.

But it was not clear that altered public policy was responsible for the change for the worse. Some social observers pointed the finger of blame at family collapse and rising illegitimacy and the resulting neglect of children. Still others emphasized the structural changes in the economy that traditional welfare programs simply did not

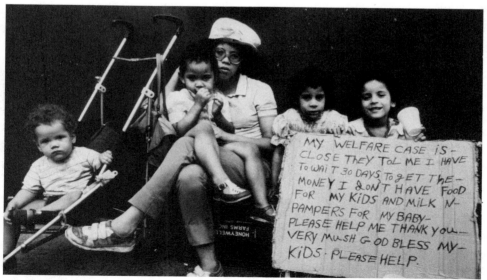

Single mothers and their children made up an increasing proportion of America's poor during the 1980s. (Blackstar/Joe Rodriguez)

address. Since the 1950s, they said, the United States had become an "information society" where an ever increasing number of jobs required ability to handle words and numbers. Those who lacked the ability simply could not find work to support themselves decently. Programs that merely served up dollars would never meet the needs of such people adequately. As for the homeless, conservatives said, most of them were mentally disturbed people released from hospitals under permissive patients' rights laws. Their problem was mental illness, a condition without known cure, not poverty.

Budget Deficits

Unable to extract the large social program cuts it wanted from Congress, the administration could not avoid massive budget deficits. But the problem was made far worse by its insistence on an enormous arms buildup. Between 1980 and 1985 military spending rose almost 40 percent, the outlays going primarily to the new weapons systems that Defense Secretary Caspar Weinberger convinced Congress the military needed to keep up with the Soviet Union.

Burgeoning defense outlays, modest domestic program reductions, and multibillion-dollar tax cuts combined to produce the most immense budget deficits in the

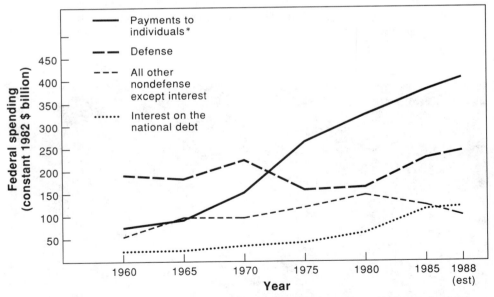

*Includes Social Security and other entitlement programs mandated by law and not subject to budgetary discretion.

Figure 6–1 The Components of Federal Spending, 1960–1988 (Constant 1982 Billion Dollars)

Sources: *Statistical Abstract of the United States, 1987* (Washington: U.S. Bureau of the Census, 1986), p. 295; *Statistical Abstract of the United States, 1988* (Washington: U.S. Bureau of the Census, 1987), p. 294; and *Budget of the United States Government, 1989* (Washington: U.S. Office of Management and Budget, 1988), pp. 6g–42.

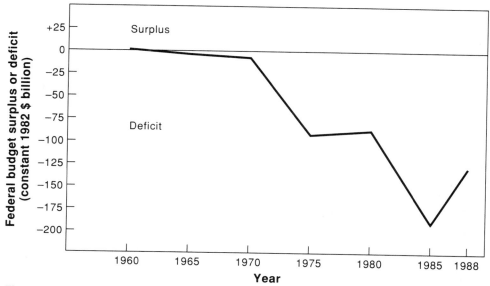

Figure 6–2 The Federal Budget, 1960–1988 (Constant 1982 Billion Dollars)

Sources: Adapted from *Statistical Abstract of the United States, 1987* (Washington: U.S. Bureau of the Census, 1987), p. 295 and *Statistical Abstract of the United States, 1988* (Washington: U.S. Bureau of the Census, 1987), pp. 291 and 294; *Budget of the United States Government, 1990*, Historical Tables (Washington: U.S. Office of Management and Budget, 1989), pp. 19–20.

country's history. (See Figures 6–1 and 6–2.) In President Carter's last year the Treasury had a shortfall of about $74 billion. In 1983, two years after the tax cut bill, it had leaped to $208 billion; in 1986 it was over $220 billion.* By the latter date the accumulated national debt was over $2 trillion, more than twice the amount of 1980. The interest on this colossal sum alone was $135 billion each year.

Each party blamed the other for the deficits. Republicans said the Democrats who controlled Congress were unwilling to cut out even useless programs. The Democrats blamed the Republican administration's military buildup and the ill-considered Republican tax cuts of 1981. Neither seemed willing to yield, and to get the budget down Congress passed the Gramm-Rudman-Hollings law in 1985, forcing modest automatic budget cuts across the board whether Congress acted or not.

The Economic Balance Sheet

Clearly this was not the result that "Reaganomics" was designed to achieve. But its effects were hidden. Economically sophisticated Americans, and some ordinary people as well, worried about the deficits and the national debt. They were a mortgage on the country's future and would be an impossible burden on its children and

---

*(These figures are in ordinary, or *current*, dollars; Figure 6–2 surveys the deficit since 1960 in *constant* 1982 dollars, which eliminate discrepancies caused by changes in the value of the dollar.)

grandchildren, people feared. But in the short run they seemed to have little effect, largely, the pundits said, because foreigners were willing to lend the United States as much as it needed to live beyond its means.

More immediately painful was the severe economic slump of the administration's first years in office. In 1979 there had been 6 million unemployed; by 1983 there were 10.7 million, representing 9.6 percent of the labor force, the highest total since the 1930s. (See Figure 5–3 in Chapter 5.) The public responded at the polls during the 1982 congressional elections by throwing out twenty-five Republican representatives, although still leaving the GOP with a Senate majority.

There was another side of the economic coin, however, one that was tied to the first. In the last Carter years, as we saw, prices had risen at a pace not seen since the Civil War era. Beginning in 1979, Paul Volcker, Carter's appointee as chairman of the Federal Reserve Board, restricted money growth sharply to counter the inflationary surge. By 1981 the prime interest rate, the amount charged the best-rated business borrowers, had leaped to over 20 percent. Such high rates discouraged consumer buying and business investment and the result was the 1981–83 slump. But another effect was to stop inflation in its tracks for the first time in almost a decade. By 1982 the rise in the consumer price index was down to 6 percent; for the next three years it averaged about 3.5 percent, among the lowest figures since the early 1960s. In effect, in cooperation with the Reagan administration, the Fed had, by policies that produced recession and high unemployment, squeezed inflation down to a manageable level.

And then the employment picture too improved. In 1983 the unemployment rate began to drop. By 1984 it was down to under 7 percent. In 1988 it fell to under 6 percent. By the time of the 1988 presidential election the Republicans could boast that under their watch millions of new jobs had been created. In many parts of the country, in fact, as the Reagan administration wound down, there were serious labor shortages, especially in entry-level positions.

How did the American people as a whole fare under Reaganomics? By the middle of Reagan's second term some of the results began to come in.

They were mixed. It was true that unemployment and inflation were down. But the Reagan era achievements in these categories just about returned the nation to where it had been in the early seventies. On the other hand GNP growth rates during the Reagan years were no better than they had been during the preceding seven mediocre years—and they were far below those of the 1960s. Another disquieting figure related to productivity growth. Between 1979 and 1986 average output per hour in private business increased by 1.4 percent a year. This was about half the average productivity gain of the period 1948–1965 and considerably lower than the productivity gains of most other industrial countries.

What about individual Americans and American families? In early 1989 House Ways and Means Committee data revealed that between the beginning of the eighties decade and 1987 American average family incomes had risen 5.6 percent. Unfortunately the gains had been highly uneven. Low-income families had *less* purchasing power in 1987 than in 1979, and upper-income families had more. The disparities were even greater for personal incomes (see Figure 6–3), revealing, according to Democrat Thomas J. Downey of New York, Chairman of the House Subcommittee on

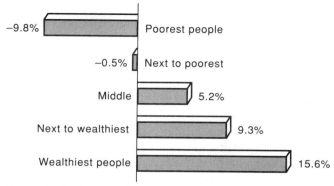

Figure 6–3 *Average Personal Income by Fifths of the Population from 1979 to 1987 (Constant 1987 Dollars)*

Source: Adapted from chart in the *New York Times*, March 23, 1989, p. A24. Data from House of Representatives Ways and Means Committee.

Human Resources, trends "inimical to the health of a democracy." Even the overall gains, the data indicated, were achieved only by the growing number of families with two wage earners. Indeed as other data showed, real wages had actually declined by about 2 percent between 1980 and 1987. In all fairness not all the deterioration at the bottom could be blamed on Reagan's economic policies. Much of it, as we noted was connected with family disruption, divorce, illegitimacy, and other social problems. On the other hand the Reagan administration had done virtually nothing to offset these trends, its critics noted.

Minorities and Women

The 1970s had been a time of mixed fortunes for the nation's nonwhite and non-European population. Higher birthrates and massive immigration, legal and illegal, from Asia and Latin America had increased their proportion of the total population. For the first time Asians could be found in large numbers in many American cities.

Some of these minority people had done very well. In south Florida, refugees from Castro's Cuba had prospered as businesspeople and professionals. In 1987 the mayor of Miami was Xavier Suarez, a Cuban refugee. Many of the Asians too had flourished. Chinese from Taiwan and Hong Kong as well as members of the pre–World War II Chinese-American community had made enormous strides in the sciences and the arts. An Wang, a Chinese-American from Shanghai with a Ph.D. from Harvard, founded Wang Laboratories, a leader in the computer industry. Yo-Yo Ma, another Chinese-American Harvard graduate, was one of the world's outstanding cellists. Koreans, Pakistanis, Indians, and Indochinese immigrants established many successful small businesses, following the lead of other immigrant groups in previous generations. Korean, Chinese, Japanese, Vietnamese, and Indian students regularly won a quarter or more of the National Merit scholarships and Westinghouse science talent awards. Many had gained admission to the most prestigious and selective American colleges and universities and white middle-class parents were beginning to complain that their own children were being crowded out.

Hispanic Americans

Cubans aside, people of Hispanic background had not done as well. In 1975 the average income of Hispanic families was $9,500 compared to $14,300 for Anglo whites. In the cities of the Northeast Puerto Ricans, although American citizens, were still primarily unskilled workers living in crime-ridden, run-down neighborhoods. In the West and Southwest, Mexican-Americans filled much the same uncomfortable niche in society.

Many Mexican-Americans were native-born citizens; thousands of others, however, were illegal immigrants. Such "undocumented" residents generally found it easy to get unskilled work in construction, in agriculture, and in factories. Although their wages were low, they were far better than those paid south of the border, and thousands risked arrest by American border guards to cross into the United States from Mexico and Central America.

So large was this migration that by the end of the 1970s there was a growing chorus of complaint that the nation had "lost control of its borders" and, especially in the Southwest, that Anglo culture was being swamped by an alien tidal wave. In some places Anglos fought back by resisting bilingual education or by demanding laws declaring English alone the nation's official language. In 1986 Congress passed the Simpson-Rodino Act imposing fines on employers who hired undocumented immigrants, but at the same time granting a general amnesty to all illegal immigrants who had arrived in the United States before January 1, 1982. The law required that newcomers apply for amnesty, but compliance was slow, and it was not clear whether the measure would end the fears of many Americans about unregulated immigration.

African-Americans

The seventies had been a time of slow economic progress for African-Americans. Thousands of African-American families clearly had made it into the middle class; some had even achieved wealth. During the Reagan years employment increases for blacks exceeded those for whites. Yet median black family incomes remained far behind those of whites.

Increasingly, moreover, a chasm had appeared between the top and the bottom of the African-American community. Below the successful African-American middle class was an expanding black ghetto underclass of husbandless women with their children and young black men without the skills or work habits to get and retain decent jobs. Many of these young males drifted into and out of crime; many died young from violence.

A particularly devastating aspect of ghetto life in the 1980s was the drug scourge. Drugs were not entirely a ghetto phenomenon, of course. Many young middle-class people continued to smoke marijuana. So common had it become that in many communities the authorities simply ignored the practice. Cocaine ("coke") use had spread widely among white middle-class young adults in the arts, professions, and businesses with immensely damaging results. But the use of heroin and "crack," a quick-acting form of cocaine, had come to permeate ghetto communities all over the nation. The drug plague not only ruined individual lives, it was also a source of ghetto crime and prostitution as addicts sought to find money to pay for their expensive habits. By mid-decade AIDS, a deadly blood and bodily fluid–borne disease that at first affected mostly homosexuals, had spread to addicts who injected heroin with unclean needles. AIDS further ravaged the ghettos.

The authorities did their best to combat the drug danger. The responses ranged from first lady Nancy Reagan's "Just Say No!" campaign to the federal government's attempt to oust from office General Manuel Noriega, the Panama strongman who had made his country a haven for drug dealers. Millions of dollars were spent on air and sea interdictions of drug runners and on attempts to stop drug production at its source abroad with the cooperation of foreign governments. Nothing seemed to work. By the end of the decade the drug plague was probably worse than at the beginning.

The chasm between the African-American middle-class and the underclass was physical as well as economic and social. As one social commentator observed, middle-class black families

> tend to move out of these economically and socially depressed areas to better neighborhoods where they and their children have a better opportunity to lead a better life. They leave behind the least educated and the most deprived.
> . . .As a result there is a concentration of misery in the very hearts of our largest cities.

One disquieting feature of the 1980s was the apparent resurgence of overt and public race prejudice. In cities around the country tribal hostilities between working-class whites and blacks erupted in acts of violence. The best publicized of these was the attack by a group of white youths on several young African-American men in Howard Beach, a lower middle-class white neighborhood in New York City. Fleeing from his tormentors, one of the black men was hit by a car and killed. Although three of the white youths were convicted of manslaughter and sentenced to long prison terms, the event produced deep resentment in the African-American community and measurably worsened race relations in New York City.

But the picture was not entirely bleak. During the seventies and the eighties African-Americans were able to harvest many of the civic fruits of the Second Reconstruction. Jim Crow was dead everywhere. Nowhere in the nation were there separate public facilities for blacks and whites. African-Americans now voted even in the South and had become a political force to be reckoned with in Dixie as never before since the post–Civil War era. In the North African-American political power had been converted into big city mayorships. As the eighties came to an end, African-American politicians were mayors in almost all of the nation's metropolises except New York, Boston, and San Francisco.

Clearly the problems that African-Americans faced were not derived from legal discrimination but from factors such as private prejudice, structural economic change, and community deterioration—all far less easy to handle. Yet black leaders blamed the Reagan administration for many of the setbacks.

The indictment was detailed. The conservative social attitudes of the president and his associates had created a climate that encouraged bolder expression of bigotry, they said. The Reagan administration had also chipped away at many of the legal gains of the recent past. The president supported efforts of segregated private schools to gain tax-exempt status. He at first had refused to endorse extension of the 1965 Voting Rights Act. The Reagan Justice Department had opposed the affirmative action programs of a number of cities, and the administration had tried to gut the Civil Rights Commission established in 1956 to investigate civil rights violations. Most important of all was the administration's drastic cuts in social programs. These had hurt African-Americans disproportionately. The Reagan administration, declared a National Urban League report in early 1984, was "almost universally regarded by blacks as the most hostile administration in the last 50 years."

The Feminist Tide Recedes

During the Reagan era the feminist political drive slowed, a process that could be tracked by the fate of the Equal Rights Amendment (ERA).

This proposed measure simply stated: "Equality of rights under the law shall not be denied or abridged by the United States or by any State on account of sex." It had first been proposed by Alice Paul's National Women's Party in the early 1920s soon after women won the vote. Although introduced into every session of Congress from 1923 on, it had made little progress during the next twenty-five years.

After World War II the ERA picked up the support of club women's groups, unions, liberal church organizations, and civil rights leaders. In 1945, 1953, and again in 1959, it passed the Senate (with amendments) but each time was defeated in the House. With the advent of the militant feminism of the late 1960s the ERA acquired new support. In October 1971 the House of Representatives approved it by a vote of 354 to 23. Five months later the Senate passed the ERA by 84 to 8.

To become the law of the land, the amendment had to be ratified by two-thirds (thirty-eight) of the state legislatures in a period of seven years. At first it charged ahead, being confirmed in thirty-two states in a little over a year. Then the process stopped.

In 1973 Phyllis Schlafly and other conservatives organized a "stop ERA" campaign. They aimed their appeal not only at conservative men but also at traditional women who resented the tone and manner of militant feminists, and although many worked, who saw their jobs as secondary to their roles as wives and mothers. The stop ERA forces declared that the amendment would deprive women of the protective labor and social legislation that had been enacted on their behalf since the early twentieth century. Women, moreover, would be forced to serve in the armed forces, even in combat roles. They would lose their advantage in custody battles involving children and would be denied alimony in divorces. The campaign was at times alarmist and silly. According to some opponents of ERA, for example, the amendment would forbid separate restrooms for men and women in public accommodations.

But whether fair or foul the campaign proved effective. By 1979 ERA had still not won the requisite number of ratifications. At this point Congress extended the ratification deadline for three and a half more years, but again the proposal could not gain the requisite number of states. In 1982 ERA was declared dead. Efforts were made during the next years to again secure congressional passage, but they failed. Although the ERA remained on the liberal agenda, in the Reagan era the public mood had changed. Feminism as a movement had begun to recede.

Reagan and the Environment

The president and his associates were clearly less sensitive to environmental concerns than their predecessors. Many Reagan appointees, including Interior Secretary James Watt, believed that efforts to safeguard the environment often hobbled economic growth and productivity. Lawsuits by public interest groups, massive environmental impact studies, excessive caution of the Food and Drug Administration in authorizing new drugs, and the like were economically harmful. Useful projects, they said, were not undertaken and jobs and profits lost; costs were pushed up; the public was denied important drugs and facilities. The nuclear power industry, they claimed, had been virtually destroyed by exaggerated fear of accidents.

Deeds matched words. Under Reagan the government cut the budget for the Consumer Product Safety Commission, the agency that administered consumer safety laws. It also cut back the Environmental Protection Agency (EPA), the chief government bureau responsible for protecting the natural environment against pollution and contamination. Reagan appointed Ann Burford, a conservative Colorado lawyer, to head EPA and administer $1.4 billion "superfund" to clean up toxic waste sites. She and her assistant Rita Lavelle soon came under fire for administering the agency to suit favored businesses and for failing to move effectively to eliminate the many lethal toxic dumps that dotted the nation. In early 1983 both resigned from their posts, and in December Lavelle was indicted for perjury for denying that she knew of her superior's deals concerning waste dumping.

Watt himself, meanwhile, came under attack for seeking to transfer federal timber, mineral, and water rights in the national forests to private businesses. A leading figure in the "sagebrush rebellion," an antienvironmentalist western movement to return control of natural resources to the communities where they were located, he had little respect for traditional conservation views. In October 1983, after having made a coarse remark that insulted African-Americans, Jews, women, and the handicapped all at the same time, he resigned and was replaced by William Clark. Clark was at least more circumspect in his environmental policies.

Reagan's Foreign Policy

If Reagan's domestic agenda required the scaling down of government programs, his foreign agenda required the exact opposite. Ronald Reagan had campaigned as the candidate of the most committed Cold War element in American political life. In office, Reagan and Secretary of Defense Caspar Weinberger extracted from Congress the funds for a massive buildup in the American armed forces. In 1980, the last Carter year, the Defense Department budget was $136 billion. By 1986 it had soared to $273 billion.

The military buildup was designed to offset Soviet strength and provide the United States with the clout to achieve its international goals. Yet at times these goals seemed to translate primarily into verbal bluster. Reagan was quick to attack the Soviet Union when the occasion seemed ripe. The Soviet Union, he stated in a speech to a group of Christian evangelists in Orlando, Florida, had "the aggressive impulses of an evil empire." In late August 1983, when a South Korean airliner strayed into Soviet airspace in Siberia and was shot down, the president denounced the Soviet Union as "barbarous" and "uncivilized," although he probably knew that the incident was a stupid Soviet blunder rather than a calculated slaughter of innocent civilians.

Reagan clearly shared a naive but spontaneous belligerent foreign policy mood with many Americans. Borrowing an image from the Sylvester Stallone movies about a one-man anti-Communist scourge, critics accused the president of displaying a Rambo-like attitude toward foreign affairs. In fact his record of action was strangely mixed. He sent marines to Lebanon in 1983 to help pacify that chaotic land, and when 241 were killed by a bomb set off by a fanatical Islamic fundamentalist, he withdrew them hurriedly. Soon after, as if to make up for this fiasco, he sent 10,000 American paratroopers to invade the tiny island of Grenada to overturn a Marxist regime that the administration believed was making the country a base for Castro's Cuba.

Central America

Reagan's willingness to project American power abroad was most vigorously pursued in Central America. The region was poor, socially volatile, and inclined to be anti-Yankee. It seemed ripe for authoritarian, pro-Soviet revolutions of the sort that had brought Castro to power in Cuba. Such changes, the Reaganites felt, would further Soviet ends and threaten American interests in Latin America. In El Salvador the United States sought with some success to prop up with infusions of money and military advice conservative-to-moderate governments under attack by leftists. By the last years of the Reagan administration El Salvador no longer seemed a serious trouble spot.

Nicaragua was a thornier problem. There a Marxist regime, the Sandinistas, had overturned the authoritarian government of Anastasio Somoza, a traditional Latin American strongman, and taken control in 1979. The Sandinistas, like other left-wing Latin American movements, promised to relieve the poverty of the peasantry, but they also banned domestic political opposition and provided aid to leftist guerrillas in El Salvador. The administration soon began to explore ways to topple them from power.

In 1984 the CIA began to mine Nicaraguan ports to prevent delivery of Soviet and Cuban arms. The Sandinistas succeeded in getting the World Court to condemn the American blockade effort. The American government also began to supply arms, food, uniforms, and advice to a group of anti-Sandinista guerrillas called the Contras, who hoped to overturn the regime they accused of being as authoritarian as that of Somoza.

The presence of another Marxist government in the Western Hemisphere disturbed many ordinary Americans. But a majority of citizens still remembered the Vietnam War and feared becoming involved in another endless military morass. For that reason and also because many thought the Contras unworthy of support, Congress vacillated in its response to administration requests to provide funds for them. In early 1983 the Democratic-controlled House of Representatives refused Contra military aid, but that June it agreed to provide $27 million for "humanitarian aid"—supplies, medicines, clothing, and the like. News of CIA involvement in mining Nicaraguan harbors outraged a majority of Congress. The Democratic speaker of the house, Tip O'Neill, called the Contras "butchers" and insisted they be abandoned by the United States. Congress at this point, over the president's loud protest, passed the Boland Amendment requiring the chief executive to consult Congress before spending any more money to support the anti-Sandinista war. Then after Sandinista leader Daniel Ortega visited Moscow, Congress relented and again voted $27 million in humanitarian aid to the Contras. The tug-of-war between the administration and a liberal Congress would have wide repercussions in other areas of foreign policy.

The Authoritarian versus Totalitarian Distinction

The Carter administration had made human rights violations a measure of international virtue, although it had not always applied the yardstick equally to all parties. Reagan would have none of this. He and his advisers found UN Ambassador Jeane Kirkpatrick's formula for distinguishing between "authoritarian" and "totalitarian" regimes more persuasive. The first were traditional tyrannies run by strong leaders, usually corrupt but not dangerous internationally. The second were like the Nazis and Communists: they imposed total ideological conformity on their society and were usually expansionist. The United States could afford to tolerate the former and in fact, although reluctantly, might be compelled to aid them if threatened. The latter were inveterate enemies who had to be stopped.

The theory justified bolstering tyrants such as Jean-Claude ("Baby Doc") Duvalier in Haiti and Ferdinand Marcos in the Philippines, although it did not preclude abandoning them when they lost all popular support, as both eventually did. It also excused continued relations with the repressive white regime in South Africa that denied elementary civil rights and civil liberties to its large black majority. The administration's tolerance of South African *apartheid* brought criticism from African-Americans and students as well as liberals. On scores of campuses during the 1980s protest demonstrations against South Africa, demands that American corporations and universities divest themselves of economic holdings in the country and that the United States join in imposing sanctions on the racist nation became the new version of the civil rights movement. Despite the protests the administration, fearing to precipitate social collapse from which African radicals and the Soviet Union might profit, refused to take overtly hostile steps against the regime in Pretoria. Rather, the president said, the United States must seek "constructive engagement" with the South African government to gradually move it toward racial justice without producing a catastrophic breakdown. Nevertheless Congress eventually voted sanctions.

The Middle East

In the Middle East the United States played an ambiguous role. The Reagan administration was an even better friend of Israel than its predecessors. Israel, in fact, became an unofficial ally of the United States. This connection made America the target of the most militant Arab nationalists, such as Libyan Muammar Qaddafi and Syria's Hafiz Assad, as well as of Islamic fundamentalists like Iran's Ayatollah Khomeini. The United States did not lose all its friends in the Arab world, however. The more moderate Arab nations, especially Egypt, Saudi Arabia, and the oil sheikdoms of the Persian Gulf region, loathed the extreme nationalists and the Islamic fundamentalists and looked to the United States for support.

The United States had several simultaneous objectives in the Middle East. It wished to protect the oil supply of the Western nations and avoid repeating the energy crisis of the 1970s. It also hoped to exclude the Soviet Union from a major role in the region. The key to stabilizing the region was to find some way of ending the continuing hostility toward Israel of all of its Arab neighbors except Egypt. This hostility, in turn, was clearly exacerbated by the forty-year-long problem of the Palestinians, who ever since Israeli independence had been refugees wanted by no one, not even their fellow Arabs. Many of the Palestinians supported the Palestine Liberation Organization (PLO), a group hostile to Israel's existence and dedicated to carving out some sort of independent Palestinian state from Israeli territory, by violence and terrorism if necessary.

For much of Reagan's first term the Middle East cockpit was Lebanon, a small Arab-speaking state with a large Christian population. In 1982 Israel, some said with United States approval, invaded Lebanon to expel the PLO and, the Israelis claimed, protect Lebanese Christians against their Muslim rivals. The Israelis rooted out the PLO, but the invasion soon turned into the Israeli equivalent of Vietnam, and the Israeli army gradually withdrew. Lebanon quickly collapsed into chaos. Christians fought Muslims, and Shiite Muslims under Khomeini's influence fought Sunni Muslims. Thousands died in the almost daily bombings and shellings, with neither side giving quarter. The Syrians introduced troops to fill the power vacuum left by the Israeli expulsion of the PLO, but they only added another element of disorder.

In 1983, as mentioned, the United States sent marines to the troubled nation as part of an international peacekeeping force. The effort to impose order offended the more militant Lebanese elements, especially the Party of God, a Khomeini-sponsored Shiite group. They soon made the United States a major target of their hatred. In April 1983 a car bomb exploded near the U.S. Embassy in Beirut killing fifty people. In October a bomb-laden vehicle driven by a fanatical anti-American crashed into the marine barracks in Beirut killing 241 U.S. servicemen.

Even after the United States withdrew its forces, the hostility of Islamic militants to America continued. During the months that followed, U.S. airlines, U.S. airline passengers in Europe and the Middle East, and U.S. service personnel in Europe became the targets of hijackings and terrorist attacks mounted by extremist groups, some apparently in the pay of Libya's Qaddafi, Syria's Assad, or Iran's Khomeini.

In Lebanon itself American reporters, businessmen, officials, and professors at the American University in Beirut were seized as hostages to coerce the United States into abandoning what the militants perceived as a pro-Israel, anti-Arab policy. The media played up the suffering of the hostages' families and, already sensitized to hostage taking by the Teheran embassy incident of 1979–81, the American public became emotionally caught up in the plight of the captives.

Despite their sympathies Americans had no reason to believe that the president would ever deal with terrorists who attacked innocent civilians. Reagan projected a tough image against international blackmailers. As he had announced during his debate with Carter in October 1980: "there will be no negotiation with terrorists of any kind." Surely he would not yield to terrorist blackmail.

Reagan's Reelection and Second Term

Reagan had made mistakes during his first term. He had promised to balance the budget, but deficits had soared out of sight. He had promised to make Americans once more respected in the world, but American civilians and service people were under attack all over Europe, and many American tourists were afraid to travel in the Mediterranean area. He had promised prosperity, but by early 1983 unemployment rates had reached forty-year records. One of the president's more disconcerting qualities was his weak grasp of detail. He often made statements that proved untrue. At one point, for example, he claimed that American submarines did not carry nuclear weapons. Of course they did. At another he announced that "growing and decaying vegetation" were "responsible for 93 percent of the oxides of nitrogen" that polluted the atmosphere. They were not. This tendency to misstate facts proved so embarrassing that his advisers began to steer him away from press conferences where he had to respond spontaneously to questions posed by reporters.

Yet as his first term wound down, the public continued to give him high marks. In early 1984 his approval rating was 54 percent according to a Gallup poll. In part this was because a sharp upturn in the economy finally began to push unemployment down. Inflation too had been tamed. But it was also because the white, middle-class American public could not find it in its collective heart to dislike Reagan. He seemed so "nice," such a good guy. The public particularly admired his bravery and good humor in those hours and days in 1981 after an obsessed young man tried to assassinate him in Washington. As he was brought into the hospital for chest surgery to remove the bullet, Reagan quipped to the doctors, "I hope you're Republicans," and "I forgot to duck." Critics ruefully called him "the Teflon president"; nothing distasteful stuck to his skin.

The renomination of the Reagan-Bush ticket in 1984 was a foregone conclusion. The battle to head the Democratic ticket, however, was hard fought. Front-runner from the outset was Walter Mondale, a former U.S. Senator from Minnesota, Carter's vice president, and a protégé of Hubert Humphrey. Mondale successfully cultivated many of the elements of the old New Deal coalition: the industrial trade unions, teachers, Catholics, racial minorities. His party rivals included Senator John Glenn of Ohio, the former astronaut; Jesse Jackson, a civil rights associate of Martin Luther King; and Gary Hart, the young, Kennedyesque senator from Colorado.

Glenn, a wooden speaker, quickly fell by the wayside. Jackson, an eloquent African-American minister, surprised everyone by making himself a credible candidate of a "Rainbow Coalition" of blacks, other racial minorities, poor whites, and left-liberals demanding a return to positive government on behalf of the nation's outsiders. Unfortunately Jackson made some antisemitic remarks that damaged him with many Democratic voters. Hart was the candidate of the "Atari Democrats," the well-educated young men and women of the baby boom generation who were sufficiently liberal to remain in the Democratic party but wanted to get away from the traditional focus on minorities and the poor. For a time Hart gave the Mondale forces a bad scare, but by the time of the Democratic convention the former vice president had the nomination sewed up.

The convention in San Francisco seemed to heal most of the party's wounds from the nomination campaign. Jackson delivered a speech in which he apologized for his unwise remarks. The keynote speaker was Governor Mario Cuomo of New York, who eloquently recounted his parents' rise from immigrant status to middle-class success. The Democrats, he said, were like a happy and compassionate family that provided help to all its members. Mondale himself, hoping to capitalize on a supposed "gender gap" between men and women in their support of Reagan, chose as his running mate Congresswoman Geraldine Ferraro of New York, the first woman on a major party presidential ticket. He also impressed observers with his courage when he declared in his acceptance speech that as president he would ask Congress for a major tax increase to bring down the runaway budget deficit. For a time after the convention the polls showed Mondale running neck-and-neck with Reagan.

Walter Mondale and Geraldine Ferraro at the 1984 Democratic National Convention.
(UPI/Bettmann Newsphotos)

The polls quickly turned around. Taking advantage of the American public's distaste for taxes, Reagan denounced Mondale's tax promise. "Democrats," he declared, "see an America where every day is April 15th." For Republicans, on the other hand, "everyday is the Fourth of July." The Democrats were their own worst enemies. Mondale lost whatever chance he had of winning in the South by first choosing Bert Lance, a Georgian and former aide to Jimmy Carter, to head the Democratic National Committee and then, when faced with criticism, withdrawing his name. Ferraro was not the asset she promised to be. Questions were raised about the tax returns she filed jointly with her husband, and her explanations suggested to many people that something fishy was involved. Mondale did well against the president in the first of two debates, but Reagan recouped in the second, and soon forged far ahead in the polls. By the end of September it was clear that the president would win and win big.

And he did. The Reagan-Bush ticket took every state in the union except Mondale's own Minnesota and won 59 percent of the popular vote. The president had won by large majorities in almost every voter category: the elderly, the young, women, Catholics, Protestants. Jews gave him larger percentages than they gave most Republicans; even union households, usually Democratic bastions, gave him almost half their votes. The president's coattails proved short, however. The Republicans gained only 14 seats in the House and lost two in the Senate.

Few presidents have ever been as successful in their second term as in their first. By the time they complete their fourth year in office, their opponents have become bolder and more adept at frustrating them; dissensions have appeared among their supporters; they often have enacted their legislative programs and have little new to offer. In Reagan's case the second term problem was exacerbated by his age. Born in 1911, by the time of his second inaugural Reagan was seventy-five, the oldest president ever to hold office. Although well preserved for a man of his years, age compounded by surgery for colon cancer and prostate problems had taken its toll. Never an attentive administrator he increasingly allowed the day-to-day running of his office to be handled by former Secretary of the Treasury Donald Regan, who in 1984 had exchanged places with James Baker to become White House chief of staff.

The Iran-Contra Affair

The president's inattention caused the administration grave difficulties in foreign affairs and resulted in an appalling loss in public standing.

Easily touched by individual suffering, Reagan was concerned about the Lebanon hostages and sensitive to their families' accusations that the administration was remiss in its efforts to recover them. Although he feared making the hostages a public issue and a test of administration capacity, when presented with a scheme to trade American arms for the hostages' release he went along despite all his talk of not dealing with terrorists.

The plan was concocted by CIA Director William Casey, National Security Council head Admiral John Poindexter, and Marine Corps Lieutenant Colonel Oliver North, Poindexter's aide. It seemed, in North's later words, to be "a neat idea." The Iranians had been fighting a desperate war against Iraq, a Persian Gulf neighbor, since 1980. Ever since their break with the United States following the shah's overthrow, they had been short of planes, guns, and ammunition and had been forced to throw waves of young, untrained men against their well-armed enemy, suffering horrendous losses in the process. They were eager to buy arms, but other nations disliked their fanaticism and most refused to sell up-to-date weapons to them. Their desperate need for modern weapons might be used, Casey and his colleagues felt, to get the Iranians to secure the hostages' release.

And there were other possibilities in such a secret arrangement. The United States had no reason to favor permanent enmity with Iran; that only helped the Soviet Union. The three men believed there were moderate elements in Teheran who, after the aged Ayatollah's death, might wish to reestablish relations with the United States and who might be attracted by an offer of arms. In fact it was this part of the deal that they emphasized when presenting their scheme to the president.

And there was still another likely bonus: some of the profits from arms sales to Iran could be used to finance the Contras. Because Congress was unwilling to provide money for the Nicaraguan "freedom fighters," aid would have to come from other sources or communism would continue to grow in the Western Hemisphere. North had been secretly soliciting private contributions for the Contras from rich Americans for some time. He had even secured a contribution from the sultan of Brunei, a pro-American, oil-rich Asian ruler. But far better would be a secret diversion of profits to the Contras from an Iranian arms deal. One of our major enemies would, unknowingly, be contributing to our fight against another of our enemies! The fact that these machinations ignored the Boland Amendment, made a mockery of American no-deals-with-terrorists principles, and were based on ignorance of Iranian politics did not deter the plotters.

In May 1986 Robert McFarlane, former national security adviser, led a secret American arms sale delegation to Iran carrying a cake and a Bible as gifts for their Iranian contacts. The Americans were treated rather offhandedly by these low-level officials, which suggested strongly that the anticipated diplomatic gains were probably illusory. Yet the Americans persisted. In all the Americans negotiated five arms deals with the Iranians, a process that yielded several million dollars, some portion of which was shunted to the Contras by North and Poindexter. The hostage yield proved disappointing, however. Only three Americans were released and, in fact, several more were kidnapped after the first hostages were let go.

The Scandal Breaks

In November 1986 a Lebanese newspaper published an account of the arms for hostages deal with Iran, and a tidal wave of criticism crashed over Reagan and his advisers. Within the administration itself Secretary of State George Shultz and Secretary of Defense Weinberger had objected to the arrangement when it was first discussed, but the president himself had been unwilling to see the scheme for what it was—a violation of his own resolve not to pay international blackmail. His first public response to the stories was that while we had sold "small amounts of weapons and spare parts" to Iran our only purpose had been to make contact with Iranian moderates.

At the end of November, while disclaiming full knowledge of the Iran-Contra scheme, he fired North and announced Poindexter's resignation. The following day he promised to appoint a special committee headed by former Senator John Tower of Texas to investigate the matter. Soon after, he appointed a special Watergate-type prosecutor to flush out any illegal acts. Meanwhile, a perfunctory investigation had been launched by Attorney General Edwin Meese that seemed aimed, critics would later say, at allowing the conspirators time to cover their tracks rather than finding out what had really happened.

The Iran-Contra affair finally peeled off the president's Teflon skin. The public had given Reagan credit for courage and boldness. Just the previous April he had ordered American air strikes against Libyan cities to teach Qaddafi, the suspected sponsor of much of the anti-Western terrorism, a lesson. Qaddafi had been squelched. Now the president had made a deal with the Iranians, another Mideast terrorist sponsor! Reagan was not acting like Rambo; he was acting like Casper Milquetoast. What anti-terrorist credibility could the United States now have in the world?

The administration's reputation soon suffered further blows. In February the Tower Commission absolved the president of direct knowledge of the diversion of funds to the Contras but reported that he had been confused and unaware of what his subordinates were planning. His "management style," the report said, was deeply flawed. The commission blamed White House Chief of Staff Regan for failing to prevent "the chaos that descended upon the White House." Regan tried to hold on to his office, but by this time Nancy Reagan, always protective of her husband's reputation, had turned against him and he was forced to resign. Replacing him was Howard Baker, a respected former Republican senator from Tennessee.

During the next few months, while a joint House-Senate congressional committee prepared to hold public hearings on the scandal, the president gradually conceded he had made mistakes. On March 4 he accepted "full responsibility" for the arms sales to Iran. But two weeks later he denied knowledge of the diversion of arms profits to the Contras. The televised congressional hearings began on May 5, and for the next three months scores of high federal officials appeared before the committee to describe their part in the complex affair. CIA Director Casey, who almost certainly was deeply implicated in the fiasco, died of a brain tumor in early May and was spared the ordeal. But Poindexter and North, especially, were severely grilled by the investigators, who charged that they had conducted a rogue operation—in effect a private manipulation of foreign policy—that ignored constituted authority and violated constitutional safeguards.

North was a well-spoken, clean-cut young marine officer who tried, with some success, to turn the attack against his attackers. Playing the role of an unashamed American patriot, he made the Iran-Contra scheme seem a bold attempt to counter the spineless Central American policies of the doves in Congress. The young officer made such a good first impression that many Americans watching the hearings forgot that he was defending a series of moves that were not only illegal but also, in the end, damaging to America's image as a bold defender of the Free World. For a time the country was seized by "Olliemania," a conviction, as one reporter wrote, that the colonel "somehow embodied Jimmy Stewart, Gary Cooper, and John Wayne in one bemedaled uniform."

The November 1987 report of the House-Senate Iran-Contra Committee blasted the plotters.

> The common ingredients of the Iran and contra policies were secrecy, deception, and disdain for law. A small group of senior officials believed that they alone knew what was right. . . . When exposure was threatened, they destroyed official documents and lied to cabinet officers, to the public, and to elected representatives in Congress.

Later Independent Counsel Lawrence Walsh obtained criminal indictments against a number of the participants.

Reagan and Soviet-American Relations

For a time the president's weakening grip affected Soviet-American relations. During his first term, as discussed, Reagan fired off regular volleys against the "evil empire." Soviet-American antagonism did not cease after 1984. In fact, in 1986 it took on new intensity as the United States and the Soviet Union became involved in a war of spies. When the United States arrested Soviet agent Gannady Zakharov, the Soviets responded by arresting *U.S. News & World Report* Moscow correspondent Nicholas Daniloff. Eventually one was traded for the other.

During Reagan's first term, Soviet-American relations were seriously impaired by the American arms buildup. Reagan sought to base a new class of intermediate range Pershing missiles in Europe to counter a Soviet buildup of equivalent missiles. The move mobilized a coalition of antiwar, antinuclear, and anti-American groups in Europe and America to march in protest. Despite the opposition the missiles were delivered and put in place on the soil of European NATO countries in the last months of 1983.

Star Wars

More disturbing to some groups was the president's strategic defense initiative (SDI) plan, soon labeled "Star Wars" by its opponents and the media. First announced in March 1983, the theory behind SDI was that a system could be built that would intercept and destroy en route any Soviet nuclear missiles fired at the United States. As such it would offer an alternative to nuclear retaliation. Fear of such retaliation, it was assumed, would serve as a deterrent to any attack. If either of the superpowers launched nuclear warheads at the other, it might destroy its opponent but would be certain to be destroyed in turn. The desire to avoid such mutually assured destruction (MAD) had prevented nuclear war for almost forty years, and there were many knowledgeable observers who believed that it was still the only effective defense against a humanity-destroying nuclear exchange.

SDI immediately came under attack from politicians, scientists, and academics. The indictment was broad ranging: it was impractical; no matter how sophisticated the technology, some attacking missiles would get through and cause untold destruction. It was not technically feasible; computers fail, rockets misfire, electrical circuits short. And there would be no way to test the Star Wars equipment; it would have to work the first time. Moreover there was the cost; it would absorb as much as a trillion dollars in the decade ahead. And Star Wars would only escalate the Cold War further. The Soviets were certain to try to find ways to equal it or counter it.

The criticism seemed compelling to many. Congress appropriated funds for preliminary research into Star Wars technology, but refused to make a full commitment. Yet whatever the misgivings of Americans and however the administration denied that it was merely a bargaining chip, SDI did probably goad the Soviet Union into major arms concessions.

Gorbachev

During most of Reagan's first term Russia was undergoing a rapid turnover of leadership. In 1982 the sixty-eight-year-old Yuri Andropov succeeded Leonid Brezhnev as Kremlin ruler. Less than two years later he died and was succeeded by the sickly Konstantin Chernenko. Chernenko lasted little more than a year and was followed in March 1985 by Mikhail Gorbachev. A healthy man of fifty-four, Gorbachev promised continuity in Soviet leadership for the first time in a generation.

He also promised a new era in Soviet life. Well-traveled, open in personal manner, impressed with the need to shake Soviet society out of its doldrums, Gorbachhev favored *glasnot* (intellectual openness) and *perestroika* (economic restructuring) to make the Soviet Union—left far behind economically and technologically by Western Europe, Japan, and America—competitive in the world. At home Gorbachev permitted greater freedom of expression. He allowed a number of prominent dissenters, long refused visas, to leave the Soviet Union. He sought to reform the production system by introducing quasi-capitalist incentives and greater local autonomy to factory managers. He tried to discourage widespread Soviet alcoholism by making vodka more expensive. He had no intention of turning the Soviet Union into a Western democracy or surrendering the ultimate tight control of the Communist party, but he saw that the rigid, old bureaucratic system inevitably consigned his country to second-class status in competition with the industrialized democracies and must be changed.

Essential to Gorbachev's reform program was détente with the United States. The Soviets could not now afford to begin another major arms race with America, especially one involving advanced computer technology. Soviet science was simply not the equal to the West's in this area and, short of extraordinary efforts, could not compete. SDI thus posed a major threat to Gorbachev's plans for a revitalized Soviet Union, as did the arms race generally. The competition must be stopped.

Arms Negotiations

In late 1983, in protest against the Pershing missiles Soviet negotiators walked out of the nuclear disarmament talks with the United States long underway in Geneva. But in January 1985 the two superpowers agreed to resume the Geneva talks with SDI included on the discussion agenda. Soon after Reagan declared that his ultimate goal was "the complete elimination of nuclear weapons" from the world. The statement and American willingness to discuss Star Wars suggested that SDI was mostly a bargaining chip to be surrendered in exchange for major Soviet arms concessions.

The new Soviet-American arms talks began in Geneva in March 1985. Gorbachev announced that the Soviet Union would cease to deploy intermediate range nuclear missiles and called on the United States to do the same. He also asked for a summit meeting with the American president to consider the arms race question.

The Geneva meeting between Reagan and Gorbachev in November 1985 was a disappointment to the friends of arms reduction. The two nations signed some minor agreements on scientific and cultural exchanges and authorized the resumption of direct air flights between the two nations that had been suspended at the time of the Soviet invasion of Afghanistan, but they achieved little on the disarmament issue. Nevertheless Reagan said, "We are headed in the right direction."

In October of the following year the two superpower leaders met again, this time in Reykjavík, Iceland, to consider once more the arms limitation issue. The Americans were ill-prepared. At one point Reagan promised that the United States would surrender *all* its nuclear armaments if the Soviets did the same—and if the Soviets accepted continued Star Wars research and development. The president had not consulted America's NATO allies, had not, apparently, checked with his advisers, and did not seem to know really what he was offering. In fact, since the Warsaw Pact countries far outstripped NATO in conventional arms, the arrangement would have handed the Soviet Union an enormous military advantage. Fortunately Gorbachev did not take the offer seriously. Instead he insisted that Star Wars be stopped, and when Reagan refused, the Iceland summit meeting broke up on a sour note.

The INF Agreement

Despite the abortive Iceland meeting, neither side allowed the arms reduction issue to rest. Gorbachev continued to need a major reduction in military expenditures to improve the ability of the Soviet economy to provide consumer goods for civilians. After the Iran-Contra scandal Reagan needed some major triumph if he was to rescue his administration's reputation and finish his presidency in a burst of glory. Not everyone looked forward to arms reductions. In both the Soviet Union and the United States hawks and Cold Warriors perceived arms reduction as a trick of the other side to gain a military advantage. American conservatives such as Senator Jesse Helms of North Carolina and the journalist George Will criticized the propensity of well-intentioned Americans to believe *any* arms reduction agreement a victory.

Yet the arms reduction process continued. In February 1987 Gorbachev offered to sign "without delay" an agreement to eliminate all Soviet and American intermediate range nuclear forces (INF), those weapons that NATO had deployed just a few years before. A whole class of nuclear weapons would be junked, and he would not ask that Star Wars be abandoned.

In the United States critics of arms reduction denounced the proposal. The American NATO commander in Europe said that it would expose NATO troops to the far more numerous Warsaw Pact conventional forces without the nuclear deterrent they formerly wielded to offset the imbalance. Although the administration insisted that Soviet compliance with any arms reduction treaty would be subject to strict verification procedures, critics continued to express doubts of Soviet trustworthiness.

Despite the doubts, the two parties were able to come to an agreement in time for a major summit meeting in Washington in early December 1987. The occasion became a major media event with the administration pulling out all the stops to make the biggest splash possible. Gorbachev was going to be used to restore a flagging administration's popularity and prestige. The Soviet leader had no objection. For his part he would use the event to consolidate his standing among his colleagues in the Kremlin.

The Gorbachevs arrived in Washington and were treated as visiting royalty. Raisa Gorbachev, like her husband, seemed a different sort of Soviet person, well-dressed, articulate, and sprightly. The Russians pulled out all the stops to charm the American public. Gorbachev told jokes and smiled a lot. He held a meeting in the Soviet Embassy for a contingent of American intellectuals and entertainment figures and flattered them by suggesting that they could help construct "interrelatedness, global peace, democratization." On the way to a White House bargaining session he ordered his chauffeur to stop on the Washington street so he could shake hands with startled pedestrians.

Reagan hoped he could induce Gorbachev to open the emigration doors for Soviet dissenters and announce a date for Soviet withdrawal from Afghanistan. The Soviet leader refused to do either, and Reagan had to be content with the INF elimination treaty. The two men did agree to meet in Moscow during the summer of 1988 to sign, if possible, an arms reduction agreement dealing with strategic, long range nuclear missiles. Many observers doubted, correctly as it turned out, that such a treaty would be ready in time.

Although he did not get all he had wanted, Reagan was immensely pleased with the results. He had been deeply impressed by Gorbachev and concluded that at long last the Soviets had abandoned their quest for world domination. His response appalled some on the far right who now declared that the president had become an unwitting tool of the communists. To almost everyone's surprise a majority of the announced 1988 Republican presidential candidates declared they opposed Senate ratification of the treaty as signed, and some observers predicted that it would have a hard time getting through the Senate confirmation process unscathed.

The predictions were wrong. Just before Reagan arrived in Moscow for his final summit with the Soviet leader in June 1988, the Senate ratified the treaty. Actually the Moscow summit turned out to be largely a public relations gesture; nothing further was accomplished in the arms reduction process, although the Soviets did announce a timetable for leaving Afghanistan. Yet taken as a whole, the summits had achieved one important administration end: by summer of 1988 Reagan had regained most of his lost popularity. The Iran-Contra affair appeared to have blown over. The Teflon principle was once more alive and well.

Continuing Economic Concerns

As Reagan's second term opened in 1985, the country's economic performance continued to present a mixed picture. Unemployment and the inflation rate remained low. But other measures of the nation's economic well-being were less positive.

Agriculture was seriously depressed during the Reagan years. Once more farmers were caught in a squeeze. During the inflation of the 1970s and early 1980s farm prices had been high and moving constantly higher. As usual in such circumstances farmers had borrowed money and bought new equipment to increase output. Then the government got a tight grip on inflation. In May 1985 farm prices were more than 10 percent below those of a year before and farmers were in trouble.

The administration tinkered with the situation. Reagan lifted the wheat export embargo that his predecessor had imposed on the Soviet Union after Afghanistan but rejected as "budget busting" a congressional measure to provide farmers with debt relief. The administration, moreover, in line with its deregulatory urge, pushed through a new farm bill that reduced federal supports for farm prices. In 1986 the farm belt was seething with discontent against the Republican administration it had so enthusiastically endorsed five or six years before.

More Deficits

During Reagan's second term, the budget deficit continued to soar, reaching over $220 billion in 1986. Even worse American exports continued to fall further behind imports. In 1984 the American trade deficit had reached $107 billion. In 1987 it leaped to $170 billion, the highest in history by far.

For over a century the United States had had a trade surplus; ever since World War I, seventy years before, it had been a creditor nation. By the mid-1980s Americans were buying far more from other nations than they were selling to them, and paying for the excess by going into debt. By 1990 by one estimate Americans would have to pay out over $100 billion each year in interest to foreigners who had lent the United States money. Meanwhile foreigners were exchanging their IOUs for American real estate, factories, and stocks and bonds. Some perceptive observers feared the United States was fast becoming an economic colony of Japan and Western Europe.

There were several common explanations for the increasing inability of the United States to compete in the international economy. One was the high price of American dollars relative to other currencies. This made all American goods expensive in yen, marks, francs, and pounds. The high value of the dollar, in turn, resulted from the high interest rates of the Volcker years at the Federal Reserve Board.

Competition in Technology

But there were other reasons as well, ones that promised to hurt American exports even after the dollar began to fall, as it did in late 1987 and early 1988. American goods, it was said, were no longer as desirable as those of its major industrial competitors.

Automobiles imported from Japan line a New Jersey dock. (JeanPierre Laffont /Sygma)

The charge had much substance. Compared to the Japanese and the West Europeans, and with the exception of aircraft and computers, the United States often produced products that were inferior to its competitors'. Americans may have pioneered the video cassette recorder, the pocket calculator, the long-playing record, and other consumer electronics, but the Japanese had learned to make them cheaper and better and had swept American-made items off the shelves. At one time the United States sold thousands of American automobiles abroad; by the 1980s the big three American car manufacturers were finding it difficult to hold on to even their markets at home.

A tragic event of 1986 underscored America's technological weakness. Ever since the last manned moon expedition in 1974, the National Aeronautics and Space Administration had come to rely on the reusable space shuttle as the chief vehicle for its activities. The shuttle was supposed to pay its way in a time of reduced budgets for space exploration by carrying commercial payloads into orbit. On January 28, 1986, an unusually cold day in south Florida, the shuttle *Challenger* exploded in a ball of flame shortly after lift off from Cape Kennedy. Seven crew members, including Christa McAuliffe, a Concord, New Hampshire, school teacher who was chosen to publicize the shuttle program among school children, died in the blast.

An investigation determined that the cold weather had damaged the shuttle O-ring seals, allowing combustible gases to be released. For two years the American space program virtually shut down while the flaws were repaired. Having neglected to develop other rocket launching systems, during this period American communications firms turned to other nations for needed launch services, thus depriving the United States of millions of dollars. Meanwhile the Soviets continued to widen the space program gap that the United States had allowed to open. Although the shuttle launch program resumed in 1988, by that time America had clearly lost its lead in space. Many experts wondered if it could ever regain it.

There was another side of the picture that was not so unfavorable to American ingenuity and innovation. Several of America's major international competitors imposed barriers on foreign goods. Japan, for example, in order to protect its farmers, refused to import American rice and beef, although they were both cheaper than the domestic product. The Japanese, in fact, refused to buy very much of anything from abroad, despite efforts of their own government to increase consumption. At the same time, American firms insisted, they often resorted to industrial espionage to steal American technology or turned to "dumping" products in the United States at a loss in order to undercut American manufacturers and gain control of the American market. In March 1987 President Reagan responded to alleged Japanese dumping of semiconductor chips with high duties on a wide range of Japanese electronics products.

Many Americans deeply resented "unfair" Japanese trade practices. In Detroit automobile workers and their spokespeople demanded high tariffs on Japanese cars. At one point, to dramatize their displeasure, autoworkers publicly destroyed a Japanese automobile with sledge hammers. The government resisted strong protectionist moves as likely to set off an international trade war and seriously weaken the free world economy. It imposed a quota system on Japanese car imports, but made it temporary. Most economists endorsed the administration's restraint, but in the 1988 presidential nominating campaign at least one Democratic candidate, Congressman Richard Gephardt, of Missouri, made protectionism the keystone of his platform.

The Stock Market

One of the more buoyant features of the economy in 1986–87 was the tremendous stock market surge. Fueled by foreign stock buyers seeking outlets for their dollars and by Americans swept up in a speculative frenzy, the Dow-Jones industrial stock averages leaped to over 2700 by the late summer of 1987. The surge created hundreds of billions of dollars of paper wealth and produced a feeling of euphoria in financial circles.

The 1980s bull market, like its 1920s predecessor, was sustained by a mood of unrestrained materialism. Thousands of the brightest young Americans made becoming millionaires before the age of thirty their fondest goal. Enrollments in Masters of Business Administration programs soared; so did law school applications. The new class of *yuppies* (young upwardly mobile urban professionals) worked hard in finance, the media, and corporate law, and seemed to avoid personal commitment to families and spouses. Players in the fast track, many were drawn to alcohol, marijuana, and cocaine to relieve the tensions in their lives. In 1984 Jay McInerny's novel *Bright Lights, Big City* told their story through the misadventures of a young man in New York just after college who cannot pull his personal life together and wanders in a daze of "coke" and despair.

The bull market was also pumped up by the take-over game. By the early 1980s clever financiers like Michael Milken and Ivan Boesky had discovered that many large corporations were worth more as separate pieces than as a whole. If they could win control of such companies they could sell off the valuable parts and make immense profits. To achieve control the "corporate raiders" needed capital to buy up the firms' stock. Their device was the "junk bond," a high-interest security. These were sold to provide the raiders with cash for the buy-out or exchanged for the stock of the target corporation. The take-overs often made millions for the promoters, but left many firms with enormous fixed debts that threatened their solvency.

None of this manipulation was illegal in itself, but at times the take-overs were accompanied by criminal use of insider information. In 1987 the Justice Department indicted Boesky and lesser raiders for picking up millions through insider information.

On October 9, 1987, the stock bubble burst. After several weeks of moderate decline the Dow-Jones averages plummeted 500 points on *Black Monday,* the largest one-day drop in the history of Wall Street. Wall Street's collapse shook the foreign stock exchanges; several lost an even larger proportion of their value overnight. Over the next few months all the exchanges proved volatile before settling down.

For a time experts feared that the 1987–88 market downturn would mark the beginning of a long international economic slide. Holding American budget deficits responsible, they insisted that the government take drastic steps to cut them. The jolt of Black Monday brought Congress and the president together to try to break the long-standing budget deadlock, but the two sides could only agree on minor tax changes and increases in the spending cuts mandated by the Gramm-Rudman-Hollings law.

The major difficulty, as in the past, was the impasse over new taxes versus spending cuts and social programs versus defense. Part of the problem, however, was the Tax Reform Act of 1986. This measure made the federal tax system fairer by scaling back tax deductions for interest payments and some kinds of real estate taxes and reducing the amounts deductible for business entertainment and other expenses largely incurred by upper-income people. In exchange for such concessions, it lowered the maximum income tax rates from 50 to 28 percent. It also dropped millions of lower-income people from the income tax rolls. To raise taxes promised to violate the many bargains made to get the reform bill through Congress.

Fortunately the worst did not happen. There was some good news for the American economy in early 1988. In the last weeks of 1987 the American dollar began to fall against the major foreign currencies. The effect was to make American exports cheaper and foreign imports more expensive. The 1988 trade deficit was 137 billion, down significantly from 1987. No one could tell whether the trend would continue; no one could tell whether America had once again become competitive in the world's markets.

End-of-Term Issues

Reagan and the Supreme Court

As the Reagan administration approached its end, the desire of the president and other conservatives to entrench their principles in the Supreme Court grew more compelling. By the midpoint of his second term Reagan had been able to appoint two conservative justices, Sandra Day O'Connor and Antonin Scalia, to the highest federal court. After Chief Justice Warren Burger decided to step down, he was able as well to elevate associate justice William Rehnquist, a conservative, to his place. Yet the moderates and liberals continued to get their way on many social issues that came before the court. Then in 1987 Justice Lewis Powell, a political moderate who had often been a swing vote on key issues, resigned for reasons of health. Reagan now had a chance to truly tip the balance to the political right and quickly nominated federal appeals court Judge Robert Bork for Powell's slot.

The Bork nomination became a battle royal between liberals and conservatives. Liberals claimed that Bork had no regard for the right of privacy, that his view that the Supreme Court must always be guided by the "original intent" of congress was seriously outdated and reactionary, and that he was hostile to civil rights. Conservatives claimed that he was a brilliant and thoughtful traditionalist who would turn the Court away from the disruptive "judicial activism" of the recent past and return it to a more appropriate role. In the end the Senate by a wide margin rejected the nomination.

The chagrined president now hastily nominated another conservative federal judge, Douglas Ginsburg. But Ginsburg admitted that he had smoked marijuana as a law school professor and soon withdrew his name. Finally Reagan nominated Judge Anthony Kennedy. Although a conservative, Kennedy seemed a reasonable man and was confirmed without a serious fight. It now looked as if, no matter what the fate of the political right at the polls, one of the three branches of government would be firmly locked up for the conservatives for many years to come.

Nicaragua Again

As the Reagan administration wound down, Nicaragua once more became a major issue. Most Americans still shied away from a major military involvement in Central America. A poll in early 1986 showed 62 percent of the voters opposed to giving aid to the Contras. Even among Reagan supporters only 35 percent favored contra military aid. Yet the administration continued to press for the overthrow of the Sandinistas and continued to demand that Congress provide military supplies for the freedom fighters.

In late 1987 it began to look as if a peaceful solution to the Nicaraguan problem might be achieved. In early 1987 the five Central American presidents, led by Oscar Arias Sanchez of Costa Rica, proposed a peace plan to bring the Contras and

Sandinistas together in face-to-face negotiations, restore democratic rights in Nicaragua, and end the threat of American intervention. The Arias plan aroused enthusiasm around the world and won the Nobel Peace Prize for the Costa Rican president.

At home most Democrats and many moderates approved the scheme. The right, including the administration, remained skeptical. Although Sandinista President Ortega agreed to meet directly with his Contra enemies and restored some civil liberties to the country, Reagan continued to denounce his regime and demand further funding for the Contras. At one point Speaker of the House James Wright declared that he believed the president would only be content with a military victory and that he did not want a peaceful solution. By the early months of 1988 it remained unclear whether Nicaragua would continue to be a festering sore or whether the healing process had begun.

The 1988 Presidential Election

For a whole generation now the presidential election process had become longer, more expensive, and more distracting. By the 1980s campaigning for the major party nominations began almost two years before election day and involved a half-dozen or more serious candidates in each party hurtling from coast to coast to collect delegates from the thirty or so caucuses and primaries that were held early in the election year.

For 1988, the year that marked the end of the Reagan administration, both parties were seeking presidential candidates. In the Republican camp the two leading contenders were Vice President George Bush and Senate Minority Leader Bob Dole of Kansas. Both men were approximately in the Republican center. There was no Republican left anymore; it had virtually disappeared since Reagan's advent.

The Democrats started with eight serious candidates: former Colorado senator Gary Hart; Governor Michael Dukakis of Massachusetts; Senator Paul Simon of Illinois; Congressman Richard Gephardt of Missouri; former governor Bruce Babbitt of Arizona; Senator Joseph Biden of Delaware; and the Reverend Jesse Jackson, like Hart, a major contender from 1984. Hart was the frontrunner at the beginning, but in the summer of 1987 he destroyed his chances by involving himself with a young woman who was not his wife and then denying their relationship. Many Americans took this as a sign of poor judgment if not dubious personal morals. Hart resigned from the race. In December 1987 he decided to return, but did poorly thereafter and ceased to be a serious contender. By this time Senator Biden, having been caught plagiarizing other men's speeches and inventing a law school record for himself, also withdrew.

By late spring George Bush had far outstripped Dole and sewed up the Republican nomination. The Democratic race lasted longer with Jesse Jackson, representing the party's most liberal wing, running closely behind Dukakis in the primaries. Jackson's appeal to African-American voters resembled John Kennedy's to Catholics in 1960: he was one of them and he symbolized their hopes for full political acceptance. But many white Democrats perceived him as too radical; others simply would not vote for a black man. In the end Jackson fell behind Dukakis.

At the Atlanta convention in July Dukakis easily won the Democratic nomination. Jackson's supporters demanded that he be given second place. But Dukakis and the party leaders, fearing that a Dukakis-Jackson ticket could not win, refused. Instead, the Massachusetts governor chose as his running mate Lloyd Bentsen, a conservative senator from Texas who balanced the ticket ideologically and gave the Democrats a fighting chance to win the big Texas electoral vote. Jackson promised to campaign for the party candidates in the fall.

By the time the Republicans assembled in New Orleans to confirm Bush's nomination, the Democrats were ahead in the opinion polls. Bush hoped to don the mantle of the still popular Reagan and identify himself with Republican prosperity and other administration accomplishments. But initially many voters perceived him as a rich Yale "preppie" who lacked the common touch. Party leaders worried that he could not attract the "Reagan Democrats," blue-collar Democratic voters who had defected to Ronald Reagan in 1980 and 1984. He also seemed stiff and uncaring, qualities that seemed to repel women voters especially.

Bush succeeded in allaying some of these feelings in an effective acceptance speech following his formal nomination in New Orleans. But he wounded himself by choosing as his running mate the forty-one-year-old senator from Indiana, Dan Quayle. Soon after Quayle's selection it became known that in 1969 he had joined the Indiana National Guard to avoid active service in Vietnam. Critics said that he had used his family's money and influence to enter the guard at a time when there were few openings and most other men could not choose that option. To the skeptics Quayle seemed a draft-evader and the son of privileged wealth.

Despite Quayle, Bush quickly took the lead. The Republican managers went on the attack with a negative campaign that depicted Dukakis as an extreme liberal who endorsed abortion on demand, had freed on parole a dangerous black criminal, and would saddle the American people with new taxes for expensive social programs. At the same time, to distinguish himself modestly from his predecessor, Bush talked of a "kinder, gentler nation" and "a thousand points of light" representing voluntary private efforts to improve the lot of the nation's underprivileged. He also repeated over and over again the promise: "no new taxes."

Dukakis tried to fend off the Republican attacks. He warned that America's world economic lead would dwindle further if steps were not taken to reverse its decline and said the economy was as full of holes as Swiss cheese. He emphasized his "competence" to handle the difficult tasks of governing. But many people found him too passionless, too cerebral. The Republicans, moreover, could claim that the country was prosperous and at peace. Long before November Dukakis was running far behind.

The election was a resounding Bush-Quayle victory. The Republican ticket was elected by a popular majority of 48.8 million to 41.8 million. In the electoral college Bush received 426 electoral votes to his opponent's 111. The Dukakis-Bentsen vote was concentrated in the Northeast, the upper midwest, and the Pacific Northwest, the more liberal regions of the country. The new Republican regional coalition of the South and West had held fast.

And yet there was no sign of a mandate such as Reagan had received in 1980. Indeed, the Democrats increased their majorities slightly in congress. For the first

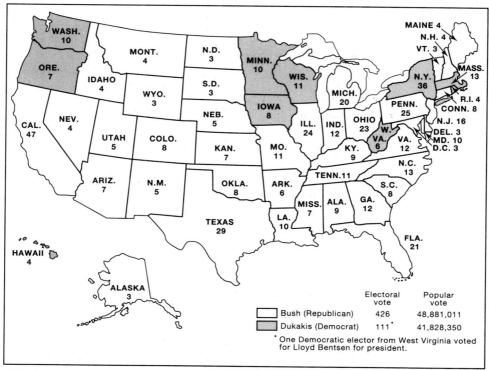

Figure 6–4   The 1988 Presidential Election

time since 1960 the party winning the presidency had actually lost congressional seats.

The End of the Reagan Era

Ronald Reagan left office on January 20, 1989. His administration had spanned eight eventful years. But what did they mean?

The public mandate of 1980, confirmed in 1984, had been an experiment to see if less government would work better than the system that had evolved under the New Deal–Fair Deal–Great Society programs and had been consolidated, if not extended, under Republican presidents. Reagan had helped to stop the growth of government and had returned economic responsibility to individuals. But he had not succeeded in dismantling the social service state he had inherited from his predecessors. In the end he had proven to be as pragmatic as president of the United States as he had been as governor of California. In foreign affairs too he had revealed himself as a practical man. Having labeled the Soviet Union the evil empire, in his last months he negotiated the most sweeping nuclear arms reduction in U.S. history. Like Dwight Eisenhower and Richard Nixon before him, he had, whatever his intentions, legitimized the role of government in America that the Democrats had bequeathed.

As the nation approached the 1990s immense problems remained. The United States faced the prospect of relative economic decline in the face of powerful challenges from abroad. These were not from its adversaries in the Marxist camp, but from its fellow capitalist nations. Could the United States compete with Japan and the Pacific rim? Could it compete with the West Europeans? In 1992 Europe was due to become a single economic unit, one with 320 million consumers and a total GNP greater than that of the United States. Would the American giant be able to keep up with the new European colossus?

And what about the quality of American life? Could something be done to elevate the sodden underclass that mocked the nation's ideals? Could crime and drugs be eliminated from the cities' streets and neighborhoods? Could the natural environment be rescued from steady deterioration and the natural beauty of the mountains, lakes, beaches, and forests be restored and maintained? Could the country's antagonistic cultural, racial, ethnic, ideological, and religious components live together in relative harmony? Could American education be made equal to that of any other nation on earth and Americans rescued from the ignorance and provinciality that threatened their leadership? These were the challenges of the 1990s and would probably remain those of the twenty-first century.

FOR FURTHER READING

Reagan's background is brilliantly analyzed in Garry Wills, *Reagan's America* (1988). Robert Dallek in *Ronald Reagan and the Politics of Symbolism* (1984) seeks to psychoanalyze the Reagan movement.

The story of the political New Right has been told in the following skeptical or hostile works: Alan Crawford, *Thunder on the Right: The "New Right" and the Politics of Resentment* (1980); Thomas Ferguson and Joel Rogers, *Right Turn: The Decline of the Democrats and the Future of American Politics* (1986); Sidney Blumenthal, *The Rise of the Counter-Establishment: From Conservative Ideology to Political Power* (1986). A less partisan treatment is Paul Gottfried and Thomas Fleming, *The Conservative Movement* (1988). For the neoconservatives see Peter Steinfels, *The Neo-Conservatives: The Men Who Are Changing America's Politics* (1979). The New Right states its own case in Robert W. Whitaker (ed.), *The New Right Papers* (1982); Martin Anderson, *Revolution* (1988); and Richard Viguerie, *The Establishment vs. the People: Is a New Populist Revolt on the Way?* (1983).

For the Christian right see the rather overwrought Flo Conway and Jim Siegeleman, *Holy Terror: The Fundamentalist War on America's Freedoms in Religion, Politics, and Our Lives* (1984). More judicious studies include, Erling Jorstad, *The Politics of Moralism: The New Christian Right in American Life* (1981); Robert C. Liebman and Robert Wuthnow (eds.), *The New Christian Right: Mobilization and Legitimation* (1983); and Richard John Neuhaus and John Cromartie (eds.), *Piety and Politics: Evangelicals and Fundamentalists Confront the World* (1987).

Two works by conservative preachers convey the views of the new Christian right: Tim LaHaye, *The Battle for the Mind* (1980) and Jerry Falwell, *The Fundamentalist Phenomenon: The Resurgence of Conservative Christianity* (1986).

The televangelist phenomenon is described by Larry Martz, *Ministry of Greed: The Inside Story of the Televangelists and their Holy Wars* (1988) and Jeffrey K. Hadden and Charles E. Swann, *Prime Time Preachers: The Rising Power of Televangelism* (1981).

The conservative economic views of Reagan's supporters can be followed in Jude Wanniski, *The Way the World Works: How Economies Fail—and Succeed* (1978); Alan S. Blinder, *Hard*

Heads, Soft Hearts: Tough-Minded Economics for a Just Society (1987); and Paul Craig Roberts, *The Supply-Side Revolution* (1984). Also see George Gilder, *Wealth and Poverty* (1981). For the views of the man who helped engineer the Reagan tax cuts see David Stockman's *The Triumph of Politics: The Inside Story of the Reagan Revolution* (1986).

Critical appraisals of Reaganomics include Robert Lekachman, *Vision and Nightmares: America After Reagan* (1988); Barry Bluestone and Bennett Harrison, *The Deindustrialization of America* (1982); and Benjamin M. Friedman, *Day of Reckoning: The Consequences of American Economic Policy under Reagan and After* (1988). Also see Martha Derthick and Paul Quirk, *The Politics of Deregulation* (1985).

Reaganite social policies were influenced by works such as Charles Murray, *Losing Ground: American Social Policy, 1950–1980* (1984).

A vivid, if biased, compendium of what Americans were thinking about in the Reagan years is Studs Terkel's *The Great Divide: Second Thoughts on the American Dream* (1988). For the yuppie phenomenon of the seventies and eighties see Paul C. Light, *Baby Boomers* (1988).

Reagan's ability to manipulate the media is described in Mark Hertsgaard, *On Bended Knee: The Press and the Reagan Presidency* (1988).

One good place to begin any consideration of Soviet-American policy during the Reagan period is Mikhail Gorbachev, *Perestroika: New Thinking for Our Country and the World* (1987). Also see, however, Alexander Haig, *Caveat* (1984) and Strobe Talbott, *Deadly Gambits* (1984).

For the best account of the Iran-Contra affair see William S. Cohen and George J. Mitchell, *Men of Zeal: A Candid Inside Story of the Iran-Contra Hearings* (1988). Also see *The Tower Commission Report* (1987). How the Iran-Contra fiasco immobilized the Reagan administration is described in Jane Mayer and Doyle McManus, *Landslide: The Unmaking of the President, 1984–1988* (1988).

As the Reagan administration wound down former members wrote *kiss-and-tell* books that revealed interesting details on how the government was run during the 1980s. Some of these are Donald T. Regan, *For the Record: From Wall Street to Washington* (1988); Larry Speakes, *Speaking Out: Inside the Reagan White House* (1988); and Michael K. Deaver, *Behind the Scenes* (1987).

Index